Dependency Culture

Dependency Culture

The explosion of a myth

HARTLEY DEAN
and
PETER TAYLOR-GOOBY

 HARVESTER
WHEATSHEAF

New York London Toronto Sydney Tokyo Singapore

First published 1992 by
Harvester Wheatsheaf
Campus 400, Maylands Avenue
Hemel Hempstead
Hertfordshire, HP2 7EZ
A division of
Simon & Schuster International Group

Typeset in 10/12pt Times by
Inforum Typesetting, Portsmouth

Printed and bound in Great Britain by
Biddles Ltd, Guildford and King's Lynn

British Library Cataloguing in Publication Data

Dean, Hartley
  Dependency culture: The explosion of a myth.
  I. Title   II. Taylor-Gooby, Peter
  361.6

  ISBN 0–7450–1225–6
       0–7450–1226–4 (pbk)

2 3 4 5   95

CONTENTS

TABLES AND FIGURES

PREFACE

The Victorian Poor Law made no bones about the fact that its primary objective was to punish poor people who asked for state help, so that potential workers only became a charge on the state when they were driven to the workhouse by absolute destitution. The idea that the main object of social security is to regulate the lives of poor people rather than to relieve their poverty fell into disfavour in the post-war heyday of the welfare state. More recently it has returned, as mass unemployment increases the pressure on welfare budgets and the weakness of the British economy calls into question our ability to maintain social spending.

This book arose out of three related concerns. We wished first of all to develop a systematic critique of victim-blaming terms like 'dependency culture' and 'underclass'. Secondly, we were anxious to explore questions of dependency and discipline in relation to the functioning of the British social security system and the relevance of recent social security reforms to current social trends. Thirdly, we hoped to outline an alternative approach to welfare dependency, an approach which would situate the role of state welfare in relation to a broader appreciation of human interdependency.

The book provides a comprehensive overview of the debates which have surrounded the use of terms like 'dependency culture'; it advances new arguments concerning the relationship between social security reform and the effects of social change; and it contributes new theoretical insights to current concerns with dependency, human need and citizenship. It will be of value to students and researchers in the fields of social policy, sociology and related academic disciplines, and also to professionals and practitioners in such fields as social work and welfare rights. The work is firmly grounded in and reports in some detail the findings of a major piece of empirical research undertaken by the authors with the assistance of funding from the Economic and Social Research Council under grant ref. R 00023 1776.

The authors would like to express their sincere appreciation to the Economic and Social Research Council for its generous support. Our thanks are also due to the following agencies for their co-operation in that research: Bellenden Neighbourhood Advice Centre; Canterbury Citizens Advice Bureau; Canterbury Probation Service; The Cyrenians; Isle of Sheppey Citizens Advice Bureau; Department of Social Security; Melting Pot; Southwark Citizens Advice Bureau; Southwark Law Project; Streatham Citizens Advice Bureau. A particular debt of gratitude is owed to the eighty-five social security claimants without whose assistance the research would not have been possible.

We also wish to thank the Open University Press for their kind permission to reproduce in Chapter 2 material from H. Dean, 'In search of the underclass' which first appeared in P. Brown and R. Scase (eds.) (1991) *Poor Work: Disadvantage and the division of labour* (Open University Press, Milton Keynes). Roger Jowell, Sharon Witherspoon and Lindsay Brook of Social and Community Planning Research carried out the British Social Attitudes Survey discussed in Chapter 3, and we are extremely grateful to them for providing the data. Finally, we should like to extend our appreciation to Clare Grist, our editor at Harvester Wheatsheaf, for the support and attention which she has given to this project.

The views expressed herein are none the less entirely those of the authors, who of course accept full responsibility for any errors of fact, omission or interpretation.

Hartley Dean
Peter Taylor-Gooby

ABBREVIATIONS

CSO	Central Statistical Office
DE	Department of Employment
DHSS	Department of Health and Social Security
DSS	Department of Social Security
EC	European Community
ESRC	Economic and Social Research Council
ET	Employment Training
FPSC	Family Policy Studies Centre
GDP	gross domestic product
NIESR	National Institute for Economic and Social Research
OECD	Organisation for Economic Co-operation and Development
OPCS	Office of Population Censuses and Surveys
SSRC	Social Security Research Consortium
VAT	Valued Added Tax
YT	Youth Training
YTS	Youth Training Scheme

CHAPTER 1

INTRODUCTION: THE BIRTH OF A MYTH

Social security must be designed to reinforce personal independence rather than extend the power of the state.   (DHSS 1985a)

I'd like a little bit of extra money so that if the kids do need a pair of trainers or a pair of shoes, I can go and get them without having to hint at me mother to go halves with me. I would like to be more independent.   (Carol, quoted in Oppenheim 1990: 50)

Social welfare is about the *regulation* of need, about the classification of individual needs into categories and the allocation of different levels of resources to different kinds of need. This book is concerned with social security claimants of working age. Since the inception of state policies dealing with poor people at the end of the feudal era, government has been concerned to ensure that welfare does not deter those who might enter paid employment from doing so. This principle underlay the punitive treatment of 'sturdy beggars' in sixteenth-century Britain, the eighteenth-century Speenhamland wage-subsidy system, the nineteenth-century Poor Law with its principles of less eligibility and denial of citizenship rights to those in receipt of state aid, and the work-test associated with twentieth-century social security benefits. It formed a cornerstone of Beveridge's regime of national insurance unemployment benefit with means-tested back-up for those without insurance entitlement. 'The correlative of the State's undertaking to ensure adequate benefit for unavoidable interruption of earnings . . . is enforcement of the citizen's obligation to seek and accept all reasonable opportunities of work' (Beveridge

1942: 58). The principle remained an important part of policy, but received little attention during the three decades of welfare state expansion after the Second World War. More recently, radical changes in policy have intensified the surveillance of claimants and brought the issue of work incentives to the top of the welfare agenda.

An analogous set of principles governs the use of welfare as an alternative to family dependency. Most benefits include provision to enable claimants to maintain spouses as dependants. Means-tested welfare is not available to married or cohabiting partners if their spouses have an income adequate to maintain them as dependants. Insurance provision covers some categories of widowhood, but the lack of any substantial benefit system directed at single parents testifies to the reluctance of government to encroach in meeting needs which are seen as properly the duty of the family.

In any society but the most primitive survival requires co-operation. Human civilisation is built upon complex chains of interdependence: those who disagree must carve their own pencils. However, legitimate and habitual forms of dependence take on the status of rights and are understood as independence. The market is the standard source of income for those of working age, either through direct employment or indirectly through family dependency on someone who is employed. The resulting social construction of dependency defines wage-labour or family relationship as independence, so that it becomes difficult to recognise the possibility of exploitation or subjugation in these contexts. The use of state welfare is understood as dependency. The operation of this process in the recent development of social security policy is the theme of this book.

Social security and dependency culture

The experience of constraint in welfare spending following the oil crisis of the mid-1970s, coupled with the election in 1979 of a radical reforming government committed to a programme of reducing state intervention, directed attention at arguments about dependency. Cuts in benefits for those whose state dependency was seen as unjustified and tighter regulation of access to benefits in the first place curbed spending and transferred a number of people from state to market and family dependency, helping the government in achieving its policy aims. The impact of the recessions of the early 1980s (which took unemployment in the United Kingdom to the highest level since 1938) and of the 1990s in increasing the numbers in a position to claim benefits reinforced the urgency of an attack on welfare dependency. In a keynote speech on social welfare, the Secretary of State for Health and Social Security declared that 'dependence in the long run decreases human happiness and reduces human freedom . . . the well-being of individuals is best protected and promoted when they are helped to be independent' and later that 'the indiscriminate handing out of benefits . . . can . . . undermine the will to self-help' (Moore 1987: 4, 9).

The official critique of dependency was reinforced by the notion of dependency culture which developed in analysis of the impact of social security in the late 1980s. In a recent review of policy, McGlone defines the 'dependency culture' thesis as follows: 'the government believes that the payment of certain types of social security encourages people to become dependent on benefit and lowers their desire to find work or behave in a responsible manner' (1990: 171). This argument links three ideas. First is the claim that people respond to financial incentives in a simple economistic calculus of cash benefit against effort, so that the evasion of work is in direct proportion to the size and accessibility of the reward for not working – social security benefits for unemployed people. The second idea rests on a more sociological approach to motivation. The values of significant others and of the neighbourhood, status-aspirations, social esteem and milieu are important influences on the choices people make. If this is so for clothes, holidays, children's forenames, architecture, academic traditions, drama and motor cars, why not in relation to work and family ethics?

The third aspect of the dependency culture argument is the moralistic edge to the condemnation of inappropriate dependency. Not only is claiming by people of working age seen as economically inefficient, as the reluctant collectivist tradition in social welfare has argued since the depression of the 1930s, its analysis immeasurably strengthened by the work of Keynes (George and Wilding 1985: 52–3), it is also presented as an affront to the cherished values of right-thinking people. Such ideas have a respectable pedigree, stretching back to the description of the Old Poor Law as 'a bounty on indolence and vice' and 'a universal system of pauperization' in the 1834 report of the Poor Law Commissioners (quoted in Blaug 1963: 152). As structural approaches to poverty gained ground, strengthened by the evidence of studies such as that of Rowntree, who demonstrated that some 10 per cent of the population of York at the turn of the century could not avoid poverty however wisely they spent their income, mainstream approaches to the problem became less concerned with the improvidence of those in need. Beveridge analysed poverty in terms of the contingencies of a common life-cycle and paid little attention to measures designed to enhance incentives, although he certainly saw work as a social obligation. He assumed that 'men who have once gained the habit of work would rather work . . . than be idle' (1942: 57). The policy recommendations were for insurance-based welfare designed to meet the needs defined in his report.

The notion that social environment generated poverty was a central element in Sir Keith Joseph's research programme on transmitted deprivation in the 1970s. Only in the 1980s has the idea that government policy itself colludes in creating a milieu which reinforces a counterproductive calculus of the attractiveness of benefits compared to earned incomes entered official statements. The centrepiece of policy making in the 1980s, the report on the reform of social security, heralded by the Secretary of State as a 'New Beveridge', states:

> it is self-defeating if [social security] creates barriers to the creation of jobs, to job mobility or to people rejoining the labour force. Clearly such obstacles exist if people believe themselves better off out of work than in work . . . if we wish to encourage people to provide for themselves, then the social security system . . . must not stand in their way. (DHSS 1985a: 3)

The idea that ill-regulated benefits set in train social processes that foster irresponsible and economically damaging behaviour is particularly attractive to a government committed to spending restraint and faced by growing demands on social security from unemployed people.

The dependency culture thesis was developed most powerfully in the recent work of US policy analysts. Charles Murray, the foremost US advocate of the approach, visited London in 1987 to meet DHSS and Treasury officials and members of the Prime Minister's Policy Unit. In 1989, he addressed the Prime Minister and contributed a series of influential articles to the press. Most commentators see Murray's work as of central importance in the propagation of the idea of dependency culture in the United Kingdom (Levy 1988: 52; Field 1989; Plant 1991: 78; George and Howards 1991: Ch. 4). It is discussed in detail in Chapter 2.

The outline of the book

The resurgence of interest in the dangers of welfare dependency occurred at a time when the current of social change was set in a direction that increased the vulnerability of some groups to reliance on benefits. In this chapter we review these changes and relate them to evidence on the risk of poverty. Two kinds of change are of most importance in patterns of employment and in family structures. We go on to consider the interaction of these changes with a shift in the direction of government policy to poor people based on the time-honoured approach of 'blaming the victim'. At a time of recession and high unemployment these changes produce a sharpening of the discipline implicit in the system of social security for the poor of working age.

Chapter 2 develops the analysis of dependency understood as a marginalising category through a detailed account of the debate about the 'underclass' in Britain and America. The attempt to define the disreputable poor as a 'residuum', superfluous to the structuring of economic and social life around the core themes of paid work and family leads to a simultaneous denial of the reality of mutual dependence under a modern division of labour and within the family, and of the possibilities of exploitation that arise when that dependence is coupled with an inequality of power. Chapter 3 examines the policy shifts of the past decade in more detail and relates these shifts to popular ideas about work, family and dependency as derived from national attitude surveys. This sets the scene for the presentation of the analysis of the experience of welfare claimants, based on our own discursive study in the next chapter.

The study shows that individual claimants by and large adhere to the mainstream values of work and family ethics. State social welfare systems are experienced as intrusive and oppressive. There is little evidence of the kind of interaction between claimants that writers like Murray assume forms the basis of a culture of dependency, resting on shared values. Chapter 5 extends this analysis. There is no evidence that the new disciplinary techniques of social security strengthen work or family incentives, and every indication that they weaken the self-confidence of claimants. This sense of captivity rather than illicit dependence increasingly distinguishes the experience of claiming last-resort welfare. It indicates that reforms designed to strengthen the incentives to encourage individuals to leave benefits may have the paradoxical effect of reinforcing the pressures that keep people in that situation. The final chapter returns to the central theme of how recent approaches to social welfare have intensified the processes that depict the use of state benefits as dependency, and characterise the use of market or family as a means of livelihood as independence. The exclusive focus on dependence on the state as pathological makes it impossible to analyse the mutual interdependence of everyone living at a level above that of Robinson Crusoe (in the days before Friday) and to discuss this in the study of welfare policy.

In the rest of this chapter we discuss changes in relation to employment and the family and consider how they increase the vulnerability of particular groups to the stigmatised status of welfare state dependants.

Social change and 'new poverty'

By the mid-1970s the long-term post-war shift in the direction of greater equality in many European countries had come to an end. The change was most marked in the United Kingdom. According to an EC study, which defined as poor those whose spending was less than half the national average (taking household composition into account), the proportion of people in the United Kingdom below the poverty line increased from 7 to 12 per cent in the relatively short period between 1975 and 1985 (O'Higgins and Jenkins 1989: 3).

Changes in the pattern of poverty over the past two decades have given rise to concern that social welfare systems are facing the rise of a 'new poverty' and that the structure of benefits is ill-equipped to meet shifting needs (see, for example, Donnison 1991; Room 1991). The social welfare systems of the post-war period were based mainly on social insurance designed to meet the normal contingencies of the life-cycle of the working class. In the United Kingdom, the system of benefits that followed the Beveridge Report catered for loss of income due to retirement, sickness, disability, widowhood and unemployment. It was assumed that most workers would be able to gain sufficient insurance entitlement through employment to qualify for benefits when they and their dependants needed them. A means-tested safety-net was provided for those whose needs were not covered. The system also assumed that macro-economic policies would maintain a high level of employment, and national insurance unemployment benefit was time limited on the grounds that jobless workers would soon re-enter work. Child benefit was introduced to help cover the cost of children.

These systems were reasonably successful in containing poverty among the working class in the three decades of stability, economic growth and high employment that followed the end of the war (Ringen 1987). However, as the economic crises of the mid- and late 1970s called into question the ability of governments to finance mass welfare, changes in the economy and in the pattern of family life produced new needs which these systems were unable to meet. The most important changes were as follows:

1. A rapid increase in long-term unemployment. The insurance-based system was unable to cope with this, since entitlement to benefit expired or had never been achieved by those entering the labour market, who suffered particularly high rates of unemployment.
2. An increasing tendency to insecure or part-time employment which generated low and uncertain income and inadequate insurance records, since those below the earnings threshold were not included in the scheme.
3. A continuing increase in the numbers of one-parent families, many of whom were at risk of poverty, and for whom there was no adequate system of benefits.

The new poverty was particularly prevalent among some social groups: ethnic minorities, migrants, the lower working class and some groups of young people. It is spatially distributed in particular areas of the inner city and declining regions. The previous dominant pattern of poverty, structured around a typical working-class life-cycle, generated its own constituency to press for social welfare. Since the most obvious needs of the new poverty are concentrated among particular groups, there is no obvious basis for political pressure to devise new policies appropriate to changing circumstances. One authoritative commentator regards the construction of such policies as the foremost challenge to a new European 'social state', which will be essential to the achievement of social integration in the EC (Leibfried 1991: 3–4).

The weakness of the economy in the United Kingdom, the social changes of the 1980s (particularly the rapid increase in the number of one-parent families) and the government policies designed to cut benefit spending posed the problem of the 'new poverty' in a peculiarly acute form in the United Kingdom. Unfortunately, no satisfactory data on recent changes in the pattern of poverty is available, since the government suppresses information which might be useful to its critics. The official statistical series which showed the proportion of the population at or below last-resort social security levels of income was discontinued in 1985, but has since been extended in a slightly different form to 1987 by independent researchers. A new official series shows the proportion of the population living at various levels of income below the national average for 1981 to 1987 (extended to 1988 by Institute for Fiscal Studies researchers) but yoes not permit the relation between incomes and benefits to be judged. The quality of the material is subject to controversy. Both MPs and academics have repeatedly called for a new seri_s (Townsend 1991; Social Security Select Committee 1991: para. 19). It is at present unclear whether statistics will be made available to cover the late 1980s and the 1990s. Both series show a substantial worsening in the position of the poorest groups over the 1980s, and such independent evidence as is available from studies of consumption patterns and from local area surveys indicates that this trend is continuing (Bradshaw and Holmes 1989). Discussion of the trends in poverty in this chapter is based mainly on the discontinued series showing the proportion of people in various groups at or below supplementary benefit level, since this makes it possible to relate poverty directly to social policy.

Table 1.1 The changing composition of the poor and the changing risk of poverty, 1979–87

A) Proportion of those living on or below supplementary benefit level falling into various groups

Members of families headed by:	1979 %	1987 %
Pensioner	48	26
Low-paid worker	8	13
Unemployed person[1]	17	37
Sick or disabled person	5	5
Other	22	19
Total (thousands)	(5810)	(10580)
Members of one-parent families (*included* in the above groups)[2]	13	17

B) Proportion of the different groups living at or below supplementary benefit level

Members of families headed by:	1979 %	1987 %
Pensioner	32	30
Low-paid worker	1	4
Unemployed person[1]	49	76
Sick or disabled person	16	30
Other	42	42
All	12	20
Members of one-parent families (*included* in the above groups)[2]	33	68

Notes:
1. 'Unemployed' means unemployed for three months or more.
2. Most one-parent families are included in the 'other' category, but some are counted as unemployed, some as low-paid and some as sick and disabled.

Sources: Number in the various population groups: Social Security Select Committee 1991: Tables F1 and F2. Number at or below benefit level: for 1979, DHSS 1982: Tables 47.07 and 47.08; for 1987, Johnson and Webb 1990: Tables 3 and 4.

The information is displayed in two ways. Part A of Table 1.1 shows the percentage of the various groups living at or below supplementary benefit level in 1979 and 1987. Part B shows the proportion of those groups in the population at large who fell into poverty. While the figures in the table refer to individuals, classification into groups is by head of household. Low-paid workers who are not household heads are not included in the statistics. About 20 per cent of UK workers – six and a half million people – fall below the Council of Europe threshold (set at 68 per cent of mean earnings), the highest percentage for any EC country except Greece (Minford 1990: 10). Unless there is an equitable internal redistribution of income in households containing these workers, the statistics will seriously under-report poverty among this group. The information also excludes the increasing numbers of homeless people and ignores not only changes in arrangements for school meals, water charges and local taxes but also increases in VAT and excise duties, all of which have operated to cut the living standards of the poorest groups over the period covered, so that the picture of changes it presents is unduly optimistic.

The numbers at or below the benefit level in the United Kingdom have increased rapidly from nearly six to over ten and a half million or from 12 to 20 per cent of the population. The most important reason for the increase is the rapid rise in the numbers of unemployed people. Families headed by single parents and by low-waged workers have also increased sharply in number. The number of sick and disabled people has increased in line with the overall rise in poverty, whereas the number of pensioners has risen only slowly, so that they make up a shrinking proportion of the expanding numbers of poor people.

The second part of the table paints a rather different picture. It reflects the vulnerability of the different groups to poverty, taking into account their relative size. The families of unemployed people are the group most likely to depend on last-resort benefits in both years, as their access to insurance benefits is cut back and they become impoverished by long-term unemployment. One-parent families also run a very high risk of poverty. Over two-thirds were living at or below the means-test level by the end of the 1980s. About a third of pensioners, mainly elderly single people and including a high proportion of women, are poor in both years. The vulnerability of sick and disabled people has increased rapidly, virtually doubling to 30 per cent. The risk of poverty among the small group of low-paid workers included in the survey has also increased rapidly.

The traditional social insurance system had by no means been successful in meeting the life-cycle needs of the population: substantial numbers of pensioners and of sick and disabled people are in poverty and the risk of poverty for these groups continues at a substantial level. Single pensioners, who tend to be older, and who include a greater proportion of women, are much more likely to be in poverty than married pensioners, over 30 per cent of them were included in both years covered in the table, as against just over 10 per cent of married pensioners. Poverty among low-paid workers increased as the labour market became more insecure, and the numbers of people categorised as sick and disabled rose as potential workers left the labour-force, discouraged by the high levels of unemployment.

Alongside the 'old poverty', which the Beveridge system of social insurance was designed to handle, the 'new poverty' of unemployed people who are not covered by insurance and of one-parent families has expanded rapidly. Even over the brief span of the statistics, the proportion of the poor who are unemployed has more than doubled and the proportion who are members of one-parent families has risen by nearly a third. By far the greater part of both groups lives at or below the poverty line. The failure of social welfare in meeting their needs is underlined by the high and rising vulnerability to poverty that they experience.

Far and away the most important reason for the rise in poverty in the 1980s was the enormous increase in the level of unemployment. Unemployment affected black ethnic minorities, working-class people, younger people and those living in particular areas of the country most powerfully. Aggregated data from the Labour Force Survey for 1987–9 shows that unemployment among people of Pakistani or Bangladeshi origin was nearly three times and among people of West Indian origin nearly twice that of white people. The survey also shows that unskilled manual workers were two and a half times more likely than non-manual workers and six times more likely than professional or managerial workers to be included among the unemployed (CSO 1991a: Tables 4.10, 4.28, 4.30). Department of Employment returns show that people under 25 experience unemployment rates about two-thirds as high again as the average. Unemployment rates in the south-east and East Anglia remain markedly lower, at about 6 per cent, than those in the West Midlands and Yorkshire (8 per cent), Wales, Scotland and the north-west (9 per cent) or the northern region (over 10 per cent: DE 1991a: Tables 2.3, 2.15). There is clear evidence of the breakdown of national insurance as a means of meeting the needs of unemployed people. In 1980, 59 per cent of unemployed people received insurance benefit (Treasury 1983). By 1982, the majority of unemployed people had no insurance entitlement and by 1990 the proportion receiving only means-tested income support had risen to 71 per cent (DSS 1991a: Table 15). There was also a sharp increase in the contribution of single parenthood to family poverty. Between 1979 and 1988, the proportion of people in one-parent families living at a level below half the national average income almost exactly doubled to 57 per cent (Social Security Select Committee 1991: Table F1 – the statistics take housing costs and family make-up into account).

Although no firm statistics are available for more recent years, it is likely that the trends outlined above have continued. Unemployment has remained high through the 1980s and is currently rising in the recession of the early 1990s. The number of single-parent families continues to rise. The economic and social trends that underlie these changes continue to operate. We will consider changes in work and in the family in separate sections.

Economic change and welfare dependency

The British economy is peculiarly vulnerable to the effects of recession, for reasons that are not clearly understood (see Gough 1990: 1–5 for a discussion). Low productivity, low competitiveness, low profitability and low investment link in a vicious circle: different accounts lay emphasis on one or other of these factors (Ball, Gray and McDowell 1989: 29–33). Unemployment in the United Kingdom rose to 12.5 per cent in 1983 (by standardised OECD definitions), higher than the level in any other of the seven major OECD economies (averaging 8.5 per cent). The level is again rising, and reached 7.3 per cent in 1990 as against an OECD average of 6.3 per cent. GDP growth at 27 per cent over the 1980s lags behind the 33-per-cent average for the seven major OECD economies over the same period, despite the achievement of high growth rates between 1986 and 1988 (NIESR 1991a: Tables 14, 15). This economic vulnerability, with its consequences for social welfare needs, must be set against the background of changes in the labour market.

In common with many advanced economies, that of the United Kingdom is undergoing a shift in employment between the manufacturing and the service sector. The contribution of the manufacturing sector to employment in the United Kingdom peaked at a level of about 8.9 million jobs in 1966, from which it declined to 4.8 million by 1991. Service industries supplied 11.2 million jobs in 1966 and expanded to supply 15.5 million by 1991 (DE 1991a: Table 1.2; DE 1972: Table 103). In itself, the sectoral shift in employment has no particular implications for social welfare. Some commentators see the change as part of a shift towards a post-industrial society, in which industry can fulfil needs with a vastly smaller labour-force and in which greater leisure and higher income generate new demands for entertainment and education. However, in the United Kingdom the shift has been allied with four other changes affecting work that weaken the position of the groups most vulnerable to poverty. First, the decline in the manufacturing sector is in terms of its absolute contribution to the economy of the United Kingdom rather than simply in the numbers employed. Secondly, some of the service sector jobs that are replacing manufacturing work do not provide stable secure incomes. Thirdly, the changes contribute to spatial imbalance in the availability of work. Fourthly, the decline of the trade union movement has weakened the capacity of workers to organise against the most damaging effects of the changes. These changes are discussed in the following paragraphs.

Manufacturing industry is contributing less to the national product of the United Kingdom. The proportion of GDP derived from manufacturing fell from 28 to 22 per cent between 1979 and 1989, whereas that contributed by the service sector rose from 48 to 63 per cent (CSO 1991c: Table 14.7). Technical improvements often associated with the introduction of new technology have led to real improvements in productivity. The long-term record of the United Kingdom economy in terms of productivity is not impressive (Ball, Gray and McDowell 1989: 22). However, substantial strides were made in the decade, with an increase in overall productivity per person employed in manufacturing of 28 per cent over the 1980s, a level greater than that in any of the seven major OECD economies apart from Japan (NIESR 1991a: Table 14). This improvement was achieved at the cost of an overall decline in manufacturing sector employment. The absolute decline of manufacturing is brought out

vividly in balance of trade statistics. The value of imports in manu-
factured goods and raw materials increased from 106 per cent of
exports in 1980 to 130 per cent by 1989 (CSO 1991c: Tables 12.5,
12.6). The fact that trade with other EC countries contributed
some three-fifths of the total deficit is a cause for particular concern when closer links are being made with the Community. Sectoral shifts in the economy weaken the position of the most
marginal manufacturing sector employees.

The big areas of increase in employment within the service sector are in: retail and wholesale distribution, where employment
rose from 2.6 million to 3.1 million between 1981 and 1991; hotels
and catering, where it rose from 0.9 to 1.2 million; recreation and
cultural activities, where it rose from 0.3 to 0.5 million; and banking, finance, insurance and professional services, where it rose
from 1.2 to 2.7 million (DE 1991a: Table 1.4). These areas are
likely to continue their expansion – by over 10 per cent in the
decade to the year 2000, according to one estimate (CSO 1991a:
12). The public-sector-dominated education, medical care, social
welfare and public administration sectors have remained static and
employment in transport and communications has declined.

The second point concerns the fact that the sectoral shift is
associated with the expansion of part-time and insecure patterns of
work. While many service sector jobs provide good incomes, particularly in the financial and professional sector, others do not.
Included in the above totals are part-time jobs, which have increased by 15 per cent over the decade in distribution, 42 per cent
in hotels and catering, 52 per cent in recreation and 58 per cent in
financial services. Thus the new developments involve the substitu-
tion of part-time for full-time work. A number of writers analyse
this change as part of a shift towards a distinction between a core
and a periphery in the occupational structure, the core consisting
of secure, well-paid jobs, the periphery of those employees who
are easily replaced and may be dispensed with in times of slack
demand. McDowell uses this model to estimate the size of the core
at about two-thirds of the labour-force in 1985, about 70 per cent
of them male, and the periphery at one third, 60 per cent of whom
are women (Ball, Gray and McDowell 1989: 169). This distinction
bears a close analogy to the Marxist division between core work-
force and 'industrial reserve army', dressed up to suit modern
conditions. The reality of work-force structuring is likely to be

more complex, containing a number of gradations between different levels of security and reward in work, reflecting labour-market conditions in different parts of the country and confronting various groups – young workers, those approaching retirement, women, black people, those without qualifications – in different ways. None the less, there are clear differences in security and conditions of employment, and change in the occupational structure is making these distinctions more marked. The group whose need of social security over their working life is greatest is increasingly likely to be found among those whose entitlement to traditional benefits is weakest.

Many of the new jobs are filled by women employees. The areas mentioned above provided 1.6 million new jobs for women over the decade, about a third of them part-time. This accounts for almost all the increase in women's employment over the period. The ratio of women's to men's average earnings has remained throughout the 1980s within 1 per cent of the 67 per cent achieved in the late 1970s (CSO 1991a: Table 5.5). The stubbornness of pay relativities, despite equal pay legislation, confirms that employment in the new service sector jobs does not allow women to make real economic progress, although it may widen the range of job opportunities. The most substantial recent study of the labour market, carried out as part of the social change and economic life initiative of the Economic and Social Research Council in 1986 and 1987, concluded that

> there is a clear relation between sex, gender segregation and promotion which works to the disadvantage of women and the advantage of men . . . For the vast majority of women class compounds gender, accentuating the depressive effects of their domestic commitments.
> (Scott 1991: 21–2)

The significance for social security of the expansion of low-waged, part-time and often insecure work in some parts of the service sector is that it increases the group vulnerable to poverty. Many members of this group will be unable to build up adequate insurance records and gain entitlement to insurance benefits. In an economy susceptible to recession, this group contains potential recruits for the army of dependent poor people.

The third issue in economic restructuring concerns the spatial impact of changes in employment. The loss of manufacturing jobs initially affected the large conurbations of London, Manchester,

Clydeside, West Yorkshire and the West Midlands. In the late 1960s and early 1970s urban industrial decline was accompanied by real expansion at the periphery in Scotland, the north, Wales, East Anglia, the south-west and the south-east, so that it could be understood as a process of renewal through relocation. However, by the 1980s it was only the southern regions that experienced growth in manufacturing jobs, in particular East Anglia. Writers such as Massey (1984) point to an increased spatial division between routine low-wage/low-skill work, which tends to be moved to peripheral areas, and research, development and high-tech industry, which are concentrated in such places as the M4 corridor. Thus the marginalisation of groups in the labour force associated with occupational shifts also has a geographical dimension.

These changes have taken place in the context of an absolute decline in manufacturing in the United Kingdom, so that the north, west and centre of the country have experienced a particularly severe regime of unemployment and sub-employment. The growth of the service sector has been similarly uneven. Consumer services tend to follow population patterns, with some variation according to consumption power, whereas producer services locate in relation to the businesses they serve. Accordingly, much of the most rapidly expanding segments of the service sector – finance, banking, professional services, research and development, advertising and market research – is concentrated in the south-east.

The outcome of these imbalances is a clear regional pattern of job losses and gains. Analysis by the Department of Employment showed that 94 per cent of total job losses between 1979 and 1986 took place in Scotland, the north, the Midlands, Wales and Northern Ireland, while the south-east lost only 1 per cent and the south-west 2 per cent and, East Anglia gained 3 per cent (Ball, Gray and McDowell 1989: 165). The regional geography of unemployment discussed earlier follows the pattern. These statistics are aggregates for large areas. There are clear differences in unemployment levels within regions: for example, unemployment in the Thanet travel-to-work area approached 12 per cent in May 1991, as against 6 per cent in neighbouring Canterbury and a south-east regional average of 6.5 per cent. The Thanet level is close to the average for the remaining designated development areas (DE 1991a: Table 2.15). The outcome is that the impact of the changes in unemployment discussed earlier bears more heavily in particular places.

The fourth change in the labour-market that affected the capacity of the weakest groups to resist the impact of changes that increased job insecurity has been the decline of the trade union movement in membership, militancy and legal standing, or, looked at another way, the rise of 'non-unionism' in work (Bassett 1989). The proportion of the civil labour force who were members of unions reached a peak of 53 per cent in 1980 and had fallen to 39 per cent by 1988, the lowest level since the Second World War (CSO 1991a: Table 11.17). Overall, membership in the service sector (58 per cent of employees covered) was as high as that in the manufacturing sector. However, this is due to very high levels of membership in the state industries recently privatised or scheduled for privatisation (energy, water, public transport) or subject to rigorous spending constraint and staff cuts (education, public administration, medicine). In the expanding service areas with large numbers of part-time workers (catering, business services, retail trade), the density of membership remains at about a quarter.

The number of days lost in strikes has fallen over recent years, although major industrial confrontations, which involve many days lost throughout an industry in one dispute, may distort the annual figures. In 1990, 1.9 million work-days were lost through industrial action as against 4.1 million in the previous year and nearly 30 million in the 'winter of discontent' in 1979. The annual average for the 1980s was 7.2 million, against 12.9 million in the 1970s (Bird 1991: 379). Five major pieces of industrial relations legislation have destroyed the closed shop, made sympathetic strike action illegal, emasculated the right to picket, made secondary picketing illegal, made secret ballots compulsory and made unions liable for the cost of lost production associated with strikes. Current proposals in the Citizens' Charter will empower any citizen to take action against a public sector union.

This discussion shows how the long-run decline of manufacturing industry and expansion of service sector work in the United Kingdom has created a pattern of employment that increases the vulnerability to dependency on last-resort social welfare of those unable to gain access to secure and well-paid jobs to dependency on last-resort social welfare. The experience of recession and unemployment in the 1980s increases the likelihood that this group will suffer poverty without access to adequate social protection. Changes in patterns of family life also increase the risk of poverty for some people.

Family life and welfare dependency

Two factors are important in changing patterns of welfare dependency. Changes in birth and death rates have a continuing effect on the age-structure of the population and thus on the relative size of the groups of pensioners and people of working age and on the need for pension provision and for health and social care. At the same time, changes in patterns of family formation, divorce and employment have led to smaller families, to a widening gap between the incomes of single- and dual-earner households, and to an increase in the proportion of single-parent families. The widening diversity of family life imposes greater pressure on the capacity of families to provide incomes and social care. These tensions are especially intense at a time of recession, unemployment and welfare cuts. The number of people of working age vulnerable to welfare dependency has increased.

Recent demographic changes involve two main factors. First, the chances of survival into advanced old age have improved. The result of this change coupled with fluctuations in the birth-rate in the early years of the century is that the proportion of elderly and very elderly people has increased. The number aged over 65 rose from 6.2 to 9.1 million between 1961 and 1991 and is expected to rise to 11.4 million by the first quarter of the next century; the number aged over 80 increased from 1 to 2.2 million and is expected to rise to about 2.9 million over the same period (CSO 1991a: Table 1.2). Old people require pensions and the very elderly group make far greater demands on health and social care services than do younger age-groups.

The influence of ageing is compounded by the operation of the second factor. The post-war baby boom was followed by a fall in the birth-rate below that required to maintain a constant population. This shift affects most advanced countries, and its implications for social policy have been extensively discussed (see, for example, OECD 1988; Ermisch 1990; Taylor-Gooby 1991b: Ch. 3). In Britain the 'total fertility rate' has continued to decline from a post-war peak of 2.9 births per woman in 1964. It fell below the level at which population size remains constant (2.1) in 1974 and by 1990 had reached 1.8. As the generation of baby-boomers come to retire in the second decade of the next century, the proportion as well as the number of elderly people in the population will rise. The size of the group of working age, whose labour must ultimately support them, will have fallen as a result of the decline in the birth-rate. The problems of enhanced demand for social and health care and greater need for pensions mentioned above appear likely to continue into the indefinite future, so that the burden on each member of the population of working age will increase sharply.

A number of commentators have pointed out that the pressure on state welfare can be viewed in an ominous or in a more benign light, depending on one's approach to the statistics. The aged dependency ratio (the population aged 65 or over expressed as a percentage of the number aged between 16 and 64) is likely to increase from 24 to 32 per cent between 1987 and 2027 (Ermisch 1990: Table 5), and this implies that the cost of providing for elderly people will rise, assuming other factors remain constant. However, the burden may be exaggerated. Ermisch calculates that current standards in health and social care could be maintained over the next forty years with only a 12-per-cent increase in current levels of expenditure (1990: 43), since the elderly population remains a minority in the total population, and total health and social care spending is relatively low in this country. Disney points out that economic growth will play a large part in absorbing the cost of future pension commitments (1985). After all, society successfully coped with a 50-per-cent increase in the numbers of people of pensionable age between 1951 and 1991, a larger increase than that anticipated over the next four decades. A careful analysis of economic activity rates by Falkingham shows that demographic changes are likely to reduce pressures on social welfare spending elsewhere – for example, on unemployed people – and may result in an upward movement of the age of retirement (1989: 229–31). Others note that current patterns of dependency among the elderly may change with improvements in the health of elderly people.

Changes in population structure do not impose insuperable problems for social policy. It is noteworthy that it is in the United Kingdom, a country which faces a relatively mild problem of increased dependency, but which has distinguished itself in commitment to welfare cuts, that demographic change has been used most explicitly to justify reductions in pensions. The situation in relation to social care is less clear. The current policy of 'care in the community' relies largely on the voluntary sector and on the unwaged work of carers, who are mainly women. A recent survey indicates that one in seven of the adult population provides such care (OPCS 1987). One estimate puts the value of the work of carers (calculated at the rates of pay of home helps) at somewhere between £15 and £24 billion a year in 1987, as against less than £4 billion spent on the whole of personal social services (FPSC 1989). Changes in family structure and in patterns of women's employment may reduce the availability of such care in future years, increasing the cost to the state.

Families are becoming smaller, separation and divorce are more common and more middle-aged women are engaged in full-time work. Elderly people are less likely to be in a position where they can call on the exclusive support of female kin. In addition, unpaid care-work may impose substantial financial pressure on carers, so that they become dependent on state benefits. Analysis of general household data for 1985 by Maria Evandrou shows that poverty is concentrated among particular groups of carers: those who are sole carers and who share a household with the dependent person are over one and a half times as likely to live at or below the supplementary benefit poverty line (Evandrou 1990: Table 13).

Demographic change is not directly linked to increased dependency among able-bodied people. In the long term the increased pressure on the population of working age may generate opportunities for paid employment. However, there are indirect links to dependency through the exclusion from the labour-market of some of those who provide care, which exacerbates reliance on last-resort benefits under the present system of state welfare.

Demographic change interacts with social factors in producing changes in the pattern of family life. The most obvious change is the greater diversity of family forms. The decline in fertility coupled with an increase in the number of married women who enter the labour-market has resulted in smaller families, completed earlier in people's lives. The number of single-person households has increased both among younger and among elderly people. These changes open up the possibility of a widening income gap between dual-earner, single-earner and no-earner households. To some extent this division has been mitigated by the relatively low pay available to most women and the poor child-care facilities which bar many women with dependent children from full-time work. The economic activity rate for women over 16 rose from 44 to 54 per cent between 1971 and 1991, while that for men fell from 81 to 74 per cent (CSO 1991a: Table 4.6). However, women with dependent children were much less likely to be in or seeking employment and roughly two-thirds of them were in part-time jobs (OPCS 1990b: Table 11). The United Kingdom has a higher proportion of women in employment than in any EC country except Denmark, but women in the United Kingdom work shorter hours on average than those in any EC country except the Netherlands (CSO 1991a: Table 4.8, 4.18). The difference is attributable principally to the lack of state-supported child-care facilities in the United Kingdom.

The gap between dual- and single-earner households is thus not as great as it might otherwise be, although good data on the division is not conveniently available. The best approximation is the Family Expenditure Survey, which publishes information on the relation between the number of workers in a household and average income, without indicating the marital status of the individuals. Between 1979 and 1989 the average income of two-worker households rose from 135 to 142 per cent of that of single-earner households (CSO 1991b: Table 22; DE 1979: Table 46). The division is likely to be mapped over the family life-cycle, since motherhood reduces women's participation in employment.

The gap between households which have access to incomes from employment and those with no earner is exacerbated by the organisation of the social security means-test, which effectively treats couples as a unit, unlike the national insurance unemployment benefit. People with unemployed partners must take home more than the couple's benefit entitlement to make working worthwhile. Evidence from the General Household Survey shows that women whose partners are unemployed are twice as likely to be unemployed themselves as those whose partners are in work (OPCS 1990a: Table 9.55). As the insurance system for unemployed people collapses under the pressure of long-term claiming, employment becomes less attractive for some groups.

The main factor contributing to the diversity of the family is the increasing number of single-parent families. Under the present welfare regime, this has an immediate and direct relevance to poverty and to welfare dependency. The number of one-parent families more than doubled from just over half a million in 1971 to over 1.2 million by the end of the 1980s. The proportion of all families headed by a sole parent rose from 8 to 17 per cent (OPCS

1990b: Table 9). This rate is rather lower than that in the United States, where about a quarter of all families with dependent children are one-parent families, equivalent to that of Sweden and Denmark and slightly higher than that in France and Germany (Ermisch 1990: 17). About a tenth of single-parent families are headed by fathers. The most common factor leading to single parenthood is marital break-up: three-fifths of single mothers are divorced or separated (OPCS 1990b: Table 9).

One-parent families run a very high risk of poverty. The first major sample survey of one-parent families in the United Kingdom, carried out in 1989, found that only 15 per cent of those interviewed had not claimed income support at any time during the period over which they had been single parents. Only 40 per cent had any income at all from earnings, and about a quarter of these gained relatively small amounts, below the benefit disregard level (Bradshaw and Millar 1991: 95–97). Table 1.1 shows that the numbers in poverty increased rapidly over the 1980s, but the group of single parents living at or below last-resort assistance level expanded in size at a rate considerably in excess of the overall increase. By 1987 nine out of ten individuals in one-parent families were in poverty on this definition. Benefit constraint and rising unemployment in the late 1980s and early 1990s will have damaged the position of this group further. The proportion of one-parent families claiming means-tested support has continued to rise, increasing from 64 to 68 per cent between 1987 and 1991 (DSS 1991a: Table 15).

The changes of the recent past have increased the vulnerability of some marginalised groups to welfare dependency. Changes in population structure and the associated restructuring of pensions are likely to increase divisions in living standards among retirement pensioners. The demands placed on those providing social care are likely to increase the use of benefits among the poorest members of this group, and this effect will probably become more marked as the number of elderly people needing care rises. Changes in employment patterns tend to widen the gap in incomes between dual-earner and no-earner households. The clearest link between family change and the development of the new poverty lies in the circumstances of one-parent families. This group has expanded rapidly over recent years and suffers a very high incidence of poverty. Current trends in divorce and separation indicate that the numbers of single-parent families will continue to rise. The social divisions implicit in this development pose a serious challenge, which current social policy is unable to meet.

The dependency of single parents on state welfare is seen as pathological by those who defend the 'dependency culture' thesis, while dependency on market income or on a male family breadwinner is not. This approach leads to calls for the further reduction of welfare support for lone parents. One writer, who emphasises the contribution of births outside marriage to the total number of one-parent families, writes: 'as long as the benefit level is well above the threshold, the dynamics of social incentives will continue to work in favour of illegitimacy as over time the advantages of legal marriage become less clear and the disadvantages more obvious' (Murray 1990a: 31). Others, who acknowledge that divorce is a far more significant route into lone parenthood, suggest that 'divorce should be made harder not easier to obtain' (Raison 1991: 275). Current policy makes a slightly higher rate of child benefit and of income support available, but is unwilling to undertake the · substantial expansion of child benefit or the establishment of a specific benefit for single parents which is essential to lift this group out of poverty, or indeed the provision of child-care facilities on a scale adequate to enable them to find paid jobs (Coote, Harman and Hewitt 1990: 51–6). At the time of writing, legislation to strengthen the system of maintenance payments by absent parents is under discussion. Evidence from Australia, where such a scheme is in operation, indicates that it is unlikely to improve the position of the majority of single parents (see Chapter 3).

Government policy, inequality and dependency

The long-run changes in patterns of work and of family life described above took place in the context of economic and political shifts that further damaged the position of poor groups. The major economic shift was the recession consequent on the oil-price rises of 1975 and 1979, which struck the economy of the United Kingdom with especial force. The political changes concern the return to office in 1979 of a government committed to a radical programme of reducing the role of the state in welfare. The development of the official view that poverty among people of working age is largely the product of dependency culture and is to be eradicated by punitive welfare policies has already been discussed. The detail of how those policies involve cuts in benefits, a weakening of social welfare entitlement, a harsher regime of surveillance and a real increase in the costs of living for this group and are associated with the abolition of the greater part of the structure of regional and job-creation policies is analysed in Chapter 3. Here we wish to draw attention to the fact that they formed part of a more far-reaching government strategy of inequality that operated for the most part outside the traditional pattern of welfare state services.

During the 1980s, inequality in the United Kingdom grew more marked as a result of an increase in the spread of market incomes, shifts in the pattern of employment by household and a decline in the redistributive impact of taxation and social benefits. The Family Expenditure Survey shows that the market incomes of the bottom tenth of the income distribution by household fell from 30 per cent of the median in 1979 to 25 per cent in 1989, whereas the incomes of the top 10 per cent rose from 204 to 233 per cent (DE 1979: Table 48; CSO 1990: Table 24). The combined impact of cuts in income tax, especially for high earners, and of increases in VAT, national insurance contributions and local taxes has been to redistribute the burden of taxation downwards. Over the period from 1978/9 to 1990/1, the changes resulted in net losses for a married couple with two children at any level of income below one-and-a-half times average earnings (Hansard, Written Answers: vol. 176, cols 700–8; vol. 164, cols 634–56).

The net result of these changes was that the redistributive impact of taxation and social welfare benefits over the 1980s was weakened. State intervention continues to redistribute to the poorest groups; otherwise those with no other form of income would face serious problems. Official estimates by the Central Statistical Office, which take into account household size, housing costs, the various forms of taxation paid and the contribution of cash benefits and publicly provided services, indicate that ahe share of national incomes going to the poorest tenth of the population fell from 9.5 to 7.6 per cent between 1979 and 1987. The share going to the richest tenth increased from 35 to 41 per cent (CSO 1991a: Table 5.16). Unfortunately, no statistics for more recent years have been published.

Despite these changes, much of the structure of state welfare spending on mass services remains intact. Those who focus attention primarily on state spending on the main services for the bulk of the population tend to conclude that the attack on state welfare in the 1980s has had little effect. One authoritative study concludes:

> the welfare state . . . is very robust. Over the thirteen years from 1974 to 1987, welfare policy successfully weathered an economic hurricane in the mid-1970s and an ideological blizzard in the 1980s. The resources going to public welfare were maintained. (Le Grand, 1990: 350)

Attention to patterns of overall inequality and to the experiences of the most needy groups falls outside the scope of such inquiries. It shows a rather different picture. The policies pursued by government in the 1980s failed to counteract a trend towards greater inequality. This further weakened the position of the most vulnerable groups and reduced the likelihood that substantial political force could be mobilised to defend their interests.

Conclusion: the irresistible rise of dependency culture

The changes in employment and in family structures discussed in this chapter operate over the long term. Among their effects is a tendency to isolate particular groups of people of working age, who become vulnerable to poverty and are ill-defended by the traditional structure of insurance-based welfare. The recessions of the mid-1970s, early 1980s and early 1990s have focused attention on the welfare needs of the marginalised poor. The new right administration established in 1979 desired to cut spending and to reinforce the supremacy of the market and family institutions that it assumed were the natural settings in which human needs should be met. In this social, economic and political context the view that government nourished and sustained the assumed dependency culture of poor people through misplaced generosity was an idea whose time had arrived. One result is an attempt to characterise last-resort benefit claimants of working age as an underclass, superfluous to the essential commercial and social life of society. In the next chapter we turn to this debate, and to the notions of dependence and independence that are implicit in it.

CHAPTER 2

CULTURE, STRUCTURE AND FAILURE: THE UNDERCLASS DEBATE

the changes made in the scope of welfare provision since 1979 . . . amount to a mini-revolution, and have played a part in creating an underclass. (Field 1989: 90)

while the Government claims that it is targeting help on those in greatest need, it is simultaneously increasing the numbers caught, in the Government's terminology, in a 'dependency culture'. (*ibid.*: 131)

This belief, expressed by Frank Field, veteran poverty campaigner and Labour MP, typifies an increasingly popular view that, by the end of the 1980s, a new 'underclass' had emerged in Britain: an underclass separated in terms of income, life chances and political aspirations from the mass of the population as welfare benefit levels fail to keep pace with changes in earnings and as the labour-market and the very basis of citizenship are subjected to radical restructuring.

Just as changes in social and economic policy were argued by some on the left to have contributed to the creation of an underclass, so the government for its part railed against the cultural values ascribed to that underclass. Politicians of the right condemned the 'dependency culture' of welfare benefit recipients, contrasting it with the 'enterprise culture' of those who seek to create wealth and opportunity. The paradox was concisely summed up by P. Brown and Sparks: 'It is an inherent feature of Thatcherism to protest against social trends which are of its own making' (1989: xiv). At the level of political discourse, Thatcherism sought to blame its victims by constructing the pejorative notion of 'dependency culture', while the opponents of Thatcherism sought to blame government policy by constructing a socio-structural notion of 'underclass'. The two notions are mirror images of the same discursive construct and each serves to feed and to taint the other.

The essence of our argument is that notions such as 'dependency culture' and 'underclass' are discursive rather than objective phenomena. In the 1990s, following Margaret Thatcher's fall from grace, it may be that such terms will for a time lose their ascendancy. Our project, however, is not a retrospective critique of Thatcherism, but an enquiry into the meaning and symbolic relevance of a discursive construct which in its form is not so much a specific product of Thatcherism (or Reaganism in the United States) as a consequence of modernity (see Giddens 1990) and a challenge to our understanding of the future scope of welfare provision.

Delinquency, dependency and the underclass

The concept of 'underclass', as Macnicol has observed, has a 'long and undistinguished pedigree' (1987: 315) and, in various guises and at various times, has been popular both in the United Kingdom and in the United States. It is a concept which, empirically speaking, is hopelessly imprecise and, as a theoretical device, has repeatedly conflated structural and cultural definitions of not only poverty, but of crime as well. It is a concept which seems periodically to be forged at points where structural and cultural explanations conflict.

The ultra-conservative American political scientist, Charles Murray, recently visited Britain to see to what extent the underclass 'disease' was spreading. He concluded that 'Britain has a growing population of working aged, healthy people who live in a different world from other Britons, who are raising their children to live in it, and whose values are now contaminating the life of entire neighbourhoods' (Murray 1990a: 4). But, responding to the question 'How big is Britain's underclass?', he conceded 'It all depends on how one defines its membership; trying to take a head count is a waste of time. The size of the underclass can be made to look huge or insignificant, depending on what one wants the answer to be' (*ibid.*: 23). For Murray, the phenomena which best predict 'an underclass in the making' are illegitimacy, violent crime and drop-out from the labour-force. It is through his perception of an underclass that he is able to posit an interrelationship between such disparate phenomena. Potentially, the underclass can be as extensive as one's preoccupations with what does or does not constitute deviant behaviour.

'Underclass' is therefore a potent term which can capture popular fears and concerns regarding, we shall suggest, delinquency on the one hand and dependency on the other. Delinquency and dependency, however they may be explained, are perceived as inherently dangerous phenomena because, as Liebow put it, 'the one threatens the property, peace and good order of society at large; the other drains its purse' (1967: 6). We would argue that the underclass concept is most interesting, not for its explanatory value, but for the way in which it has so often drawn together and illuminated preoccupations with delinquency and dependency and for the way in which it permits often unspoken associations between the two.

Michel Foucault, in his celebrated account of the prison, attempted to deconstruct the term 'delinquency', arguing that, as a particular form of illegality, 'delinquency' is not necessarily the most socially harmful; it is merely the form against which penal policy and the penal apparatus are directed. Delinquency is thus 'an effect of penality . . . that makes it possible to differentiate, accommodate and supervise illegalities' (1977: 276). It is not that the penal system has thus far failed to eliminate crime: on the contrary, says Foucault, it has

> succeeded extremely well in producing delinquency, as a specific type, a politically or economically less dangerous . . . form of illegality; in producing delinquents in an apparently marginal, but in fact centrally supervised milieu; in producing the delinquent as a pathological subject. (*ibid.*: 277)

It may be argued in a similar vein that 'poverty' may be seen as an 'effect' of social security and relief systems (Dean 1991: Ch. 4); that poverty is a particular form of material deprivation that is sustained and rendered manageable through the very policy mechanisms calculated to prevent or relieve it. There is a danger, however, of glossing over the diversity of the discursive formulations which constitute the notion of 'poverty' and we are here considering 'dependency' rather than 'poverty' (just as Foucault considered 'delinquency' rather than 'crime' or 'deviance').

Benthamite social commentators such as Patrick Colquhoun in a 'Treatise on Indigence' (1815) had insisted (in terms not dissimilar from those of modern Thatcherites) that poverty was no more than the natural and necessary condition of free labour, whereas the true social evil was 'indigence' (i.e. dependency). The nineteenth-century English Poor Law was therefore quite explicitly directed, not against poverty, but against 'pauperism', a status of dependency which poor relief set out simultaneously to define and to punish.

Nevertheless, whenever 'poverty' is rediscovered as a socio-structural 'problem', as it was in England in the latter part of the nineteenth century and has been in both the United States and the United Kingdom in the latter part of the twentieth century, so it seems are notions of 'residuum' or 'underclass' reinvented; all-embracing notions which conveniently fudge socio-structural definition with cultural caricature and can thus seek to address discursively constituted threats of dependency and delinquency as if they were objective social phenomena. Thus in England (and especially London) in the latter part of the nineteenth century there arose an image and indeed a fear of 'a minority of the still unregenerate poor' (Stedman-Jones 1971: 11): 'This group was variously referred to as "the dangerous class", the casual poor or more characteristically, as the "residuum" ' (*ibid.*).

Stedman-Jones suggests that a preoccupation with the 'residuum' was universal in conservative, liberal and socialist thought alike and that it stemmed from a fear that the 'residuum' might contaminate the 'respectable working class' or that it might even expand to such proportions as to envelop it. We would argue that the impetus to define a 'residuum' or 'underclass' has always stemmed from a concern to defend other assumptions concerning the integrity of existing social relations of production and reproduction and, in particular, of labour and the family. Proponents of the underclass concept have never been able satisfactorily to define or locate the members of their underclass other than by reference to the variety of afflictions or shortcomings which they supposedly exhibit (whether such afflictions be real or imagined, or the shortcomings culpable or innocent). In effect, therefore, the underclass is always negatively defined, not by criteria peculiar to the underclass, but by the criteria of productive work and/or family life from which, for any number of reasons, the 'residuum' or 'underclass' is excluded. What is defined is not a class, but a residue; a stratum existing under or beneath the norms of class.

Even Marx and Engels, when defining the 'lumpenproletariat', spoke of ' "the dangerous class", the social scum, that passively rotting mass thrown off by the lowest layers of old society' and were primarily concerned lest this underclass might not be drawn into the wider proletarian movement but become instead a 'bribed tool of reactionary intrigue' (1970: 25). The dilemma facing the British Labour Party in the 1990s is seen by Field as one of how to build support among the mass of better-off voters for policies which would 'spring' his posited underclass from its current position (1989: 156). The underclass, even if it is not actually a threat, is perceived as a potential impediment upon labour and the labour movement.

It is instructive, therefore, to consider the notions of 'residuum' and 'underclass' as discursive rather than objective phenomena, since they furnish a commentary upon the broader social relations which they have helped and are still helping to constitute.

The history of a discourse

Like all underclasses, the 'residuum' of Victorian England was ostensibly regarded by its various proponents in different ways. At one extreme, the hard-liners of the Charity Organisation Society, dedicated to decreasing 'not suffering but sin' (Henrietta Barnett, quoted in Stedman-Jones 1971: 271), viewed the problem of the residuum as a consequence of 'demoralisation'. At the other extreme, new liberals and socialists, influenced by secular and social Darwinist ideas, began to explain the residuum more in terms of a theory of 'degeneration' (Stedman Jones 1971).

Henry Mayhew (1861), a journalist and champion of the downtrodden, had encompassed within his definition of the 'non-working' class three very disparate groups: those with physical defects, those with mental or intellectual defects (the 'lunatics and idiots') and those with moral defects (such as 'the vagrant, the professional mendicant and the criminal'). This taxonomy of defects was founded on a general belief that

while he [Mayhew] wishes to arouse the public to the social necessity of enabling every person throughout the kingdom to live in
comfort by his labour, [he] has no wish to teach the humbler classes
that they can possibly obtain a livelihood by any other means. (from
correspondence quoted in Stedman-Jones 1971: 267)

Similarly, the pioneer social investigator, Charles Booth, who
had demonstrated to his own alarm that in the 1880s 35 per cent of
the population of Tower Hamlets was 'at all times more or less in
want' (Booth 1887: 375), was careful to distinguish the 'residuum'
as but a relatively small group within the ranks of the poor making
up he estimated only 8.4 per cent of the total population in 1891
(Booth 1902: vol. 2, 21). Booth divided the 'residuum' into two
sub-classes. Class A, whom he described as 'loafers' or as 'the
vicious and semi-criminal', he estimated to comprise less than 2%
of the East London population. Class B, whom he regarded as
merely 'feckless', improvident and beyond self-improvement, was
a larger group whose membership tended inevitably to overlap
with Class C ('irregular earners') (Booth 1902: vol. 1). Booth is by
convention remembered as an opponent of the rigid doctrines of
the Charity Organisation Society and as an advocate of 'limited
socialism', with state pensions for the 'respectable' working class,
but just as central to his prescription was the proposal that Classes
A and B, the 'residuum', should be dispersed out of London to
labour colonies:

> To the rich the very poor are a sentimental interest. *To the poor they
> are a crushing load.* The poverty of the poor is mainly the result of
> the competition of the very poor. The entire removal of this very
> poor class out of the daily struggle for existence I believe to be the
> only solution to the problem. [emphasis added] (*ibid.*: 154)

In spite of competing diagnoses and prescriptions, there appears
in Victorian England to have been something amounting to a consensus that the 'problem' had more to do with protecting the integrity and aspirations of the 'respectable' working class and the
'honest' poor than it did with the afflictions of the residuum itself.

The ground for America's discovery of an 'underclass' in the
1980s was, it seems, laid some twenty years before when the
United States rediscovered poverty (see Harrington 1962). A component part of the common wisdom which had informed 1960s'
liberalism at the time of President Johnson's 'War on Poverty' was

an implicit or explicit acceptance of the 'culture of poverty' thesis, popularly ascribed to the anthropologist, Oscar Lewis. Whereas Charles Booth had applied moral criteria in order to make a purportedly empirical distinction between a minority 'residuum' and 'the poor', Lewis applied purportedly objective 'cultural' criteria so as to conclude that at 'a rough guess . . . about 20% of the population below the poverty line . . . in the United States have characteristics which would justify classifying their way of life as a culture of poverty' (1968: 57). The term 'culture', according to Lewis, implied 'a design for living which is passed down from generation to generation' (1965: xxiv) and he claimed to have observed 'remarkable similarities in family structure, interpersonal relations, time orientations, value systems, spending patterns, and the sense of community in lower class settlements in London, Glasgow, Paris, Harlem and Mexico City' (*ibid.*). Such cultural patterns, Lewis claimed, were transmitted from generation to generation so as to reinforce a recurring cycle of poverty.

While such a thesis could be called on in aid of expanded relief programmes aimed at breaking these cycles of poverty, it also provided fuel for more conservative and eugenicist commentators, who could now point to a hereditary dimension to poverty and a pathology not only of poor individuals but of poor families. Indeed, a storm of controversy arose in 1965 when Daniel Moynihan, then Assistant Secretary of Labor, produced a White House report on the 'Negro family' which concluded that 'the fundamental source of the weakness of the Negro community' was 'the deterioration of the Negro family'. Wilson (1987) claims that it was revulsion against the racist application of the culture of poverty thesis that deterred further interest in poverty matters on the part of the liberal academic community, and that effectively deferred the onset of a debate which has more recently emerged in the United States about the American 'underclass'.

Wilson himself defines the underclass as

> that heterogeneous grouping of families and individuals who are outside the mainstream of the American occupational system. Included . . . are individuals who lack training and skills and either experience long-term unemployment or are not members of the labor force, individuals who are engaged in street crime and other forms of aberrant behaviour, and families that experience long-term spells of poverty and/or welfare dependency. (*ibid.*: 8)

This, however, is only one of several definitions and much argument and energy has been expended trying to determine the size or extent of the American underclass. Estimates, based on differing measures, vary widely from less than 1 per cent of the population to more than 10 per cent (Dahrendorf 1987: 4). In spite of this lack of agreement or precision, there is supposedly a body of evidence which 'is at the moment taken by all shades of opinion to indicate a real phenomenon' (Manning 1989: 8).

The phenomenon, as may be seen from Wilson's definition, is constituted at the point where structural considerations concerning the American occupational system intersect with cultural considerations to do with delinquency, dependency and the family. The American underclass finds itself at the focus of a social policy debate between those on the right who would abolish federal welfare and income support measures and those on the left who would expand or at least redirect them. Commentators such as Murray (1984) argue (just as John Moore has done in the United Kingdom) that welfare creates a dependency culture; it embodies a set of disincentives which undermine the labour-market and the family. Against this view, commentators of the left and centre have demonstrated that the effect of welfare on labour supply has been overestimated and that the rising numbers of female-headed families (i.e. 'unsupported' mothers) is a demographic trend unrelated to welfare programmes (for a summary of this debate see Manning 1989: 9).

However, the political and academic debate is grounded upon a set of 'common-sense' assumptions about the nature of the problem which the underclass is supposed to represent; and upon general and diverse preoccupations, not only with poverty, but with very real and pressing issues, such as race, urban crime and the ghetto. Wacquant and Wilson speak of 'the inter-related set of phenomena captured by the term underclass' (1989: 8). It is of course the plasticity of the term underclass and its ability to 'capture' a range of concerns which has made it so popular and which enabled a New York journalist, Ken Auletta, to first bring the term to prominence in the early 1980s.

Auletta played in a sense the role of a modern-day Mayhew. He concluded

> for most of the 25 to 29 million Americans officially classified as poor, poverty is not a permanent condition. . . . most of these

people overcome poverty after a generation or two. There are no precise numbers on this, but an estimated 9 million Americans do not assimilate. They are the underclass. Generally speaking they can be grouped into four distinct categories: (a) the *passive poor*, usually long term welfare recipients; (b) the *hostile* street criminals who terrorize most cities, and who are often school dropouts and drug addicts; (c) the *hustlers*, who, like street criminals may not be poor and who earn their livelihood in an underground economy, but rarely commit violent crimes; (d) the *traumatized* drunks, drifters, homeless shopping bag ladies and released mental patients who frequently roam or collapse on city streets. (1982: xvi)

Like Mayhew, Auletta maps out a taxonomy of defects which incorporates both the delinquent and the dependant and which constitutes 'both America's peril and shame' (*ibid.*: xviii). Auletta none the less paints a sympathetic portrait of the underclass and voices support for programmes directed to providing opportunities and assistance to its members. Yet, claiming to be neither a conservative nor a liberal, he acknowledges that welfare does encourage dependency and the break-up of families. The problem, he says, is that both sides of the social policy debate talk past each other: 'We could extricate ourselves from this rhetorical quagmire if we simply admitted what common sense rather than doctrine dictated: Both sides are right' (*ibid.*: 306).

The rejoinder to this assertion must surely be that, if 'common sense' can dictate that welfare recipients and street criminals are related parts of the same problem, then perhaps neither side can be right. The underclass debate has in fact cemented a consensus of belief, not about the nature of the threat, but about what it is that is supposedly threatened, namely the labour-market and the family system.

Britain's emerging underclass

The underclass debate in the United States, while coinciding with the advent of the Reagan era of welfare retrenchment, harked back in many respects to an earlier debate over the culture of poverty thesis. A broadly similar pattern may be detected in the United Kingdom, where the underclass debate was awakened by critics of social polarisation under Thatcherism, yet resonates with a variant of the culture of poverty thesis originally proposed in the 1970s by none other than Sir Keith (now Lord) Joseph, who was then Secretary of State for Social Services in the Heath government, and was later to become a close adviser and supporter of Margaret Thatcher.

Between 1972 and 1974, Joseph delivered a series of speeches in which he identified a phenomenon he called the 'cycle of deprivation'. Like Lewis, he claimed there was a process by which multiple deprivation and social disadvantage could be intergenerationally transmitted:

> Do we not know only too certainly that among the children of this generation there are some doomed to an uphill struggle against the disadvantages of a deprived family background? Do we not know that many of them will not be able to overcome the disadvantages and will become in their turn the parents of deprived families? (Joseph: 1972)

Extensive research subsequently commissioned by the Department of Health and Social Security and the Social Science Research Council demonstrated nothing of the sort (see M. Brown and Madge 1982). The intergenerational cycle of Joseph's popular imagination, if it could be said to exist at all, was in reality frequently broken by individuals and families alike: the evidence suggested that there is no single, simple explanation of deprivation and that the transmission of deprivation is influenced, not by any one cultural or structural factor, but by 'many critical chains of events' (*ibid.*: 266). None the less, the seeds of a debate had been sown.

Peter Townsend, who condemned Joseph's cycle of deprivation thesis as 'a mixture of popular stereotypes and ill developed, mostly contentious scientific notions' (1974:8), sought to explain the persistence and the patterns of deprivation in structural rather than cultural terms:

> A large, and proportionately increasing, section of the population are neither part of the paid workforce nor members of the households of that workforce . . . they have been denied access to paid employment, conceded incomes equivalent in value to bare subsistence, attracted specially defined low social status as minority groups, and accommodated, as a result, within the social structure as a kind of modern 'underclass'. (1979: 920)

Similarly, Bill Jordan, while dismissive of Joseph's cultural thesis (1974), had argued that those dependent on state income support had been assigned by the welfare state to a newly created under-class or 'claiming class' (1973).

While those on the right sought to identify a culturally distinct deprived minority, those on the left sought to identify a struc-turally defined underclass. The 'culturalists' were concerned with the 'problem family'; the 'structuralists' with 'poverty'. The term 'underclass' tended, however, to be used rather casually during the 1970s and it was only in the 1980s that the influential Ralph Dahrendorf brought it to centre stage, presenting the underclass as 'a cancer which eats away at the texture of societies and metasta-sizes in ways which can increasingly be felt in all their parts' (1987: 3). Dahrendorf sought to concert the analysis of economic restruc-turing and demographic trends with ideas about culture and counter-culture, concluding that

> something like a million British people are characterized by a syn-drome of deprivation which often leads to a 'ghetto' existence. The syndrome is also a vicious circle. Once people have got into it, they find it hard to break out. They are not clinging on precariously to a 'normal' world of jobs and life chances, but settling into a life cycle of their own. This is sufficiently different from the rest to make them feel they have no stake in the official society. (*ibid.*: 4)

Concern has been expressed that, in detecting new divisions in British society, proponents of the underclass thesis may be running ahead of the evidence (see R. Pahl 1988: 258). But, evidence apart, the hypothesis advanced by Dahrendorf is in many ways wider than that taken on board in the American debate, because his concept of underclass is accompanied by a challenge to conven-tional assumptions about the future feasibility of full-employment ('Work itself', he says, 'is a part of the problem': (1987: 9)) and about the adequacy of the protection of our modern rights of citizenship (which he claims are fundamentally violated by the existence of a powerless, disenfranchised underclass). Yet within the discourse of the hypothesis is an implicit link between, on the one hand, questions of state dependency and the limitations of the labour-market and, on the other hand the non-compliance of the excluded with the norms of society: crime, says Dahrendorf, 'is one of the modes of life of the underclass' (*ibid.*: 5). The possibility that the underclass might expand or harden is regarded as a threat to Britain's social and political stability and also to its 'moral hygiene' (*ibid.*: 11).

It was within this climate that Frank Field (1989) introduced his own account of the emergence of Britain's underclass (to which we have already referred). Field's simplistically defined underclass has much in common with Jordan's 'claiming class' of the 1970s and encompasses three disparate groups: the long-term unemployed, single parents and elderly people without occupational pensions. The only thing which the three groups have in common is dependency on state benefits and, indeed, the tax and benefit systems are Field's central preoccupation. Field clearly demonstrates the scale upon which economic inequalities have widened during the 1980s, but his choice of the term 'underclass' appears to have been made primarily for dramatic effect. The almost gratuitous use of such a term is significant none the less. Field effectively sidesteps Dahrendorf's broader arguments by accepting that an underclass culture exists, but insisting that we should not blame victims but strive in the longer term to return to full employment and a fairer welfare state. Dependency culture is by implication accepted as a real phenomenon and the 'underclass' is admitted as a legitimate term in political and social policy discourse.

The informal economy

A central and legitimate concern of social policy commentators, like Field, has been the effect of the unemployment and poverty 'traps' resulting from the interaction between low wage rates, the tax structure and means-tested benefit levels. Field argues that these traps operate heavily against the underclass and those at its margin and that

> One way open to the individual to beat these two traps is to make dishonest returns to the tax office, the benefit office or both. Participation in the black economy [sic] may produce substantial short-term gains for the individual concerned, but these gains have to be offset against the 'rights of citizenship' that go with a complete national insurance contributions record. Such exclusion from citizenship is again the mark of the underclass. (1989: 131)

Here Field gives voice to a popular assumption which links the notion of underclass to the existence of a 'hidden' or informal economy. If there were a distinct class of persons systematically engaged in illegal forms of economic activity, there is a sense in which it could legitimately be regarded as an 'underclass'. The evidence, however, suggests otherwise.

There are no reliable estimates of the size of the informal economy. Such estimates as are made are based either on anecdotal evidence or on macro-economic measures of the discrepancies between reported income and expenditure measures of gross domestic product. Such measures do not accurately identify the participants in the informal economy and, as Catherine Hakim (1989) points out, they are likely to include up to five million people whose activities are not in any respect illegal. Included in this figure are some three million regular workers whose earnings do not exceed the tax and/or national insurance thresholds and some two million workers whose 'jobs' do not count as such in official statistics and whose earnings are too trivial to count for tax or welfare benefit purposes. Hakim suggests that speculation about the scale of an ill-defined informal economy has had a stigmatising effect which reinforces distinctions, not between the employed and the unemployed but between primary or 'core' workers in stable employment and secondary or 'peripheral' workers engaged in the expanding sphere of part-time, flexible, irregular or precarious forms of 'self-'employment.

Further light is cast upon the significance of the informal economy by Ray Pahl's research findings. Of the adults included in his study on Sheppey, 5 per cent acknowledged doing work 'on [their] own account for extra money'. Of these a third were housewives without regular employment and the remainder were working, rather than unemployed (1984). Pahl went on to observe that those doing informal work were likely to be members of households in which there was already one or more full-time worker (and/or to be full-time workers themselves). The opportunities for participating in the informal economy were greater for the members of already 'work-rich' households than for 'work-poor' households, which usually lacked the material resources and/or the social contacts necessary for such participation. Pahl's argument is that employers' strategies and household work practices act in concert to compound the process of social polarisation (see R. Pahl 1988 and, for example, Roberts, Finnegan and Gallie 1985).

The intersecting notions of 'informal economy' and 'underclass' are bound up with certain complex processes of social polarisation, and may even fuel such processes. However, neither notion relates in practice to the other, since the participants in the informal economy cannot justly be characterised as members of the underclass (or vice versa), and both notions arise from assumptions which are equally inexact.

Who's to blame?

The inexactitude of the underclass notion persists in spite of some sophisticated and superficially rigorous efforts to conceptualise an underclass. The social and economic processes which have reconstituted the class structure of the United Kingdom over the past two decades (see Chapter 1 above and, for example, Sarre 1989) have called forth various attempts to reconceptualise our understanding of class and classes. In one such attempt, W.G. Runciman has posited the existence of no fewer than seven classes, including an underclass, since

> That there is below the two working classes an underclass which constitutes a separate category of roles is as readily demonstrable as that there is an upper class above the middle class . . . But the term must be understood to stand not for a group or a category of workers systematically disadvantaged within the labour market . . . but for those members of British society whose roles place them more or less permanently at the economic level where benefits are paid by the state to those unable to participate in the labour market at all . . . Many are members of ethnic minorities, many are women (particularly single mothers), and some are both, but it is not ethnicity or gender as such which defines their class position. They are typically the long term unemployed, but some may supplement whatever they receive from the state by undeclared labour, mendicancy, barter or petty theft . . . Even if they are not, except for personal as opposed to institutional reasons, living below the margin of subsistence, they are 'the poor' of today. But like the upper class, they need to be distinguished as such in institutionalised, not statistical terms, and it is because they can that they constitute the seventh of the seven classes. (1990: 388)

Runciman's class schema purports to be based on the roles which people play in terms of their institutional relations with the market and the economic power (or lack of it) which characterises such roles. The problems with this would seem to be twofold: first, the impermanence of his underclass; and second, that its conceptual definition rests upon institutional relations, not with the market, but with the state.

Runciman acknowledges that 'for the purpose of assigning roles and their incumbents to their appropriate classes, the concept of career is, on any theory, crucial' (*ibid.*: 379). But in the case of the underclass, just how does one determine what constitutes a 'career' based on receipt of state benefits? If single mothers on benefit are members of the underclass, then the evidence of the 1980s suggests that such membership tends to be remarkably transitory, since single mothers are likely to remain as lone parents on average for only 35 months (Ermisch, cited in J. Brown 1990). What is more, single (i.e. never-married) mothers represent a relatively small proportion of all lone mothers on benefit, the majority of whom are separated, divorced or widowed (see again J. Brown 1990): are these women to count as members of an underclass or is there some arbitrary point at which the trajectory of their 'careers' both past and future lifts them above such classification? Similarly, the evidence of the 1980s suggests that, of those who could be classified as 'long-term unemployed', the vast majority has experienced unemployment as a major interruption to their working life: unemployment was not a normal condition and, as Nick Buck puts it, 'They were not so much stable members of an underclass as unstable members of the working class' (1991: 21).

The more serious question raised by Runciman's conception of underclass is that, unlike other classes, it is the state rather than the market which is implicated in its definition. Without the availability of state benefits for underclass members to receive, would the underclass exist? In the purely institutional terms which Runciman seeks to observe, how would the underclass stand in relation to the market? The answer implied by Runciman would surely belie his insistence that his is a structural rather than a cultural class schema, since, when reviewing twentieth-century changes in class structure, he equates his contemporary underclass with the Edwardian 'loafer class' depicted by D'Aeth (Runciman 1990: 389–90). The implication would seem to do Runciman's argument no good at all, because without an institutional relationship to the post-war welfare state, the roles of those assigned to the underclass are defined in terms of behaviour – the intermittence of their labour and their drinking habits.

To whom, then, or to what is the existence of the underclass attributable? Is it the behaviour of its members or is it the institutional relationships made possible by the state? The main thrust of Charles Murray's argument in his earlier writing was in fact that the behaviour of the poor and disadvantaged should be understood in terms of its economic rationality, and that it was the perverse incentives created by social policy which were to blame for the persistence of poverty in the midst of affluence in the postwar United States:

> A government's social policy helps set the rules of the game, the stakes, the risks, the pay offs, the trade offs, and the strategies for making a living, raising a family, having fun, defining what 'winning' and 'success' mean . . . The most compelling explanation for the marked shift in the fortunes of the poor is that they continued to respond, as they always had, to the world as they found it, but that we – meaning the not-poor and un-disadvantaged – had changed the rules of their world . . . The first effect of the new rules was to make it profitable for the poor to behave in the short term in ways which were destructive in the long term. Their second effect was to mask these long term losses to subsidize irretrievable mistakes. (1984: 9)

Murray's answer was and is that the poor would best be served by a curtailment of state welfare; the state should get out of their way. In his later writing on the underclass, however, Murray perceptibly shifts his emphasis and is far more preoccupied with the *blame* which should attach to the poor. This shift may ironically have been influenced by the nature of the explanations which have begun to emerge from more 'liberal' and left-wing commentators in the United States. For example, Lawrence Mead has argued that the problems of the underclass should be addressed, not by the retrenchment of social policy, but through a more authoritative social policy which would enforce the common obligations of citizenship; 'The main problem with the welfare state is not its size but its permissiveness' (1986: 3). The goal of social policy should therefore be to overcome dependency by promoting 'equal citizenship', the merit of which is that

> It does not require that the disadvantaged 'succeed', something not everyone can do. It requires only that everyone discharge the common obligations, including social ones like work. All competent

adults are supposed to work or display English literacy, just as everyone is supposed to pay taxes or obey the law. (*ibid.*: 12)

This more subtle approach, which was called on in aid of new style 'Workfare' welfare regimes in the United States has been criticised by William Julius Wilson, who emphasises that the underclass with which he is concerned – the ghetto underclass – is *truly* disadvantaged, through the economic and social dislocation of the inner-city environment (1987: 159–63). Wilson equally rejects arguments that the ghetto underclass of America's inner cities, through predominantly black, can be understood solely in terms of institutional racism. Wilson's underclass is in essence defined more in terms of social ecology: jobs have been lost from inner-city neighbourhoods upon a massive scale as industry has relocated; the 'successful' black middle class has similarly moved out of the ghettos, undermining the structure and stability of community institutions; chronic and intractable joblessness among young men has reduced the size of the 'marriageable pool' available to young women, resulting in an increase in out-of-wedlock births and the numbers of female-headed families, so undermining traditional family structures; the resulting dislocations are reflected in a very high and localised incidence of poverty, welfare dependency, street crime and aberrant behaviour. Wilson's answer is a comprehensive and universal programme which would combine both employment and welfare policies; but while rejecting policies based crudely on the reshaping of incentives for the underclass, he has none the less drawn attention to dislocations at the level of individual behaviour, and this would seem to have fuelled rather than assuaged the arguments of the New Right.

So, when predicting the rise of a British underclass, Murray points first of all to the 'sky rocketing' incidence of illegitimacy (1990a: 5) and he pitches his justification for this in terms of the need which children (especially boys) have for fathers and the need which young men have for the 'civilising force' of marriage (*ibid.*: 23). Critics such as Alan Walker have objected that

Mr. Murray's underclass, like all previous attempts to individualise the causes of poverty, diverts attention from blaming the mechanisms through which resources are distributed, including the role of the Government, to blaming, in William Ryan's famous phrase, 'the victims'. (1990: 58)

Murray has ridiculed such criticism, accusing Walker of substituting 'the noble poor person' for Rousseau's noble savage (1990b: 67). Blame, Murray emphasises, is important. While he continues to assert that governments must shoulder blame for the creation of the underclass, he would not wish the underclass to be persuaded of that fact, and he is anxious 'to reintroduce the notion of blame, and sharply reduce our readiness to call people 'victims' ' (*ibid.*: 71). Blame, he argues, is as important as praise when it comes to motivating the individual, and the exercise of moral judgement is necessary to the inculcation of moral responsibility.

In every discourse, the consistent mark of the underclass stems, therefore, not from its objective relations with the state, the market or the social environment but from the acknowledgement of its culpability.

Marginalising minorities

In spite of assertions to the contrary by black American sociologist William Julius Wilson (see above), the American underclass in the United States is often portrayed as a racial phenomenon. Nicholas Lemann (1986), for example, has suggested that black sharecropper migrants from the rural south of the United States brought to the inner-city ghettos of the north an 'ethic of dependency', inculcated by the exploitative, semi-feudal conditions of labour to which they and their immediate forebears had been subjected. While this particular thesis seems to have few strong supporters on either the left or the right of the underclass debate it is common currency, however, that the posited underclass in Britain has no such racial connotations. Certainly, black people are overrepresented in the categories alleged to constitute the British underclass, but while the underclass in America is 'mostly black', that in Britain is 'mostly white' (see Field 1990: 38; Murray 1990b: 78).

Lemann, however, rather like Auletta (see p. 34 above), identifies the problem as the failure of certain black Americans to assimilate to middle-class values and as a failure of 'leadership'. Even when a racial dimension to underclass is seen as central, the persistence of the underclass is still regarded in terms of failure.

What the American and British underclasses have in common in spite of their supposedly different racial composition is that they are both conceptual repositories for non-conforming social minorities: minorities which are capable in practice of being identified with reference to overlapping criteria which, if they are in any way interrelated, are related in highly complex ways. Such criteria may include socio-economic status, family characteristics, aberrant behaviour, cultural background or even ethnicity.

By suggesting that we should not regard such minorities as victims and that we should be prepared to allocate blame, commentators like Charles Murray are opening the door to forms of prejudice and oppression fuelled as much by popular stereotypes as by policy debate. Even if, like Frank Field, we refrain from blaming such minorities, the irresistible teleology which underpins the underclass notion is that the cause of the underclass lies in its composition. Either way, the reflexive effect of the underclass concept is not to define the marginalised, but to marginalise those it defines. Underclass reinforces an entire discursive network of association between delinquency and dependency, between crime and poverty, between race and antisocial behaviour, between immorality and single parenthood, and so forth. Putative membership of a symbolic underclass may in itself bring real consequences in terms of the multifaceted identities and experiences of the minorities it affects.

Dependency and the symbolism of the underclass

'Underclass', therefore, is a symbolic term with no single meaning, but a great many applications. It is used both in global descriptions of the exclusionary processes of class-based societies and as an almost casual shorthand notation in debates about social and economic inequality. It represents, not a useful concept, but a potent symbol.

Foucault has argued that, as industrial capitalism matured, the physical means by which 'abnormal' individuals were segregated from the 'pure' community became generalised so as to function throughout society in accordance with a 'double mode': 'that of binary division and branding (mad/sane; dangerous/harmless; normal/abnormal); and that of coercive assignment, of differentiated distribution (who he is; where he must be; how he is to be characterized . . .)' (1977: 199). If we are to construe this to imply, as Foucault does, that techniques once specific to penal or remedial establishments became inherent to power relations in general, then we should argue that the underclass (or residuum) is indeed *par excellence* a symbolic device for the division and branding of the delinquent and the dependant and for their assignment to a very particular social location, status and identity. The underclass is a symbolic rather than an actual institution, capable of serving at a discursive level as a repository for those whom society would segregate or exclude.

Foucault himself has analysed the division and branding of the 'delinquent'. What we are arguing is that, in the recurring debate about the underclass, we may also see the evidence of a related and parallel process – the division and branding of the 'dependent'. The current debate about 'dependency' in relation to the underclass is thus oriented on the binary axis of work versus welfare. Independence implies the norm of the wage relation and the mutually self-sufficient family; dependency implies the 'abnormal' and, in particular, unemployment or single parenthood and the receipt of welfare benefits. Financial dependency on the state (rather than upon the wage or the family) is translated into a problem of behavioural dependency.

David Ellwood has recently reviewed and evaluated three models of behavioural dependency (1989): the rational choice model, which assumes that individuals will evaluate the options they face in accordance with 'tastes and preferences'; expectancy models, which look upon dependency as the result of a loss of confidence or the loss by the individual of a sense of control over his/her life; and cultural models, which regard dependency as a behavioural deficiency and/or the consequence of aberrant social mores. Ellwood's broad conclusion was that, when seeking to explain the statistical patterns of long-term welfare dependency in the United States, it is the rational choice model which best fits the data, since the economic and marital options open to single mothers on long-term welfare posed unreasonable choices and could therefore reasonably explain their continued reliance on welfare. Ellwood was less convinced when it came to explaining the evidence of changing family structure patterns associated with welfare dependency, in so far as individual choices in this sphere are more complex and less observable, and so expectancy and cultural models, 'although capable of making widely divergent predictions with only modest variations in assumptions' (*ibid.*: 13), may have relevance.

The assumption behind all three models, which goes unquestioned by Ellwood, is that long-term welfare dependency by single mothers is potentially problematic, both economically and for the 'traditional family'. The assumed policy objective is to guarantee that male breadwinners will earn and will marry and will be enabled to support child-bearing women and children. Ellwood concedes that 'Of course people with confidence and mainstream values form single-parent households' and that, according to current research, the typical child born in the United States will spend at least some time in a single-parent home. But, he insists, 'some behaviour such as births to unmarried teenagers is harder to understand and justify using a choice model, especially when the mothers are in no position to provide for themselves, much less their babies' (*ibid.*: 12). For Ellwood, therefore, welfare dependency remains problematic because it is not economically rational; it must sometimes be explained in terms of defective expectations and/or adverse cultural values.

It was Auletta, however, who explained unmarried teenage motherhood by quoting from conversations he had with members of the Little Sisters of the Assumption, a religious order in East Harlem running a surrogate mother programme:

> When they look into life, what do they see? It's not as if they were planning their life. Their life is planned in a sense . . . Maybe in one day the mother has to keep three appointments – food stamps, welfare, a clinic. Depending on these systems for survival creates a way of life whereby your life becomes more and more organized by the systems. And remember, these *are* systems of dependency. You can sense a taking away of the family by the system . . . 20% of the residential units here in East Harlem are vacant. An additional 10% are near abandonment. So what do people look at when they wake up? They have no hope. What is within your ability? Becoming a mother . . .
>
> A baby is something everyone considers something of worth. You don't have anything of value of your own. A baby is of value. People who are educated and work try to build something which lasts beyond them. It's the same for poor people. (quoted in Auletta 1982: 71, 72)

The Little Sisters of the Assumption thus attribute an amoral form of rationality to welfare dependency. It is rationality derived none the less from prevailing notions of what is to be valued; dependency that is displaced from the family to the system.

Similarly, for 18- to 24-year-old young people in the north-east of England in 1987, among whom almost one in three had never had a full-time job (*Observer*, 25 January 1987), the real choice even for the relatively well educated was between 'shit jobs, govvy schemes or the dole' (ESRC 1987: 17). Research indicated that a clear majority of these youngsters were 'non-political, pragmatic young adults . . . eager for employment, even on modest wages' and 'far from advancing a rebellious morality, they were conservative on most social issues' (*ibid.*). Although welfare dependency could not upon such evidence be regarded as irrational or aberrant behaviour, Leicester University's Labour Market Studies Group claimed to have found that 'People who have to exist on social security have a different set of values. Morality starts to change. Small-scale thieving is seen as part of every day life' (*Observer* 25 January 1987).

The single mothers of East Harlem and the unemployed youngsters of north-east England are all candidates for inclusion as members of a posited 'underclass', characterised not by their misfortune, by their lack of rationality or even by distinctive cultural values or expectations, but by a failure of morality. Welfare dependency is suspect, it is an underclass phenomenon, because it seems to threaten what Dahrendorf referred to as our 'moral hygiene'; because it represents in fact an inversion of acceptable dependency.

Durkheim's classic thesis had been that, as the social division of labour increases and individuals become more specialised or differentiated, so do they become more socially dependent (1964): the mutual interdependence that is characteristic of social existence becomes more complex. This in a sense was the starting point for the Fabian conception of welfare, whereby more and more

> 'states of dependency' have been defined and recognised as collective responsibilities, and more differentiated provision has been made in respect of them. These 'states of dependency' arise for the vast majority of the population whenever they are not in a position to 'earn life' for themselves and their families; they are then dependent people. (Titmuss 1963: 42)

Yet behind the notion of collective responsibility for dependent people remained an assumption in favour of individual responsibility on the part of wage earners and their families, whose dependency is surely no less 'social' merely because it is mediated through the wage relation and the family, rather than through the state. Concealed beneath what Marx (1970) referred to as the 'dull compulsion' of the wage relation lie, not the 'free' labourers of bourgeois rhetoric, but individuals who are dependent upon the sale of their labour power for the means of their subsistence. And for the reproduction of individual labour power, each individual is further dependent upon the socially determined structure of the modern nuclear family.

Ironically, therefore, those who are dependent on collective provision by an impersonal state have become *independent* of the wage relation and/or the family. Welfare dependants are not of course 'free', but are enmeshed and identified by state mechanisms of surveillance and discipline, just as delinquents are enmeshed and identified by state penality. The common ground upon which dependants and delinquents can be symbolically assigned to an 'underclass' is that they each offend against norms which are peculiar to capitalist social relations and they are socially constituted through their respective relationships with state authority.

In his quest for an antidote to the 'underclass', Ken Auletta quotes with approval the sentiments of a highly charismatic 45-year-old black woman teacher running a Chicago ghetto school, who had been featured in a CBS television documentary: 'Even when the four-year-olds begin to read 'The Little Red Hen', I point out the moral, that if you don't work you don't eat' (quoted in Auletta 1982: 309). But does this secular version of the biblical homily 'if any would not work, neither should he eat' (2 Thessalonians 3: 10) represent a moral or a rational imperative? 'The Little Red Hen' is a farmyard tale in which all the other animals refuse to help the heroine while she sows and harvests a quantity of wheat and eventually bakes some bread, so when the other animals say they will help to eat the bread, the Little Red Hen rebuffs them because they played no part in making it. The abstract conclusion to be drawn is that people must contribute to the life of a community if they are to be sustained by it: anthropologically speaking, this amounts to a recognition of rational necessity. It is only because the wage relation (something specific to capitalist social relations) intervenes between the individual and the community and mediates their mutual interdependence that the homily takes on the character of a moral fetish. State welfare benefits and indeed crime can and do provide the means to eat without the necessity for waged work, but in each case the scope of the relationship between the individual and the community (and the potential for reciprocity) is strictly fashioned, regulated or embargoed through the intermediary of highly specific state institutions. At the level of discourse and popular common sense, the creation of an underclass affirms rather than refutes the moral premise of 'The Little Red Hen'.

Conclusion

Writing before the term 'underclass' had been popularised in the United States, Liebow (1967) described in perceptive detail the life of 'Negro street corner men' in downtown Washington DC. What characterised and explained the behaviour of these men was their own perception of their failures as men, as workers, as fathers, as husbands and as lovers. The poorly-paid and menial jobs which were in practice available to them did not satisfy their aspirations to reasonable pay and status. The fluidity and volatility evinced in their relationships with women and children did not satisfy their aspirations to be patriarchal providers. Street-corner life was essentially an accommodation to failure in terms of values, sentiments and beliefs shared with the 'larger society'. Liebow concluded that the inside world of the street-corner men (that which might now be referred to as 'underclass culture') did not in fact arise from, nor did it produce, a distinctive counter-culture. On the contrary,

> It is in continuous, intimate contact with the larger society – indeed, it is an integral part of it – and is no more impervious to the values, sentiments and beliefs of the larger society than it is to the blue welfare checks or to the agents of the larger society, such as the policeman, the police informer, the case worker, the landlord, the dope pusher. (*ibid.*: 209)

The 'underclass' is no more and no less than a symbolic manifestation of socially constituted definitions of failure. The term does not usefully define a real or tangible phenomenon, but inevitably it touches upon real and important issues, to do with work, the family and citizenship. Social commentators and policy makers would do well to avoid the term, but they must address the social divisions which generate or constitute the perceived 'failures' of the unemployed, the single parent and the welfare claimant. Recent structural and cultural changes have intersected, not to produce an 'underclass', but to shift the boundaries between core workers, peripheral workers and non-workers; between the individual and the family; and between the citizen and the welfare state. Such changes have also exacerbated regional inequalities and inner-city decay and, some would argue, may have contributed in their way to rising levels of crime. We need therefore to go, not in search of the underclass, but in search of a better understanding of structural and cultural changes and their complex interrelationship and effects.

William Julius Wilson himself, in his presidential address to the American Sociological Association, has recently sought to move debate 'away from the controversy over the concept of underclass, including the simplistic either/or distinction between culture and social structure' (1991: 6). We shall endeavour in this book to observe that injunction and, although in Chapters 4 and 5 we shall consider fresh evidence which in many ways vindicates our rejection of the term 'underclass', our aim is to open up new areas of debate regarding the questions of dependency and the welfare state.

CHAPTER 3

VALUES AND DEPENDENCY

– Do you call poverty a crime?
– The worst of crimes!
(G.B. Shaw, *Major Barbara* 1905, Act III)

Our first chapter described the changing policy environment of the
1980s and 1990s and showed how the incoming Conservative administration adopted a self-consciously radical stance in its approach to
social policy. The second chapter considered the way in which the
new perspectives on social need were predicated on a particular
interpretation of dependency. In this chapter we examine the influence of notions about dependency on social policy reform over the
period in more detail and relate policy change to popular ideas
about welfare dependency as reflected in the findings of structured
national opinion studies. This discussion sets the scene for our own
analysis of dependency and social values, based on material from a
more intensive study of the experience and understanding of claimants, which is presented in the next two chapters.

Dependency culture and social policy

The association of the concept 'culture' with the attitudes and
proclivities of the poor owes much to the 'culture of poverty'
debate. At the hands of theorists such as Daniel Moynihan (1965),
Keith Joseph (1972) and Charles Murray (1984, 1990a), the debate

has long since lost sight of the seminal thesis advanced by Oscar Lewis. It was Lewis who claimed to have identified

> a sub-culture of western society with its own structure and rationale, a way of life handed down from generation to generation ... a culture in the traditional anthropological sense that it provides human beings with a ready made set of solutions for human problems. (1966: 10)

Whether or not the thesis as originally stated is valid, it is clearly quite different from the idea that state dependency constitutes cultural failure and that poverty is to be blamed upon the behaviour of the poor. Nor did Lewis claim that state welfare provision caused or perpetuated a culture of poverty. On the contrary, he believed that systematic state welfare, along with universal literacy, high technology and advanced communications, would serve to reduce the incidence of the phenomenon. The culture of poverty which Lewis portrayed was characteristic of an incomplete or inadequate stage of capitalist development and reflected the failure, not of the poor, but of capitalism itself. Presented in these terms, the thesis stands as a refutation of John Moore's claim that the 'aberrant path' of the welfare state has led its beneficiaries into a 'sullen apathy of dependence' (1987: 7).

The most perceptive of Lewis' critics, Charles Valentine (1968), had argued not that the culture of poverty thesis was necessarily flawed, but that Lewis' own empirical evidence did not support it. Valentine was concerned to devise ambitious research methods which might examine how it was that the poor, as part of a wider prevailing culture, might adapt their lifestyles or 'lifeways' in order to accommodate the tensions and contradictions which they experience.

Recent policy discussion has shifted the focus of discussion away from poor people considered as creators of their own culture, in response to the circumstances in which they find themselves, and to government policy seen as a central element in creating the environment which poorer groups inhabit. The roots of dependency culture are seen as lying in factors entirely external to poor people rather than in their own choices, lives, traditions, experiences and ways of making sense of their world. The 'benefits culture' has been looked on as something which characterises the supposed apathy or degeneracy of social security recipients rather than in terms of the adaptive lifeways by which recipients might accommodate or cope with the effects of low income and the pressures exerted by the administrative regime of the social security system itself.

We will return to the question of how the notion of culture is to be understood and examined when we consider the usefulness of different research methods towards the end of the chapter. First, we discuss the way in which the dependency culture thesis has influenced government policy in the recent past. Ideas about dependency culture have had a particular influence on government policy in relation to unemployed people, to employment and to the family. The central themes of policy follow from the determination to substitute direction for intervention in the primary social welfare function of regulating need discussed in Chapter 1, and the combination of contempt for dependency on benefits with enthusiasm for dependency on wages or on the incomes of other family members analysed in Chapter 2. In brief, policy aims at the restoration of work and family ethics. We will consider each area separately.

Employment, benefits and the work ethic

Chapter 1 described two factors outside the immediate control of government which influenced policy on benefits and the labour-market: the rising pressure on employment which resulted from the increased numbers of people seeking paid work and the increase in the proportion of insecure and low-paid jobs resulting from sectoral shifts and from the long-run decline of the United Kingdom economy. Both factors were compounded by the two recessions consequent on the sharp oil-price rises of the mid- and late 1970s and the further recession of the early 1990s, exacerbated by the Gulf War and by excessive monetarist discipline. These recessions have had a particularly powerful impact on the economy of the United Kingdom.

The aims of policy

The election of the Conservative government in 1979 signalled an abrupt break in policy. Over most of the 1970s, Labour in office had responded to economic crisis by pursuing macro-economic, training and labour-market support policies designed to create more jobs and help people to enter them. Despite the increase in the numbers of unemployed people, both national insurance unemployment benefits and means-tested supplementary benefits (which accounted for roughly half of spending on this group) were uprated to maintain their value against prices and against increases in average wages (Barr and Coulter 1990: Figures, 7.6, 7.7). The central problem of social security was how to finance these policies. The widespread belief that Labour policies necessitated high tax-rates and inflationary public borrowing eventually contributed to electoral defeat.

In the 1980s, the employment and benefit regime was reversed: welfare policies were subordinated to the overriding aim of reducing the role of government and extending the freedom of market forces. Government curtailed regional and other subsidies designed to create jobs, eroded existing mechanisms of wage-regulation, decisively weakened the power of trade unions through legislation and through the management of set-piece confrontations and opposed the attempts of the European Community to establish mechanisms for setting minimum wages and improving job security. Benefit levels were reduced to save money and bolster work incentives. Means-tested benefits were used increasingly to target resources more precisely on defined groups (and deny them to others) and the mechanisms for the surveillance of claimants' lives were strengthened.

The direction of policy is clear from the objectives for employment policy set out in the 1991 Employment Department Group Report. These include various training initiatives, measures to promote workplace safety and equal opportunities, measures 'to promote enterprise and the generation of new jobs' by fostering 'arrangements that enable pay to respond flexibly to labour market conditions', encouraging self-employment and tourism, and helping people to get jobs, in particular 'to make sure that unemployed people in receipt of benefits are available for and actively seeking work; and to discourage benefit fraud'. Nowhere is there mention of the kind of national or regional job-creation subsidies that government pursued in the previous decade, nor indeed of any measures designed specifically to create jobs, except in the one case of the tourist industry (Employment Department Group 1991: 1).

The emphasis on restriction of the scope of government intervention and subordination of social to economic policy aims is also reflected in the objectives of social security: 'it must be effective in meeting genuine needs in a way which encourages independence and incentives to work' (DSS 1991a: para. 5). The major social security planning document of the 1980s had set out the objectives of the service in a similar manner: 'the social security system must be capable of meeting genuine need', 'it must be consistent with the Government's overall objectives for the economy' and it 'must be simple to understand and easier to administer' (DHSS 1985a: para. 1.12).

The central themes in both employment and benefit policy in respect of poor people of working age are three: to strengthen work incentives, which means widening the gap between benefit levels and earnings; to direct spending accurately to defined groups of needy people, which means greater use of means-testing and of restrictions on entitlement; and to simplify administration of the system, while intensifying the measures to stop fraud and regulate claimants' lives which are required by the other two objectives. Policies to create more jobs take second place to policies designed to compel people to take whatever jobs are available, and training schemes are incorporated more tightly into the system of labour discipline. Social security for unemployed people changes its character. From being an apparatus designed to maintain the incomes of those out of work, it becomes a system designed to force people into work.

The success of the new policies

Reform of social security in the 1980s and early 1990s was predicated on the assumption that the existence of dependency culture among claimants is a major problem of social welfare, that it is the result of an over-generous benefit regime and that determined measures are necessary to eradicate it. In relation to unemployed people, the objectives of reducing benefit levels, targeting payments more precisely on some groups and denying them to others, and increasing surveillance have been gained. Other labour-market policies have also been reasonably successful. The influence of trade unions has been undermined and their membership has fallen from 13.3 million in 1979 to 10.2 million by 1988 (CSO 1991c: Table 6.20). Increasing numbers of young people are enrolled on training schemes – just under 600,000 by 1991 (DE 1991b: 360). The 'new vocationalism' has become a dominant force in educational reform, especially for working-class students (Ainley 1988).

The impacts of new policies in relation to the three goals of reducing benefit levels, targeting benefits on defined groups and establishing a harsher regime of administration and training are considered separately.

Benefit levels and work incentives

The first specific aim of policy was to cut benefit levels in relation to wages, to increase the incentive to find work. The main benefits which support unemployed people are national insurance unemployment benefit and means-tested income support. In addition, the entitlement to family credit of many of those in low-paid jobs may affect work incentives by widening the gap between the incomes of those in work and those out of work. Over the 1980s there have been a large number of piecemeal changes in the system of benefits for unemployed people. Atkinson traces thirty-eight between 1979 and 1988, of which only two were favourable to the unemployed: the introduction of national insurance dependants' additions for women in 1983, under a European Community equal opportunity ruling, and the removal of benefit disqualification for voluntary redundancy in 1985, designed to mitigate resistance to labour-shedding. The most important measures to damage the interests of claimants were the abolition of the earnings-related supplement in 1982 and of child additions in 1984, the taxation of benefits in 1983, the ending of statutory indexation of benefit in 1986, the extension of the period of disqualification for those alleged to be voluntarily unemployed from 1986 onwards and a tightening up of contribution conditions after 1988 (Atkinson 1988: 22–4).

The real value of national insurance unemployment benefit fell over the period. Calculated at April 1990 prices, the value of benefit fell from £38.41 a week to £37.35 for a single person between November 1979 and April 1990 and from £62.18 to £60.40 for a married couple. Since the incomes of the population in work had increased rapidly over this period, the reduction in benefits had a powerful effect on the relation between benefits and wages. For single people the fall was from 16.4 per cent of average male adult earnings to 12.6 per cent, and for a married couple it was from 26.2 to 20.4 per cent (DSS 1991b: Table H3.05). These calculations do not take into account the effect of changes in the tax regime or housing costs. If this is done, the net income of people on unemployment benefit is seen to fall from 22.9 per cent to 17.6 per cent of the average net incomes of a single person in work: for a married couple without children the fall is similar (from 35.3 to 27.3 per cent), but for those with children it is proportionately greater (from 43.2 to 31.8 per cent for a couple with two children: DSS 1991b: Table H3.10).

The policy of targeting through means-testing throws a stronger emphasis on last-resort means-tested benefits. The 1985 Social Security Review led to legislation in 1986 which replaced supplementary benefits with income support, and the old family income supplement with family credit. Income support rates vary according to the age of adult claimants and their family responsibilities. The new rules assume that claimants will pay a portion of housing costs and local taxes, so that changes to these have a more powerful effect of their living standards. There is considerable dispute about the impact of these changes on claimants' living standards. Official estimates stated that only 12 per cent of claimants would be worse off, but other estimates suggest higher figures – 43 per cent according to the Social Security Advisory Committee, 48 per cent according to the Policy Studies Institute and 60 per cent according to the Benefits Research Unit (see Svenson and MacPherson 1988: 41-53 for a review of the debate). The Parliamentary Social Services Select Committee commissioned a study which took into account the impact of changes in local taxes and in water rates and arrangements for housing costs, as well as changes in benefit rates. This showed that in general, married couples were slightly better off, but single people, especially those under the age of 25, and single parents were likely to be much worse off (Social Services Select Committee 1989). Changes in the means-tested benefits paid to unemployed people are likely to have cut the living standards of at least some groups among them. Family credit is designed to be paid at higher rates than the benefit it replaces, but continues to suffer from low take-up. A special study commissioned by DSS in 1988 showed that 'about 65 per cent of available Family Credit expenditure was being claimed by about half the eligible population' (DSS 1991a: para. 39).

These changes have contributed to the sharp increase in inequality and in poverty in the United Kingdom over the 1980s, discussed in Chapter 1 (see Table 1.1). Official statistics indicate that the incomes of those at the bottom remained roughly constant, while those dependent on employment enjoyed a real growth in prosperity, more marked as one moves up the income ladder. Those on average incomes enjoyed a 34 per cent growth in real income between 1979 and 1988, whereas those in the bottom twentieth experienced only 2 per cent growth (Social Security Select Committee 1991: Table D1). These calculations do not take into account the shift from direct to indirect taxation as part of general economic policy, which is likely to hit the poorest groups hardest. One study suggests that tax changes may have reduced the living standards of the poorest fifth of the population by some 8 per cent between 1979 and 1986: more recent policies will have continued this trend (Barr and Coulter 1990: 306).

As Chapter 1 showed, unemployed people make up a growing proportion of the population on benefits. The numbers declined slightly after 1986, but are again rising in the recession of the early 1990s. The group accounted for 25 per cent of supplementary benefit claimants in 1978/9 and 43 per cent in 1985/6, falling back to 24 per cent of income support claimants by 1989/90, but returning to 25 per cent by 1990/1 and expected to rise further in future years (DSS 1991a: Table 14). In 1978/9 they accounted for some 9 per cent of benefit spending. By 1985/6 this had risen to 17 per cent. By 1990/91, it had fallen back to 9 per cent as a result of the improvements' to pensioners and disabled people's benefits and the reduction in size of the group of claimants.

The success of policy in enforcing the 1834 principle of 'less eligibility' in modern dress is summed up in Figure 3.1. The graph shows how the relationship between the incomes of people in work and of unemployed people on unemployment benefit (upper line) and supplementary benefit/income support (lower line) have changed. The upper line plots standard rate unemployment benefit for a two-child family as a percentage of average net male earnings, taking into account income tax, national insurance contributions and child

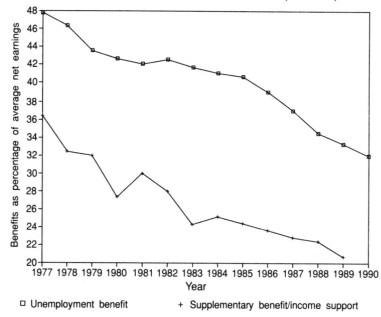

Figure 3.1 Unemployment benefits, 1977–90 (DSS 1991b: Table H3.10; DSS 1989: Table 34.36)

benefit. The living standards of those entitled to such benefits have fallen against earnings by about a quarter over the period. The lower line gives the average benefit paid to unemployed people who depend on income support, now a much larger group than that entitled to insurance benefits. Unfortunately no data which enable us to take family structure into account is published. The living standards of income support claimants have also fallen compared with average earnings, by about a third over the 1980s. The benefits paid to individual claimants will vary. Differences in family and other circumstances will generate different patterns of need. However, the fall in average benefit levels compared to average earnings shows clearly how the assertion of work incentives has taken precedence over meeting need. This is in spite of the fact that, as one recent review of evidence concluded, 'substantial research to date has failed to demonstrate that benefits have anything more than a minor effect on unemployment levels and durations' (McLaughlin, Millar and Cooke 1989: 25).

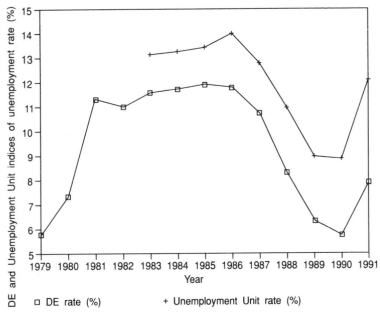

Figure 3.2 Unemployment rates, 1977–91 (DE 1991a: Table 2.1,
corresponding tables for earlier years; Unemployment Unit 1991: Table 5)

It is worth noting that the changes have not made the contribution to the reduction of public spending and hence to the pressure
on taxation that was anticipated, since unemployment has remained high over the period. Spending on unemployed people
rose from £3.1 to £9.2 billion (at 1990/1 prices) between 1979/80
and 1986/7 as the numbers of claimants rose, only to fall back to
£4.9 billion by 1990/1, with an increase to £5.4 billion anticipated
by 1993/4 on a favourable interpretation of the impact of the recession of the 1990s (DSS 1991a: Table 9; Barr and Coulter 1990: 288).
Unemployment remained below 3 per cent during the 1950s and
1960s. It rose rapidly from the mid-1970s onwards, as Figure 3.2
shows. Changes in the method of calculation of the official statistics disguise the extent of the increase, so the graph includes an
unofficial index which shows what the level would have been if the
statistics had not been altered.

The principal changes are: the removal of those registered for
work but not claiming benefit from the count and the exclusion of

those seeking part-time work (1982); the exclusion of people aged 59 or over who do not get benefit and the abolition of the requirement that men over 60 claiming benefit should register (1983); and the introduction of a two-week delay in making the count and the inclusion of self-employed people in the labour-force denominator (1986 – for a measured assessment see Price and Bain 1988: 176–7). These changes have had the effect of reducing the politically salient statistic of the unemployment rate by somewhere in the region of 3 per cent. In addition a whole series of job creation, youth training and temporary employment schemes have been used to generate an increasing number of jobs and work-placements that remove people who would otherwise be counted as unemployed from the figures. By 1988, these schemes accounted for over a million people, and the number has risen subsequently (Treasury 1988: 103). The top line of the graph is based on an index prepared from 1983 onwards by the independent Unemployment Unit, which adjusts the official figures to take account of the changes.

The procedure of adding the numbers removed from the register by the schemes to the official count and making further adjustments for changes in statistical methods may lead to some exaggeration of the true level of unemployment, since some of those added back would presumably have found their way into work by other routes if the schemes had not existed. However, since no estimate of the size of this group is available and the government has damaged the statistics so that no reliable time-series of this central economic indicator exists, it seems most sensible to err on the side of caution and to use the Unemployment Unit figures as the best we have. These show a rather different picture to the official measure: at the peak of the mid-1980s unemployment rose to 3.9 million. It then declined, but did not fall to anything approaching the levels of the previous decade. More recently unemployment has again risen, and there is a strong likelihood that the figure of 11.9 per cent in the official index for 1985, the highest since 1938, will soon be exceeded (NIESR 1991b: 3). The two measures diverge more sharply over time, as the changes in official statistical methods have a cumulative effect.

The evidence on rising unemployment reinforces the argument that government policies have been highly successful in containing spending on unemployed people, although they have not achieved a real reduction in the level of spending: spending has fallen sharply from the peak of 1986/7 whereas the number of unemployed people, as indicated by the more accurate unofficial index, has not fallen at anything like the same rate. Part of the difference is made up by the expansion of the training programmes. However, the total budget for the training and employment schemes for 1990/1 at just under £2 billion can only account for about half the fall in benefit spending since the mid-1980s (Employment Department Group 1991: Table 6.5). If unemployment is understood in terms of the broad approach of the Unemployment Unit, there have been real savings in expenditure on the group as a result of policy changes. Many unemployed people are getting less money in real terms than they would have if the changes had not taken place.

Targeting and genuine need

The second main objective of policy was to target benefits more precisely on genuinely needy groups and by implication, to exclude others. This approach led to a more stringent definition of eligibility and to the expansion of means-testing as an instrument of policy. The principal tactics used in pursuit of the curtailing of entitlement are discussed: the denial of income support rights to most 16–18-year-olds from 1988 onwards, the redrawing of disqualification periods and contribution conditions for unemployment benefit (which effectively deny benefit to anyone who has not been in employment for at least six months in either of the two tax years preceding the claim) and the categorisation of claimants for income support in the 1986 Act, which has a particular effect in reducing the entitlements of those under 25. These policies have had the effect of reducing benefit spending and, in particular, the number of younger claimants, and of transferring claimants on to means-tested rather than insurance-based benefit.

In 1979, just under 50 per cent of social security spending on unemployed people was means-tested. By 1990/1 the figure was 82 per cent (DSS 1991a: Table 12). The main reason for the change is the rise in the proportion of the population subject to long-term unemployment. For many more claimants entitlement to insurance-based benefits has been exhausted or has never been built up. The extension of targeting interpreted as means-testing is due more to changes outside the benefit system than to changes within it. However, many commentators argue that the exceptionally high unemployment levels experienced in the 1980s both in comparison with other countries and in comparison with previous years, are the result of deliberate labour-market strategy (Layard and Nickell 1990), so that economic policies make a strong indirect contribution to the spread of means-testing.

A number of measures which assisted the creation of jobs (especially in the areas of the country most affected by unemployment) and strengthened the position of those in work have been curtailed. The areas covered by regional assistance were cut back, so that by 1982 the proportion of the work-force covered had fallen from 47 to 28 per cent and by 1988 to less than 10 per cent. The level of the grants was reduced in 1982, 1984 and 1988 (D. Smith 1989: 98). The system of industrial development certificates, designed to channel industry in particular directions, was abolished in 1979. Wage regulation has never formed a major element in social policy in the United Kingdom. The Fair Wage Agreement, which required government departments and local authorities to accept tenders only from contractors who recognised national agreements, was abolished in 1982. The powers of wages councils, which set minimum wages for about 2.5 million employees, were cut back in 1986, when protection for all workers under 21 was also removed. In 1989 the government proposed abolition of the system. In any case wages council rulings are inadequately enforced (Campaign Against Poverty 1991).

The changes in the pattern of employment exacerbate these problems. The numbers of low-waged workers in poverty have increased over the period. The number of families falling below the level of supplementary benefit entitlement, but debarred from claiming by reason of employment, rose from 180,000 in 1979 to 370,000 by 1987 (DHSS 1986; Johnson and Webb 1990: Table 4). Consequently, the failure to achieve satisfactory take-up rates for family income support/family credit reduces the incomes of a substantial group of people. The numbers of part-time and insecure workers who fall outside the national insurance system is also increasing. Members of this group have few employment rights and are unable to claim unemployment benefit if they lose their jobs. A recent study estimates that the number in this category rose from about 3 to over 4 million in the 1980s (Hakim 1989: 472, 494).

Administrative reform and the new training regime

The third policy objective is to extend administrative control of claimants and to enforce a new training regime. Mechanisms to monitor the lives of claimants on benefit and to expand opportunities for the imposition of work discipline through placement on training schemes have been intensified. The DSS established specialist claims control teams in 1980 with the brief of investigating the status of the long-term unemployed more rigorously. Over 1,000 additional investigators have been employed. The Department of Employment set up regional benefit investigation teams in 1983. In 1984 DHSS undertook an intensive programme of investigation of suspected claimants in fifty-nine areas. The procedure has since been extended nationwide. Despite claims by the agencies that fraud investigations save substantial sums (£326 million out of the £5,000 million going to unemployed people in 1990/1: DSS 1991a: para. 100), there is little evidence of large-scale fraud. In 1990/1, about 75,000 of the one and a half million unemployed claimants withdrew from benefit after being contacted by fraud investigators (Employment Department Group 1991: Table 6.29). An unknown proportion of these are likely to be honest claimants scared off by the threat of prosecution. The Restart scheme, begun in 1986 and made more stringent in 1987, requires those unemployed for more than six months to attend for counselling interviews, at which they are encouraged to seek work possibly further from home or on worse conditions than they had previously contemplated. Some claimants may be persuaded to leave the benefit registers and accept training scheme places. The 1989 Act requires claimants to produce evidence that they are 'actively seeking work' and removes the right to reject possible vacancies on the grounds of low pay or unsuitability. A study in 1990 of jobs on offer to such claimants through job centres concludes that 'many more unemployed people are going to be forced to accept jobs which fail to offer them a living wage' (Cox 1990: 75).

The Department of Employment is also responsible for managing the Youth Training and Employment Training programmes, currently administered by regional Technical Education Councils, which contain a high proportion of business people. The object of the programmes is to guarantee training places to all young adults unemployed for over six months and to offer them to as many as possible of those aged between 18 and 49 unemployed for more than two years. The role of the training schemes has expanded rapidly over the period of high unemployment, especially since the introduction in 1988 of measures to deny benefits to those who do not participate. The quality of schemes varies and many have experienced high dropout rates – over 40 per cent at the early stages of YTS in 1984 (Finn 1985: 123). However, they have the effect of removing claimants from the unemployment count and of imposing a work-place discipline on their lives.

There is considerable evidence that the YT and ET schemes do not fit young or long-term unemployed people for work. Job placement rates of about 55 per cent of those who complete the schemes were reported in 1986 and 1987, roughly comparable to movement into work among those who had not been on the schemes (Ainley 1988: 99). The Employment Department Group's report for 1991 does not give a placement rate for YT, but anticipates that 'by 1993/4 90 per cent of YT leavers are expected to go into jobs, further education or training' (1991: para. 39). It is difficult to assess this objective without a projection of the outlook for non-YT trainees and without information on the kind of 'further education or training' envisaged. The latest statistics on the Employment Training scheme for long-term unemployed people indicate that about half the 215,000 people offered placements between December 1989 and November 1990 were in jobs within three months of leaving, 5 per cent were self-employed, 8 per cent in unpaid work-experience schemes, 3 per cent in further education, 3 per cent in voluntary work and 23 per cent formally classified as unemployed (Hansard, Written Answers, vol. 191, cols 631–2). The scope of the scheme is being reduced as it is officially regarded as ineffective (Employment Department Group 1991: Table 6.8, para. 21). In general, it appears difficult to demonstrate that those who go on such schemes are any more likely to find work at the end of them than people who do not. This observation strengthens the argument that the primary function of the schemes is to be understood in terms of the subjection of those excluded from the labour-market proper to work-place discipline and the erosion of expectations among unemployed people.

Policy conflicts: targeting, the poverty trap and incentives

Two main areas of potential conflict between different policy objectives exist: the mechanisms of targeting may prevent benefits from reaching genuinely needy people, and reforms may in fact reduce the impetus to work. The evidence on the low take-up of means-tested benefits especially family credit, indicates that the principal targeting device is failing in its object of directing resources to those in genuine need. It has already been pointed out that many claimants experience the new administrative mechanisms as harassment, so that the policy of reducing spending collides with both the policy of meeting genuine need and the policy of simplification. The increasing numbers of destitute, homeless people on the streets of large cities indicates that the benefit system is failing to satisfy basic needs, particularly for some groups of young people. Although precise figures are not available, the number of homeless young people in London was put at 50,000 in 1985 (O'Mahony 1988: 14). By 1989, the figure was estimated at between 75,000 and 125,000 (Salvation Army 1989; Greve and Currie 1990). A study of 16- and 17-year-olds denied income support in 1990 showed that just over a fifth admitted having stolen in order to survive, 6 per cent to having begged and 2 per cent to having sold drugs (MORI 1991; see also Hutson and Liddiard 1989: 22). Measures designed to impose stricter labour-market discipline on young adults may have undesirable social consequences. The experience of claimants will be explored further in analysis of the data from our survey in the next chapter.

The second area of controversy results from conflict between the aims of sharpening work incentives and of targeting benefit through means-testing. Means-tested benefits are withdrawn as income rises. If the rate at which a person loses benefit is particularly high, a low-waged worker may experience little incentive to find a higher-paid job or increase earnings because what is gained in better pay is lost in smaller benefits. The reforms of 1988 were designed to mitigate this effect by achieving a greater degree of co-ordination between different means-tests and by testing on net rather than gross income, so that income tax and national insurance deductions do not compound the withdrawal of benefits. The result has been a fall in the numbers facing very high benefit withdrawal rates. In 1985 the number subject to a poverty 'tax-rate' of over 100 per cent was 70,000, and the number subject to over 80 per cent was 490,000. By 1991 these figures had fallen to nought and 280,000. However, high withdrawal rates below these levels persist. The number encountering a 70 per cent rate has risen from 290,000 to 395,000 and the numbers on 50 per cent remain roughly constant at 450,000 (DSS 1991a: Table 20). Poor people in genuine need on whom welfare benefits are targeted face effective tax-rates that are higher than those levied through income tax on any earners, however high their income. In any case, the problem of incentives associated with the poverty trap may be more apparent than real. The evidence of our study indicates that claimants have strong work incentives despite the effect of loss of benefits.

This discussion shows how ideas about incentives have been a major influence on benefit and employment policy in the 1980s and early 1990s. This is a decisive break with the policies of previous periods. The most important effects have been cuts in benefits relative to wages, contributing to a sharp increase in inequality, the expansion of means-testing for the able-bodied poor, stricter policing of claimants' lives and the virtual abolition of job creation as an activity of government. Later in this chapter we will consider how these policies relate to popular attitudes and perceptions. First, however, we will review developments in another area where policy has been influenced by ideas about dependency and the family.

Family policy and social welfare

Family policy has been one of the major themes of political discussion in the 1980s and 1990s. It is a commonplace that all major parties have attempted to present themselves as 'the party of the family' though they may disagree violently on the kind of family they wish to protect (Coote, Harman and Hewitt 1990: 10–11; Wicks 1991: 2). In the United Kingdom, the family has traditionally entered official discourse as a zone of exclusion rather than a sphere of positive intervention. Its significance lies more in assumptions about the issues which need not concern formal politics because the family will take care of them than in direct and explicit measures, so that family policies tend to proceed by implication and omission rather than by action. A number of recent changes have affected the family. However, there is nothing like the same obvious and far-reaching reversal of the previous pattern of policy that emerged in relation to work and welfare.

Three arguments link the family and ideas about dependency. First, a number of writers influential with the Conservative government of the 1980s and early 1990s have argued that the two-parent family, where the husband has primary responsibility for providing an income and the wife primary responsibility for providing care for dependants and others in the home, is both natural and desirable. As the Conservative shadow spokesman for social services put it in 1977: 'if the good Lord had intended us to have equal rights to go out to work he wouldn't have created men and women. These are the biological facts' (Jenkins 1977). This approach leads to concern about dual parenthood and the roles of men and women in the home and the labour-market. Secondly, the family is seen as an institution characterised by a sturdy independence, which makes it an important bastion against subversive influences in society, yet vulnerable to dependence on the state (Mount 1982). This justifies restrictions on family support policy. The third point concerns single parenthood and paternal authority: 'in communities without fathers, the kids tend to run wild' (Murray 1990a: 11). The view that dual parenting is essential to good discipline and effective socialisation leads to policies designed to curb welfare for single parents and to restrict the access of young people to social benefits which might enable them to leave home.

The view that government must defend the two-parent, male-breadwinner family by creating a safe haven where state policy does not intrude conflicts with two developments, in relation to formal employment and in relation to changes in family structure. In both areas the tensions are unresolved. First, the labour-market changes of the 1980s have generated a rising demand for women workers. The Secretary of State for Employment declared in 1988 that 'the 1990s would be the decade of the working mother' (Wicks 1991: 18). As Chapter 1 showed, there has been a rapid increase in the numbers of women in paid employment, although labour-market participation by women with young children remains low. The conflict between the demand that married women work primarily in unwaged child-care and home-making and the demand for women as employees has not been resolved in policy. Arguments about dependency deny the claim that government should play any part in providing child-care. As the Conservative minister who chaired the Ministerial Group on Women's Issues put it in 1991:

I am antipathetic to the notion that there should be universal access to child-care: 'creches for all'. It simply exacerbates the trend that we have had of seeing that it is possible if you've got responsibilities to put them onto the state. (quoted in FPSC 1991)

Care for dependants is categorised as a family responsibility. None the less, the continuing demand among women especially among the expanding group of middle-class women professionals – for mitigation of the 'double-shift' of domestic work and formal employment may force an official response.

The second area of unresolved conflict concerns male authority and the family. The traditional model sees family dependency as entirely healthy and the intrusion of state provision into the proscribed sphere of domestic responsibilities as nurturing a harmful reliance on government. Studies of kinship obligation demonstrate the variety, complexity and unpredictability of the duties that family members feel to one another (see, for example, Finch 1989: 242). Policy makers cannot simply rely on an automatic kinship duty to care. At the same time, evidence on violence and exploitation within the home challenges the view of the family as universal haven (Edwards 1989; J. Pahl 1989). There is no necessary link between support for dual parenting and the reduction of state provision. A prominent centre-left commentator recently argued that 'research evidence increasingly shows that a child's life, over and above class circumstances, is improved by having a stable two-parent upbringing'. This claim is used to strengthen the case for doubling child benefit and expanding nursery provision to make it possible for mothers to take on full-time jobs (Halsey 1991).

Policies designed to strengthen the family by cutting away services that might substitute for close family relationships may prove counterproductive. The study of those under 18 who have been denied income support since 1988 showed that over half had been forced to leave home by their parents because they were unable to contribute to family budgets (MORI 1991). The lack of secure provision and an adequate income support system for single parents makes it much more difficult for mothers to escape from violent relationships. Policy tensions in this area are also unresolved. At the time of writing the government is contemplating some restoration of benefits to under-18s, although there are no plans to improve benefits for single parents.

Over the 1980s, government has been successful in restricting family support, chiefly by reducing the value of child benefit, removing the additions for children from short-term national insurance benefits and introducing rules which make it more difficult for single parents to claim unemployment benefit unless they can show that child-care is available, should they be offered a job. However, as Chapter 1 showed, the proportion of families headed by a single parent continues to rise, and such families are more vulnerable to poverty than any other family grouping. The growth in single parenthood is the chief reason for an increase in the proportion of total benefit expenditure going to families – from 16 to 18 per cent of total social security spending between 1979 and 1991 (DSS 1991a: Table 10). High levels of unemployment coupled with lack of support, especially in cheap child-care, mean that the majority of single parents are dependent on income support benefit; many of those in work claim family credit. Increases in child benefit payable to all mothers and not means-tested were set at a rate below inflation from 1979 to 1987. Thereafter child benefit was frozen in cash terms until 1991, when an uprating for the first child and proposals to index-link benefits for all children at a later date were announced. The policy of targeting has led to a rise from 14 to 47 per cent between 1979 and 1991 in the proportion of benefit spending on families that is means-tested (DSS 1991a: Table 20).

One of the key reforms introduced by the Social Security Act of 1986, was the replacement of the supplementary benefit single payments scheme by the Social Fund (Craig 1990, 1992). The main object of the Social Fund was to reduce expenditure on one-off social assistance payments, partly by imposing budgetary cash limits upon the fund, and partly by providing that except in certain limited circumstances assistance is given by way of loans recoverable by deductions from future benefits rather than by grants. In this way, the total cost of one-off social assistance payments has been reduced from a relatively modest 0.5 per cent of the total social security budget to just 0.2 per cent (see Becker and Silburn 1990: 3), that is to say from £335m in 1986/7 to £130m (net of repayments) in 1989/90.

At the same time, however, the new scheme reintroduced discretionary decision making as the basis upon which assistance might exceptionally be given with the cost of large and/or unexpected items of household expenditure. The legislation required Social Fund officers, when awarding payments, to take into account the existence of any other sources from which a claimant's needs might be met and 'the possibility that some other person or body might wholly or partly meet it' (Section 33(9), Social Security Act 1986). Thus, apart from directly imposing new forms of budgetary discipline, the Social Fund was seen as a way of encouraging a greater degree of dependency on the family, relatives, friends and/ or private charity. Recent research suggests that the impact of this is perhaps less than originally feared (see Becker and Silburn 1990, SSRC 1991) but, as Gary Craig has put it, 'there is also clear evidence that such unmet need is being driven underground, into individualised and private "solutions" – loan sharks, help from family/friends, "doing without" ' (1992).

The most important development in policy for single parents is the proposal to set up a child support agency which will have the responsibility of assessing and collecting maintenance for income support and family credit claimants, and for anyone else who chooses to use its services (DSS 1990). This income will then be set against benefit rights. The object is to enforce paternal responsibility and to reduce state spending on single parents. Considerable controversy surrounds the proposal to cut benefit for single mothers who do not reveal the name of the father of the child. The government's Social Security Advisory Committee expressed particular concern about the position of 'those women who do not name the liable parent for fear of violence' (Low Pay Unit 1991: 12). It is uncertain whether this proposal will succeed in making fathers pay more maintenance for their children. Any success in achieving this narrow objective will be at the expense of the poorest families (Bennett and Chapman 1990). Some commentators suggest that it will be difficult to extract substantial increases in maintenance. A study of the 1987 Australian Child Support Scheme, on which the United Kingdom scheme is modelled, indicates that 'only a small percentage of sole parents are in a position to benefit', principally because it has only been possible to secure adequate maintenance orders from less than 10 per cent of absent parents (Harrison 1991: 91). Whether the United Kingdom scheme will be any more successful in improving the lives of single parents remains to be seen. Some aspects of the programme resemble the arrangements for surveillance of the lives of claimants that developed over the 1980s in relation to unemployment.

A number of measures are designed to impose a greater degree of parental responsibility in order to strengthen the role of the family in socialisation. The 1991 Criminal Justice Bill makes it obligatory for parents of juvenile offenders to attend court with them. The courts will have powers to bind over the parents of offenders under 18 to exercise proper care and control over their children. Parents will be liable for their children's fines. Previous measures increased the penalties for parents who fail to ensure that their children attend school. In the field of social security, the main changes have been the weakening of benefit rights for young people. New regulations in 1983 time-limited benefit entitlement for young people living in board and lodging accommodation; the 1986 Act introduced lower rates of benefit for those under 25; and in 1988 benefit rights were denied to those under 18 who were not on Youth Training Schemes.

Other changes contradict these measures, in particular the imposition of individual local tax liability on all adult members of the household (so that the tax burden rises when young people remain in their parents' households) and the provision for 'non-dependant deductions' under the housing benefit scheme. This reduces the assistance which parents may receive towards their rent on account of notional rental contributions by adult children, regardless of whether or not such contributions are actually paid. These factors are often seen as contributing to the rise in the number of homeless and destitute young people (Greve and Currie 1990). Despite the measures taken and the increase in youth unemployment over the period, there is no indication that the proportion of 16–18-year-olds living with their parents has increased.

These policies have failed to reconstitute parental authority as benign autocracy, or to halt the rise in the number of single-parent families. There has been some success in limiting the increase in social spending in this area, and in targeting benefits more precisely through means-testing. The evidence that take-up rates for the principal benefits involved are unsatisfactory (about 90 per cent and 65 per cent on an expenditure basis and barely 80 per cent and 50 per cent on a claimant count basis for income support and family credit respectively: DSS 1991a: paras. 38, 39) suggests that the system is, however, unsuccessful in targeting on genuine need. An increasing proportion of one-parent families lives in poverty. The numbers claiming last-resort means-tested benefits had risen from 560,000 in 1985/6 to 855,000 by 1990/1 (DSS 1991a: Table 14).

Family policy has been strongly influenced by ideas about dependency culture. In contrast to the area of work and welfare, the result has been inaction, rather than the reversal of the direction of policy. The result is that social change continues to have a strong impact on the family, but that government refuses to acknowledge the new patterns of need arising from changes in work and household structure. Social security has failed to change in order to meet the needs of single parents, despite the rapid increase in numbers, with the result that this group is the fastest growing group in poverty, as the evidence of Table 1.1 showed. Policy is confined to measures to enforce maintenance more rigorously, which appear unlikely to make much difference to living standards. Despite the increased pressures on women to participate in paid employment, the government refuses to play a major role in child-care, so that work opportunities are effectively curtailed, especially for those who can only command low wages. Young people are denied benefits in order to strengthen family structures. The result is a greater risk of poverty for those who are unable to live at home.

The view that welfare provision fosters dependency culture has guided work and family policy. The main object of our study is to examine the experience of claimants, in order to understand how the new approaches affect the lives of those whom they are designed to influence. In the following chapters we discuss evidence derived from detailed discursive interviews. First, however, we consider some findings from a structured national survey that show how far the preconceptions that drive policy change are shared by claimants and by the population at large.

Dependency culture and public attitudes

This section looks at the attitudes of the public at large to see whether they share the views of policy makers about benefits for unemployed people and single parents and about work and family ethics. It then goes on to examine the attitudes of the group who are arguably most vulnerable to dependency culture – long-term claimants who are unemployed or single parents – to consider whether they display a particular pattern of attitudes that distinguishes them from the rest of the population.

General attitudes to state welfare

Over the 1980s, support for state welfare has grown unequivocally, despite official arguments that have emphasised the virtues of the market. The attitudes of different groups, including supporters of the party of government, have grown closer together. The most authoritative evidence for this statement comes from the annual British Social Attitudes Survey, but this is reinforced by other evidence (see Taylor-Gooby 1991b: 111–13). The survey shows that, between 1983 (the earliest year for which data is available) and 1990, the proportion of the population stating that they would like to see more welfare spending even though this would involve tax increases has risen from a third to more than a half: by the end of the period there is little difference between the proportions of Conservative and Labour voters endorsing this view (50 as against 55 per cent). When attitudes to particular services are examined, it is provision for the mass of the population – the health service, education and pensions – that commands the strongest level of support, increasing over the period.

This pattern of attitudes is usually taken to indicate declining support for government social policies among the electorate at large, counterbalanced by sufficient enthusiasm for economic and taxation policy to win elections (see for example, Heath, Jowell and Curtice 1985: 91–6). In relation to benefits for unemployed people and single parents, a slightly different pattern emerges. Benefits for the mass need of retirement and for the highly deserving group of disabled people are popular throughout. Labour voters are more inclined to support child benefit, unemployment benefit and single parents' benefits, although the level of support for unemployed people has declined as unemployment rates fell over the period. Child benefit has risen rapidly up the priority ordering in recent years, indicating widespread concern at the freezing of the benefit in 1987.

One question in the survey focuses directly on the major plank in the government's policy towards unemployed people: widening the gap between benefits and wages in order to enhance work incentives. The proportion agreeing with the view that 'benefits are too high and discourage people from finding work' fell from 35 to 29 per cent of the sample between 1983 and 1990. However, there is considerable suspicion as to whether the system operates satisfactorily either to police claims or to meet genuine needs. Substantial majorities in both years agree both that there are many fraudulent claims and that many of those eligible fail to claim their entitlement.

Attitudes to the family ethic are best explored through the 1989 survey, which included a number of questions on the topic. These showed considerable attachment to the institution of marriage and to the two-parent family. Although less than a fifth of the sample agreed with the view that 'the main purpose of marriage these days is to have children', over four-fifths agreed that 'people who want children ought to get married'. Less than a quarter thought a single father could bring up a child as well as a married couple, and less than a third that a single mother could. The family ethic does not extend to the view that paid employment is the prerogative of the male breadwinner. In response to a battery of questions on this issue, there is clear agreement that women have the right to seek paid employment and that this does not damage their family (Jowell, Witherspoon and Brook 1990: 271).

There is little support in popular attitudes for the government's policies towards unemployed people, just as there is little endorsement of its restrictive approach to social policy in general. The objectives that underlie family policy receive rather stronger endorsement, although there are no questions on the detail of policy, especially the measures to secure maintenance and to extend means-testing for single parents. We move on to consider whether any evidence of a dependency culture can be found among the attitudes of the claimants themselves.

Dependency culture and long-term claimants

We used the 1989 British Social Attitudes survey to examine in some detail the attitudes of long-term unemployed people of working age and of single parents who claimed benefits. We defined these groups in practice as those who claimed income support and had been unemployed for a continuous spell of six months or more immediately preceding the interview and those who claimed income support, child benefit and single parents' benefit and did not define themselves as unemployed. These definitions are stringent: the first excludes those who have had interruptions in their spell of unemployment and those who define themselves as looking after a home, sick, disabled, retired, on a government training scheme or in education. The second excludes single parents who define themselves as unemployed or who do not claim single parents' benefit (some 10 per cent according to official estimates: DSS 1991a: para. 38). In the survey sample of 3,029, just 65 people fitted the conditions of the first group, and 45 the second.

The groups identified arguably contain those who are most likely to have developed the cultural characteristics of dependency. We examined how their attitudes related to those of the mass of the population. A more detailed discussion is given in the research report (Dean and Taylor-Gooby 1991).

The long-term unemployed group are realistically gloomy about their prospects for finding work. Less than a quarter expect to find a job in six months and most simply say 'never'. There is strong evidence of a willingness to retrain. Over three-quarters said that they would strongly prefer to work even if they were guaranteed a reasonable living income when unemployed. Thus they share the work orientation of the mass of the population. This parallels the findings of studies based on the British Election Survey (Heath 1991).

An interesting contrast with mass attitudes emerges in response to questions which ask the respondent to identify the most important problem of unemployment. Those in work tend to see the most important problem as lack of money – 58 per cent put this as the most significant issue. Among the unemployed group support for this view was rather lower, at 33 per cent, although it still came first in the priority order. Nearly as many (27 per cent) rated loss of confidence as the main problem. This indicates that the impact of work on self-esteem is experienced more strongly by unemployed people than others imagine, reinforcing the evidence of work-orientation.

Equally clear contrasts emerge in response to questions about perceptions of unemployed people. Most employed people think that unemployed people could find work, although only a minority go so far as to say that they are fiddling: unemployed people reject both views forcefully (Table 3.1). Long-term unemployed people share mainstream values, except when it comes to the condemnation of unemployed people. This is further evidence for the view that they do not hold a distinctive dependency culture; if they did

Table 3.1 Perceptions of unemployed people

	Agree %	Neither %	Disagree %
Unemployed people could find a job if they wanted to			
Employed	54	19	26
Unemployed	21	31	48
Most people on the dole are fiddling			
Employed	32	29	38
Unemployed	26	29	43

they would contradict most mainstream values but concur with judgements that attributed dependency to unemployed people.

In response to questions about the value of marriage and about women's roles in relation to paid employment, the single-parent claimant group shared the views of married couples dependent on employment in the sample. Both groups endorsed marriage and also stressed that women had equal rights and responsibilities to take jobs and contribute to family income. The groups differed in response to three questions concerning single parenthood and marriage (Table 3.2). Single parents challenge whether marriage is

Table 3.2 Single parenthood and marriage

	Agree %	Neither %	Disagree %
Married people are happier than unmarried people			
Married	29	48	19
Single parents	9	47	39
A single mother can bring up a child as well as a married mother			
Married	29	16	53
Single parent	59	25	16
A single father can bring up a child as well as a married father			
Married	25	16	53
Single parent	36	45	19

Table 3.3 Welfare and responsibility

	Agree %	Neither %	Disagree
Welfare makes people less willing to look after themselves			
Employed	34	23	41
Unemployed	30	17	53
Married	34	24	41
Single parents	17	21	57
The welfare state encourages people to stop helping each other			
Employed	31	26	42
Unemployed	27	26	47
Married	31	27	42
Single parents	13	49	39
Many on social security deserve no help			
Employed	27	27	45
Unemployed	19	23	58
Married	20	25	48
Single parents	15	14	71

essential to happiness and disagree that single parents are less successful in bringing up children than are with married couples. This indicates greater support for diversity in family patterns, but does not endorse the view that single parenthood should necessarily be linked to state dependency.

A further series of questions covered welfare dependency in more general terms. These show that the employed groups do not, by and large, see welfare as undermining self-help or mutual aid, or as charity for undeserving groups. Unemployed people and single-parent claimants hold these same views even more strongly (Table 3.3). This further supports the view that those whose circumstances might incline them towards a culture of dependency do not in fact display the appropriate values.

Government policy that identifies dependency culture as one of the main problems of state welfare and devises strategies to root it out finds no echo in popular attitudes. Large-scale national surveys detect little evidence of such a culture among unemployed people or single parents on benefit.

Studying claimants' experiences

The studies upon which the previous section are based depend upon the analysis of answers given by individuals to the questions devised in advance by a researcher and included in a pre-coded questionnaire. Such an approach is at best partial for two kinds of reason, one to do with methodology and the other to do with the scope of the investigation. Our own study, based on discursive interviews, enables us to examine in detail how the new policies were interpreted by the claimants themselves in the context of their own lives. Both approaches are necessary to provide a full picture of the experience of claiming. This chapter therefore concludes with a discussion of the advantages and disadvantages of each method.

Structured surveys and discursive interviews

The technique of structured survey suffers from three main limitations. These result from the way in which questions are formulated, the context in which they are asked and the way in which patterns of answers are analysed to support particular arguments. Survey questionnaires must inevitably reflect the assumptions of the social scientists who design them, both in what they include and in what they omit. A whole process of review, pre-testing and piloting is undertaken in order to minimise this problem and the professional standards of the British Social Attitudes Survey team are widely respected. None the less, there can be no guarantee that aspects of the topic under study that are of importance to particular individuals are included or that individuals actually hold well-formulated views on the subjects about which they answer questions. It is considered polite in our society to respond when someone asks you a question, and belittling to confess ignorance. One result is that people will produce quite convincing patterns of response to questions on subjects which they have never seriously considered. These problems demand careful questionnaire design and caution in analysis, but cannot be entirely resolved by such measures (Bateson 1984: 24–7).

In *any* interview situation forced replies to formal questions may fundamentally elude the essence of what a person conveys, as is vividly illustrated by journalist Beatrix Campbell, who has described speaking to a young unemployed woman at a local unemployed centre in south Yorkshire. With two companions, this 19-year-old was roaming the country looking for work, stopping in night shelters and hostels, possessing little more than the clothes she stood up in:

> Her passivity was formidable, but we talked a bit . . . During her account of her travels she never said a word about how she felt. Did she ever get depressed, I asked, like the proverbial television interviewer? Silence. 'Does it ever get you down?' I repeated. 'I suppose it does', she said. 'Have we finished, can I go now?' I wanted to ask her more, but she didn't want to talk much about the detail, which didn't seem very important to her. And yet detail in these things is everything. More, the detail is the bearer of your real feelings about it all, and yet your real feelings can't be disclosed. Why should she disclose her real feelings to me, after all? I've got a notebook and a pen, and more than one pair of shoes, and I'm not revealing *my* feelings. So why should she? (1984: 182–4)

The second problem of the method derives from the way in which questionnaires are administered. We have already seen that the fact of being asked a question imposes constraints on the answer, namely that there will probably be one, even if the question is not obviously relevant. The circumstances in which the interview takes place are likely to exert a further influence. Interviews may be carried out on respondents' doorsteps or in their homes by people who are trained to appear neutral and to offer as few cues as possible, in order to avoid contaminating the results. An experienced survey practitioner points out that 'even apparently trivial reactions can affect answers. For example, following a respondent's reply with the word "good" can introduce bias in subsequent answers' (Hoinville, Jowell and associates 1980: 100). Complete neutrality is impossible, both because an individual must fit into some category and because factors which lead to some responses in some people may produce different responses in others. It is commonly assumed that any interviewer bias will be randomised in large surveys, so that the results will be rendered less precise rather than skewed in a particular direction, but the problem remains.

The third set of issues concerns the interpretation of survey findings. Interpretation requires an engagement with the data based on a theory about how particular responses hang together. In the preceding discussion of the Social Attitudes Survey, dependency culture is understood to generate a rejection of work and family ethic among particular groups of claimants, and the answers to certain questions are assumed to provide good evidence of this. Just as the construction of the questionnaire requires the selection of a particular perspective from those that are available, so does the interpretation of the results (Marsh 1982: 123–4).

These problems do not invalidate structured survey as an investigative method. They suggest that conclusions carry more conviction when they are reinforced by evidence produced by different methods. There is no royal road to truth. The use of discursive interviews loosely structured around a schedule of relevant issues allows the person interviewed more freedom to interpose perspectives not initially offered by the researcher. The researcher may also pursue particular themes that seem salient in the ideas of the person interviewed and thus arrive at an understanding of why it is that the person holds the views offered. Unstructured interviews have their own problems. The possibility of interviewer bias requires more consideration since the interviewer plays a more active role in the construction of the interaction. In general, discursive interviews allow good opportunities for people to express their views in ways which depart from the preconceived pattern of the researcher. For this reason they are commonly used as an important element in defining the themes to be covered in a structured questionnaire survey. In our study, the bulk of the analysis rests on discursive interviews organised around a loose schedule of themes derived from discussions with claimants. These interviews are of particular importance because they enable the research to approach the topic from another perspective and because they contribute to an understanding of the pattern of attitudes.

The investigation of values

A further reason why discursive interviewing is particularly appropriate to this study arises from the issue under investigation. Attitude surveys provide information on the attitudes of respondents understood as their beliefs about and evaluation of the particular object, issue or policy mentioned in the question. The focus of the study is dependency culture and the assumption is that the pattern of values that underlie attitudes may be analysed on the basis of the response to attitude questions, so that a picture of a culture is built up as the preponderance of the values expressed by individuals in a particular category.

There are two problems with this approach. First, it presents culture as the sum of individual attitudes. Secondly, it assumes that different attitude areas are of equal value as clues to culture. Culture is a general term for the symbolic, learned non-biological aspects of human society. It is a property of a group. The arguments that distinguish dependency culture from mainstream culture imply a duality, possibly a plurality, of co-existing cultures of which this is one. A sub-culture is a lifeway or lifeworld of meanings and interactions that give sense to circumstances and behaviour, shared by a group. This gives rise to problems with the use of national random sample attitude survey material as a way of exploring the sub-culture of dependency. The material is gathered in one-to-one interviews with people who for the most part are unlikely to be members of the culture. The method is unable to explore the collective nature of culture as it exists within a particular group. In addition, the method focuses exclusively on an interview at one point in time, whereas culture persists and contains ideas about the past and expectations for the future. Attitude data as analysed above cannot do justice to the collective or to the temporal nature of culture.

One approach to this problem involves the identification of cultural sub-groups and the use of ethnographic or participant observational methods, so that the researcher seeks to understand the shared meanings of the life of the members of the group from a position as close to their own as can be achieved. In the case of dependency culture, there are a number of problems with this approach. First, the existence of the culture is in dispute, so there is no clear way of identifying the appropriate group for study. Secondly, dependency culture theorists do not postulate one definitive group of dependent claimants. Social benefit claimants who might participate in the postulated dependency culture also participate in social life in a variety of other roles, as members of a family or an ethnic group, as residents of a particular area, as at a particular age and stage in the family life-cycle. These factors may influence their

behaviour, values and views in ways that are difficult to disentangle. For example, two people may be equally candidates for
dependency culture because they both rely on benefits and do not
seek paid work. One may do so because that person's primary role
in life is as a parent and he/she sees this as a full-time job; the other
may be slightly disabled, exhausted after forty years' manual work
and effectively retired early. To disentangle the assumptions and
perceptions of such individuals through participation in their social
groups over a period of time would be rewarding but demanding.

These factors strengthen the case for the choice of discursive
interviews as a way of examining the cultural orientations of claimants. Rather than seeking a group of dependent claimants in which
to participate, the research sought out working age claimants from
their various social locations and explored their relations with
other claimants, their expectations and their understanding of
their past through lengthy discursive interviews. These interviews
made it possible to explore the cultural issues of relationship to
others in the same position, as well as their anticipation and
remembrance.

Conclusion

This chapter has discussed how ideas about dependency culture
have influenced social policy in the 1980s and 1990s, how far they
have been reflected in popular attitudes and the attitudes of long-
term claimants as recorded in structured survey data and how they
may be also approached through discursive interviews. The Conservative government of the period reversed the main direction of
social security and employment policy, and repudiated any attempt
to restructure family policy in line with changing patterns of family
life and women's employment. The emphasis in relation to benefits
was on targeting on 'genuinely needy' people and widening the gap
between benefit levels and wages rather than increasing levels of
provision. The benefit regime for single parents and young adults
became harsher. Job-creation subsidies were removed.

These policies have been successful in holding down the level of
benefits and increasing the numbers at the poverty line. The emphasis on means-testing has also been relatively successful at diverting

resources to particular groups, but has failed to meet the needs of many of those who live in poverty. Policy overall has signally failed to reduce the level of unemployment, reverse the trend to the restructuring of the family or reduce the number in poverty. The aims of meeting need and spending less appear to contradict each other, as do the aims of preserving the traditional family against social change and refusing to intervene within it.

The pattern of popular attitudes displayed in survey data shows strong support for the retention and expansion of state provision, and the level of support has risen as spending constraint grows more stringent. There is no evidence of an alternative dependency culture among welfare users, even when the focus is narrowed to the core group of long-term able-bodied claimants. This picture is circumscribed by the shortcomings of the structured attitude survey as a method and is limited in what it can tell us about the culture of respondents. Discursive interviews offer an alternative picture of the reality of the lives of social welfare claimants. Our study uses a discursive interview survey of claimants in order to develop an understanding of claiming as they experience it, to provide opportunities for discussion of relationships with other claimants, expectations and past experience, and to generate material from an alternative perspective to triangulate with the broad-brush picture of claimants presented above. The study is the largest discursive interview study of the claiming experience to focus on dependency culture and the issues that surround it. The main findings are presented in the next two chapters, and the details of how the research was carried out are contained in the appendix.

CHAPTER 4

THE CLAIMING EXPERIENCE

It is hard being on social. I don't wish to be on it. If I had my own choice I wouldn't be on social security. It doesn't really do nothing for me. . .

It ain't exactly a brilliant life, you know what I mean? Sometimes I get annoyed when people say 'you people on social get things done for you' and all this sort of thing: most of them that says it to me, they're not even on social themself, so they don't really know what it's like. . .

I don't feel as if any of it – none of it – is a right; it's a privilege. But they actually make me dependent, because . . . I feel that the system is such that it wants to make me dependent by this resentment, this grudging, secondrate – I put it more than secondrate, it's worse than that, but that's the member of the population that you become. You are a problem . . . you are just a problem to all these other good people.

These quotations come from three interviews with long-term income support claimants conducted in 1990 as part of an ESRC-funded study (Dean and Taylor-Gooby 1991). This chapter and the next will be based mainly upon the findings of that research. As the above quotations show, our aim is to give voice to the feelings, fears and aspirations of the people who are 'dependent' on state social security benefits. We shall show how the experience of claiming social security benefits measures up to the image of the 'dependency culture'.

The questions which our research sought originally to address were essentially threefold: to establish whether and in what sense there is a 'dependency culture' characterised by distinctive behavioural or attitude patterns among social security benefit recipients of working age; to examine the relevance of competing ideas about social security with regard to its effects upon work incentives, social discipline and active citizenship; and to appraise the consequences of those recent changes in social security policy which have been intended or justified as an attack upon the 'dependency culture'. Chapter 3 has described the reforms of the 1980s, which were designed to reinforce work incentives, to encourage dependency upon liable relatives and/or the wider family and to increase the scrutiny to which benefit claims and claimants are subject. In Chapter 3 we also reviewed some national survey data on work incentives, the family ethic and social welfare. Our study in this chapter enables us to extend the research to examine the values of working age welfare claimants in detail.

Our research was based on eighty-five in-depth discursive interviews with social security benefit recipients of working age. This makes it, so far as we are aware, the largest investigation of its kind in the United Kingdom to date. The sample was drawn from South London and north and east Kent, partly with co-operation from independent advice-giving agencies, local press and media and partly with co-operation from the Department of Social Security. In view of the qualitative nature of the research, this was not intended to be a statistically representative sample, but it was balanced in terms of gender, age and race. It also contained a sufficient number of each kind of working age social security recipient likely to have been affected by recent changes in the social security regime, including of course both non-employed persons and single parents, to enable us to examine the effect of the new policies.

The composition of the sample and the methodology of the investigation are discussed in the appendix. Here we shall be concerned principally with our findings and, in this chapter, with claimants' experiences of the claiming process and their general orientations towards work, the family, the state and the wider community.

Mainstream values

'Dependency culture' is characterised by a departure from the pattern of values which guides the behaviour of most people.

Where our research found such tendencies to be in evidence, they were in fact relatively isolated and were not intelligible in cultural or sub-cultural terms. The behaviour and attitudes of most or all social security claimants, we have found, are ultimately intelligible in terms of mainstream orientations and/or the contradictions between citizenship expectations and the nature of the claiming experience.

Our investigation appeared to suggest that respondents in the sample by and large subscribed to a core of 'mainstream' values in relation to work, the family, the state and other people which might broadly be characterised as a possessive individualist orientation – though 'possessive' is not here used in quite the same sense as in MacPherson's (1962) celebrated expression 'possessive individualism': respondents were not necessarily rapaciously acquisitive, but tended to be preoccupied with the security of their personal hold upon or individual 'possession' of the material means of subsistence. However, dependency culture may only apply to some claimants. To examine whether a minority among our sample was departing from the values of the rest of the population in such a way as to constitute a distinctive dependency culture, it is first necessary to delineate mainstream culture.

Our interview transcripts confirmed, sustained and developed a picture of what constituted the mainstream possessive individualist values referred to above. These values operate in four principal domains, each with a primary and a secondary component, as follows:

1. Work is valued primarily as a means to self-esteem or identity and only secondarily as a means to material reward. Where material rewards are valued, there is virtue or 'worth' associated with the effort involved or the pride taken in one's work.
2. The family (in its individual nuclear manifestation) i valued primarily for its affective relationships and emotional rewards and only secondarily as a means to reciprocal material security. To the extent that material security is valued, its importance is restricted to obligations which are seen to arise during a very specific socially constructed stage of the life-cycle – childhood.
3. The state is regarded primarily as an external authority (or adversary) and only secondarily as a means to collective security through citizenship. To the extent that collective security

is valued, it is apprehended in terms of contractual rather than co-operative principles of reciprocity.
4. 'Other' people are regarded primarily from the vantage point of privatism and exclusive social associations and only secondarily from any awareness of broader collective interests and inclusive social associations. To the extent that 'liberal' attitudes (i.e. social tolerance/compassion) are embraced, these are more libertarian than solidaristic in nature.

Most of the claimants we interviewed aspired in most instances to primary rather than secondary values as characterised above and, subject to the qualifications outlined and so far as was apparent from the interviews, there were no claimants who did not intelligibly fit the hypothesis. However, recent social security reforms may place strains upon such aspirations. It is the resulting breaches of people's expectations as workers, as family members, as citizens and as members of a wider community which can best account for such instances of behaviour and attitudes as were observed to be at odds with mainstream values. We shall examine each of the four domains of mainstream values, in relation to work, the family, the state and other people.

Labour discipline

In Chapter 3 we illustrated the ways in which many of the social security reforms of the 1980s were intended or justified in terms of increasing work incentives. For unemployed claimants in particular the penalties for 'voluntary' unemployment and the rules relating to 'availability' for work were made more stringent. In more general terms, changes in the structure of means-tested benefits were intended to increase the incentives for claimants, including single parents on benefit, to take low-paid employment.

The impact of changes

The claimants in our sample were asked whether they were aware of those changes to the social security system which might encourage people to work, or whether they felt they had been affected in this way. Barely a third of the sample (32 of our 85 respondents) were really aware of those changes in the social security system which relate to work incentives, and less than a third (27 respondents) actually felt they were under pressure to obtain work. A handful of respondents (6) indicated they felt generally pressured by the system, but did not seem to be especially conscious of recent rule changes, and a similar number were aware of recent rule changes, but did not find them unduly oppressive or else regarded them (often with derision) as being ineffective. A majority of the sample (44 respondents, including 27 of the 33 single parents in the sample) appeared to be immune to, or unaware of, any particular or specific pressure relating to work incentives.

This shows that the changes to the social security system have not been especially effective in increasing work incentives. As will become clear, however, this does not mean that claimants are not motivated to work, or that the changes have been entirely without consequence.

Other recent changes in employment and social security policy have been concerned with training programmes or skills promotion and the claimants in our sample were therefore asked whether there were any training or educational opportunities which were or had been available to them or in which they might be interested. Well over a third of the sample (34 respondents) had recently been or were currently engaged in some form of training or non-recreational educational activity or were planning shortly to do so. Over a fifth of the sample (18 respondents) were definitely interested in pursuing education or training, but were unable to obtain any or were not aware of anything appropriate. Under a quarter of the sample (20 respondents) were not aware of any training/education which was currently available and were not especially interested. Only two respondents admitted that they were aware of or had been offered training which they had declined through lack of interest or because the offer was inappropriate.

Although the level of commitment to the idea of training and education was therefore generally high, it was in fact proportionately higher among single parents than among the non-employed members of the sample. This may reflect the different significance which a spell on benefits can have for single parents (who may expect to enter or return to the labour-market at some

definite stage in the future) as opposed to non-employed persons
(many of whom are anxious to return to work as soon as possible,
but who cannot determine how soon such an opportunity may
arise). More predictably, perhaps, an interest in training or education was also proportionately higher among the younger age
groups in the sample than for the oldest age group.

Of the respondents who had been or were engaged in or proposed to go on some form of training or educational activity, just
over a half referred to government schemes (YTS, ET or, in some
instances, courses run in connection with Job Clubs and the Enterprise Allowance Scheme); around a third referred to specific non-
governmental vocational education courses (such as in typing or
accountancy); and a handful of respondents referred to academic
courses (GCSE, Access or degree courses). Respondents were not
generally asked what they thought about the relevance or efficacy
of government training schemes, but of those who had experienced
them only two said they had found the experience helpful, while
most said they had found the schemes in some way unhelpful,
unsatisfactory or irrelevant. Other respondents who had not directly experienced such schemes volunteered similar condemnatory
opinions. Characteristically, respondents complained about the exploitative nature of training schemes, and their failure in some
instances to guarantee usable qualifications or to provide the specific kinds of training which would be helpful to respondents. Job
Club courses (intended to promote job-seeking skills) were criticised for their irrelevance and the patronising treatment afforded
to participants: 'they treat you like little school kids'. There can be
little doubt that there is considerable support among social
security claimants (and not only those who are registered unemployed) for access to training and educational opportunities,
but that current government provision falls short of people's
expectations.

Obstacles to employment

An attempt was made to establish what reasons respondents gave
for their (or, in some instances, their partners') inability or difficulty in finding suitable employment. Of the respondents who addressed this question, around a half identified a single or primary

cause, while the other half cited a combination of factors, or gave quite complex explanations. The most commonly cited cause, mentioned by a third of those specifically answering the question, was the constraints of caring responsibilities for children or dependent adults. The other causes mentioned (in descending order of frequency) related to either: the respondents' lack of experience and/ or qualifications; the inadequacy of the wages on offer in such jobs as were available; the age of the respondent; health or medical factors; factors directly relating to social security, such as the stigma or discrimination associated with their claimant status and/or with being long-term unemployed, or the lack of money available to them for travelling to interviews; or the respondents' lack of references from past employers and/or their criminal records.

Recent evidence from other sources has indicated that unemployed people as a whole, including those not registered as available for work, are no less motivated to work and may even be more highly motivated than the employed population (Gallie and Vogler 1990). Our own non-directive interviews with social security claimants did not contain a specific 'test' of work commitment, but much of the discussion in the course of our interviews related directly or indirectly to the motivation of respondents to seek or to take up paid employment. The picture to emerge was that three-quarters of the sample (64 respondents) were clearly anxious to find work: of these, more than half (35) were currently seeking or had recently sought employment or training and the remainder (29) were temporarily prevented or constrained from seeking work (e.g. because of caring responsibilities or medical factors). Other respondents (6), while clearly not immediately anxious to find work, none the less expected to do so at some later date or would do so if a suitable opportunity presented itself. This confirms the findings of our analysis of the British Social Attitudes Survey in Chapter 3.

About one sixth of our sample (14 respondents) would seem not to have been particularly or at all motivated to find work: of these, some (4) none the less said in the course of the interview that they hoped to come off benefits in the foreseeable future. Of those remaining (10), some had health problems, some had caring responsibilities and one was a 52-year-old man who had just taken early retirement with an enhanced pension from the recently dismantled Inner London Education Authority. The only other 'unmotivated' respondent was a highly articulate and unusual man in his late 50s who, having been unemployed for several years after an erratic overseas career as a technician in the oil industry, now claimed to have rejected the work ethic and the entire 'ethos of capitalism': having consciously adopted an anarchist (not a socialist) perspective, he was forced none the less to admit that he had had to 'work through' his feelings of guilt about welfare dependency and that this was a process which had involved 'a certain amount of pain'.

The discursive content of each interview was carefully studied for evidence of the nature of each respondent's motivation to work or the value which employment had for each respondent (whether or not she/he was motivated at present to seek work). This revealed that a majority of the entire sample (45 respondents) had demonstrated that any desire they had to work stemmed primarily from some internal drive or ambition or for a desire for the self-esteem, stimulus, satisfaction or enjoyment associated with employment. Far fewer respondents (23) had seemed to demonstrate that their desire to work was primarily pragmatic in nature and that it was related to a desire for a better standard of living and/or to provide for their own family. Just two respondents seemed to demonstrate that their desire to work stemmed directly or negatively from the pressures of the claiming experience: one of these respondents was a middle-aged man with osteoarthritis who continued to seek work because the DSS Regional Medical Officer insisted he was capable of 'light work', but who longed to be just 'left alone'; the other was a young, illiterate single parent with negligible prospects of full employment who felt particularly stigmatised by the claiming experience (having been prosecuted by the DSS for a minor fraud involving an overpayment of just £33) and concluded pathetically that 'we should be responsible for ourselves really . . . it would be nice to show other people you can go out [i.e. and work]'.

It would seem therefore that for most claimants their motivation to work is quite unrelated to and largely independent of any pressures exerted upon them by the social security system. As one unemployed respondent put it, 'I don't need encouraging'. It would further seem that the small minority of claimants for whom such pressures may take precedence is likely to include those whom the labour-market is in practice least likely to accommodate.

Of greater significance than the incentive effects of the social security system in the minds of the claimants in our sample were the disincentive effects of the 'poverty trap' associated with the inter-relationship between means-tested benefit rules and rates on the one hand and the low prevailing level of wages on the other. Once again, the discursive content of the interviews was studied for evidence of the respondents' awareness of such issues. More than half of our interview transcripts (46) contained relevant passages and most of these included discussion by respondents of how much they would have to earn before it would be worth while going out to work (or into full-time work), or explicit or implicit criticisms by respondents of the limitations imposed by the current level of earnings 'disregards' under the income support scheme. Some respondents additionally or separately complained about the low level of wages available to them and/or were specifically critical of the family credit scheme (a means-tested benefit to supplement low wages): as one such respondent put it, 'when I work, I don't want to bother with having to claim'. Only a handful of respondents (but including both the respondents whose partners were actually receiving family credit) expressed approval for the family credit scheme, while a similar number of respondents acknowledged that, if benefit levels were set too high, people (but *not* necessarily the respondents concerned) might not want to work.

It was striking that single parents seemed to feel particularly discouraged by the social security system from working; a full two-thirds of the single parents in the sample indicated as much. This was consistent with other recent research findings (see J. Brown 1989). Our evidence also suggests that the more aware or knowledgeable claimants are as to the workings of the social security system (see p. 130 below), the more likely they are to blame the poverty trap upon the workings of that system rather than upon inadequate wage levels, while claimants who are confused or uncertain about their entitlement to benefits are more likely to focus their attention upon the difficulties of achieving a living wage.

Claimants' aspirations

Turning to the question of what work (if any) respondents were currently engaged in, only eight respondents (seven of them women) were engaged in declared part-time employment, of whom two combined it with voluntary work and one with undeclared part-time employment. A further four respondents admitted they were engaged in occasional or regular undeclared employment (of which more will be said later: see p. 119) and seven respondents said they did regular voluntary work. Four-fifths of the sample (68 respondents) were doing no work at all, confirming the contention of several respondents that the system does little or nothing to encourage the desire of many claimants to undertake part-time work (c.f. McLaughlin, Miller and Cooke 1989).

While discussing the matter of work incentives, the claimants in our sample were asked what kind of work they would like to do and, while respondents generally responded in terms of the kind of work they were accustomed to or were qualified to do, more than two-fifths of the sample (38 respondents) also spoke about their wider aspirations or pipe-dreams. The largest group of these respondents (15) said they would like to take up a particular skilled occupation or trade (such as driving, computing or carpentry); a similar number said they would like to work in some caring occupation (such as social work or child-care); a much smaller number said they would like some form of self-employment and just two respondents said they would like some kind of managerial responsibility. Such replies are interesting because they imply, not only that there is a wealth of unfulfilled ambition among the ranks of social security recipients, but that the fulfilment which such recipients seek is more likely to be regarded in terms of personal satisfaction or even altruism than in terms of autonomy or power.

When asked how much longer they thought they would remain in receipt of benefits, a half of our sample (43 respondents) either did not know or feared they would remain on benefits indefinitely. Slightly fewer respondents (38) either had plans to come off benefits at some future time or stage, or had firm hopes of coming off in the foreseeable future. Three respondents, at the time of interview, had in fact already started in employment. Single parents were proportionately more likely than non-employed respondents to have expectations of coming off benefits in future, and it was the oldest age group in the sample who were the most uncertain or pessimistic about their future prospects. Respondents from a professional/managerial or from a skilled manual occupational background were proportionately more likely than other groups to be pessimistic about their future prospects, while those from a clerical/retail/catering occupational background seemed, proportionauely speaking, the most optimistic.

Claimants by and large wanted to come off benefits, and their expectations of doing so were shaped either by their own plans for some future stage of their life cycles or by their estimation of their prospects in the labour market. In terms of both empirical probability and the respondents' own perceptions, dependence on social security benefits was for most claimants a finite stage, rather than a fixed status: it was hopefully a temporary experience, not acceptable as a permanent one.

The pressure to work

Occurring as it does in the context of low wages and low job security, the pressure upon social security recipients to 'price themselves into jobs' may therefore erode the self-esteem and undermine the self-motivation of the unemployed and, perversely, increase their preoccupation with secondary/material considerations. The claimants we spoke to, both non-employed and single parents, were for the most part highly motivated to work, but the pressures upon these two groups were different.

Some single parents indicated that it was important for them to stay at home until their children reached a certain age, but they looked upon this as a temporary state of affairs and intended to go or return to work in due course. However, single parents who were ready to seek employment felt directly constrained from so doing by both the benefits system and the deficiencies of the labour-market. As one such respondent put it, 'It's quite a luxury to go to work really': a luxury she was no longer permitted and could not afford.

For non-employed respondents (which includes both registered unemployed persons and those excluded from the labour market for different reasons – see appendix) the pressures were different. Some would illustrate their desperation by saying that if they were offered *any* job (even a job 'shovelling shit') they would take it. But others would recoil from work that was too menial or uncongenial: 'I can never see myself sweeping the street, that's more degrading than going to the social, I think'. Such reservations, though certainly not confined to respondents with skilled or professional occupational backgrounds, were of particular salience to them: as one respondent put it, 'am I going to make a very good cleaner in a leisure centre when I've been trained to be the goddam manager?'. Another respondent put it simply but eloquently:

> We don't all want to sit at a desk pushing a pen and we don't all want to be diesel mechanics [the respondent's original occupation] and we don't all want to be ditch diggers . . . we all want a job that we like. If that's not available, well we can take any old thing, and by taking any old thing you just make yourself worse and worse and worse.

The point was underlined by a young unemployed man (with a partner and child) with no qualifications and no pretensions other than to be a labourer:

> I'd hate to work in a factory . . . I don't want to sit there putting things in a machine or packing boxes, that's no good to me, I'd get fat and lazy . . . If I'm working, I want to *work*, that's why I like building work. What I'm asking for is a good job, good pay and I'll work *hard* for it.

One respondent was bitterly critical of the pressure exerted on him to go on government training schemes because it undermined his self-motivation and interfered with his capacity to decide for himself that he wanted to work: 'it's not easy to have the necessary self-respect to organise myself, because you're not supposed to have any self-respect if you are on somebody else's money'. In this connection, two respondents (one consciously, the other unconsciously) made out a case for something in the nature of a basic income guarantee: 'If they paid me £150 or £200 a week, right, and said it was unconditional, within six months to a year I'd have a job; I'd feel I was wanted – do you understand?'

A few respondents were keenly aware of the political philosophy which underpins recent social security reforms, but even when they applauded it they struggled to define the sense in which they found it somehow counterproductive and demotivating:

> If I'd come to that view 20 years ago . . . I would have said 'right, it's dog eat dog' (which is what I consider the Tory philosophy is) . . . 'the gloves are off'. I would have loved it. But I feel, you know, that I've come to the point that I'm not in that peak fighting condition as it were to be able to tackle that situation on an even footing . . . so I'm very disadvantaged and . . . there's an inevitability about the situation. But there's little I can do about it.

Family dependency

As has been outlined in Chapter 3, some of the reforms to the social security system implemented in the 1980s were designed to encourage claimants to rely more for assistance upon family, relatives or friends. The introduction of the discretionary Social Fund in place of the supplementary benefits single payments scheme contrived quite deliberately to throw income support recipients back on to the resources of their wider families. The renewed attention given to the enforcement of contributions from liable relatives and the various attempts to restrict the independent entitlements of young people were similarly focused upon the responsibilities of families.

Reacting to enforced family dependency

In our interviews with social security claimants we sought to probe the attitudes of respondents to these changes. To the extent that such changes have involved fairly subtle shifts in emphasis in policy interpretation or may not have been publicly justified upon such grounds, it was difficult to test the awareness of respondents as to the changes themselves. However, respondents' feelings on the issue did generally emerge in the course of most interviews, as did some indication of the reliance which they in fact placed on help from family, relatives and friends.

Two-thirds of our sample (57 respondents) either implicitly or expressly disapproved of the idea that they should rely on help from family or friends. Of these respondents, well over a half (34) did not or could not turn to their family or friends. Only 4 respondents expressed any approval for the idea (and of these, 3 in fact did not or did not have to rely on family or friends). Around a fifth of the sample (18 respondents) expressed neither approval nor disapproval and, of these, only 6 had not turned to family or friends for help. In all, therefore, a majority of the sample (43 respondents) indicated that they did not generally seek help from family or friends.

Predictably, perhaps, the youngest age group in the sample was proportionately more likely to rely on family or friends than were the older groups, but the oldest age group was more likely to disapprove of having to do so. Women respondents were proportionately more likely than men to say that they relied on family or friends, but were not significantly more likely to say or imply that they disapproved of having to do so.

Closer study of the discursive content of the interviews revealed more about the strength and nature of respondents' views in relation to family dependency and pointed to a great many internal contradictions in the positions adopted by some respondents (but see p. 136 below). None the less, some two-thirds of the sample (60 respondents) indicated in what they said, if not that they disapproved of enforced family dependency, that there were limits to what was acceptable in this regard. Of these, two-thirds (41 respondents – nearly half the total sample) had objections in principle, while the remaining third (19) objected on pragmatic grounds because their families were simply not in a position to help them. The principled objections which seemed to reflect the predominant view of familial obligation revolved around the sense of 'pride' which respondents took in managing independently of either their parents or their grown-up children: as one respondent, the partner of an unemployed man, said, 'it seems to me to be wrong . . . they [one's parents] have brought you up for so long, you've married and left . . . [but] . . . because of the way things are [being on benefits], you've gone but it's like you're living at home and asking for your pocket money every week'; or as one single parent with both older and dependent children put it, 'you shouldn't have to be beholden to your children, it's wrong'.

The claimants in our sample were asked what family, relations and friends would be available to them 'if push came to shove' and they needed some extra financial help or a loan. Almost a quarter of the sample insisted there was nobody to whom they could turn. A similar proportion mentioned a combination of relatives and/or friends. Of those who identified a particular source of help (44 respondents), half referred to their parents or parents-in-law, and much smaller proportions referred to sons and/or daughters, to friends, to brothers and/or sisters, and only one respondent mentioned an ex-partner. Men were proportionately more likely than women to have nobody to whom they could turn, as were older people compared to younger people.

Of the 33 single parents in the sample, only about one fifth (7 respondents) had formal maintenance arrangements with their ex-partners (or the fathers of their children); of these arrangements, 4 were satisfactory and 3 were badly observed. Of the remaining single parents, 3 received only informal or irregular maintenance and the partners of a further 3 had died. Thus almost two-thirds of single parents with former partners still alive reported that they received no or negligible maintenance. While some single parents felt aggrieved that they received no or insufficient maintenance from their ex-partners, most were aware that this would not bene-fit them while they remained on social security benefits and others were adamant that they wanted as little as possible to do with their ex-partners (see p. 129 below).

Regardless of the nature or quality of the relationship which single parents retained with their ex-partners, their dilemma was concisely summed up by one young single parent who, though on good terms with her child's father, was thankful not to be finan-cially dependent on him because 'it would be a lot harder and it would be more frustrating and stressful because you would have a man around you not really helping, or maybe perhaps can't really help you. That's the thing people don't take into consideration'.

There was a sense in which the burden of financial obligation was seen as standing in the way of the kind of affective familial relationships which many claimants value.

First and last resorts

In the context of discussing with the claimants in our sample the matter of dependency on family and friends, respondents were asked what they would do in the event of an immediate and per-manent cessation of their benefits. The off-the-cuff answers re-ceived were more generally revealing than had been anticipated. In fact less than a fifth of the sample said they would turn to family, friends or to charity, whereas a third of the sample said they would try and get a job or go out to work (legitimate or otherwise). Smaller numbers of respondents said they would turn to crime (or, in one case, to prostitution); that they would sell their house or possessions or draw on their savings; that they would just have to walk the streets or starve or resort to institutional care; and one respondent said he would commit suicide. Some respondents (11) just had no idea what they would do: of these, the majority were passive or despairing at the prospect, but a few were positively aggressive, saying they would go down to the DSS and have it out with them, or shoot them, or blow them up (though one respondent said, having made such a remark, 'that's fantasy I'm sure . . . That sounds terribly pathetic, embarrassing, I'm ashamed, deeply ashamed of it'). Single parents were more likely than non-employed respondents to say (or to believe) they would or could find some kind of work.

Younger respondents were more likely than older respondents to be able to turn to their families. The more despairing or resentful responses to this question were most likely to come from older respondents and/or from men. Although this had not been the intention, this question focused the minds of many respondents upon the extent of their dependency on state benefits and, when answering a later question about state dependency (see Chapter 5), several respondents referred back to what had been said in reply to this one.

Conversely, respondents were asked what effect an increase in benefits would have: usually respondents were asked to suppose their benefits were increased by half as much again. Of the 77 respondents who answered, less than one eighth (9) said it would mean less dependency on family or friends, whereas nearly four-fifths of the sample (33) said it would mean a better standard of living; a few respondents said it would mean both these things. Thus, almost a half of those responding could envisage some immediate improvement in their living standards. Some respondents (8) said such an increase would make no or not much difference in their particular circumstances, while twice that number stressed that it would not so much improve their living standards as relieve their anxiety and/or reduce their indebtedness.

What became clear, therefore, was that family (or the wider kinship networks which the term was usually taken to encompass) is not seen by most claimants either as a first line of defence after the state, or as a first charge upon 'surplus' resources.

The state and the family

The pressures exerted by recent social security reforms which might incline people to turn more to their families in preference to the state would seem to run contrary to prevailing primary values, and to be potentially disruptive of contemporary, socially constructed life-cycle patterns.

As has been explained, we have observed that social security claimants would often imply or express the view that, in adulthood, it is wrong to rely for material support upon one's parents (who have already shouldered the burden of raising one through childhood) or one's adult children (whose responsibilities now lie with their own partners and/or children). The point was most vividly put by the wife of one unemployed respondent who had contributed to the interview in order to describe her experiences of claiming benefits as a single parent when her husband had been in prison, and to whom the recent reunification of her 'own' family had clearly been a great relief: 'I think it's totally disgusting. Why should other people [i.e. parents/relatives] look after us? *We're* a family now.'

From this perspective, claimants seemed to be looking to the state to protect the integrity, not of the institution, but of the relationships which constitute the individual nuclear family unit (c.f. Ashford 1987). Several respondents referred to ways in which the inadequacy of benefits was disruptive of family relations, because of 'rows' between partners over money (c.f. Craig and Glendinning 1990a; Ritchie 1990) or, as one young unemployed man now living on his own in a hostel explained:

> there was two children, my girlfriend and myself living on £50 a week and that was to pay our bills . . . clothe the children . . . bits and bobs . . . and really the money had gone and I would have none . . . So really, that's what broke me living with her . . . we couldn't afford to live together . . . really, the government is terrible.

There seemed moreover to be a clear boundary to be drawn between the perceived responsibilities of the family and those of the state (c.f. Finch 1989). Family responsibilities were synonymous with parental responsibilities to dependent children and were concerned with caring in a non-material sense, while the state's responsibility was to guarantee the financial and material security of the nuclear family unit. Some of the angriest reactions to be elicited from or recounted by respondents were from parents who at some stage had felt the state was reneging upon its responsibility to underwrite their own dependability as parents. One respondent, whose house was due to be repossessed because the income support scheme will not cover interest repayments on a second mortgage, spoke in the most bitter terms about how, 'if they won', he would 'stand and fight on the doorstep' to defend his children. Two respondents described with indignation how, when left without benefit to feed their children, they had actually resorted to the dramatic ploy (much fabled in the popular imagination) of threatening to leave their children at the DSS offices: the statement they sought to make was, not that they did not care for their children, but that the state was failing in its duty to make such care possible. Parents should care, it is implied, but in the last instance it is the state which should provide.

However, the sanctity of the nuclear family unit must not be invaded by the state. This was most often expressed through references to 'privacy' or to the 'personal'. As one single parent put it, 'as long as my child has food, love, warmth, I see that as priority', and while, for example, she agreed in principle that fathers should contribute to the maintenance of children, she deeply resented the practices by which such liabilities are enforced, because 'your personal life is your personal life and has nothing to do with them [the DSS] whatsoever'. What is more, once a family bond, whether with parents or an ex-partner, had been severed, respondents preferred by and large to manage on their own, albeit with state assistance: 'I suppose I'm a proud person, really I'd rather use my money I get from social.'

The adversarial state

We have already argued in Chapter 3 that the social security system has become more punitive. Some of the rule changes to which we have specifically referred in this chapter are in themselves overtly coercive. At the same time, however, there have been changes associated with the detection and punishment of social security fraud and abuse resulting in a greater level of scrutiny and surveillance for all claims and claimants. Coupled, as they have been, with a more restrictive approach to entitlement and a greater attention to the categorisation of claimants by status, such changes amount to an altogether more hostile benefits regime for many claimants.

Grievances

Our research sought to address these issues by asking claimants first of all about their 'grievances' in relation to social security. Respondents were asked whether they had had any 'problems' with their claims for social security benefits and, if so, what they had done about them. Only 5 out of 85 respondents reported that they had had no or no significant problems. Of the other respondents, the largest group (49) had at some time sought some independent advice and/or had appealed to a social security tribunal or other adjudicating authority; a smaller group (30 respondents) had tried to sort their problems out themselves; and one respondent admitted she had done nothing about her problem.

Clearly, it was to be expected that claimants who had been referred to the research staff by independent advice agencies or who had volunteered to be interviewed as a result of media coverage would be those with grievances to voice, and indeed only one member of this group of 31 respondents said he had had no significant problems with his claim, compared with 4 out of the other 54 respondents. The indications none the less are that the vast majority of social security claimants experience problems or have some form of complaint or grievance against the system, and that a majority of those with such problems have sought some assistance or attempted some action as a consequence.

Of the claimants in our sample who talked about the steps they had taken to deal with their problems with the social security system, most (46 respondents – just over half the sample) had sought independent advice or assistance, sometimes from a combination of sources. Of those who identified a single source, most had been to independent advice-giving agencies (Citizens Advice Bureaux, law centres or other voluntary agencies), although a few had been to social workers or local authority consumer/debt advisers and two had been to their MP. A handful of respondents (6) had obtained advice or assistance from friends or members of their families. However, almost a third of the sample said they had never sought any form of advice. The oldest age group in the sample was that which was proportionately most likely to seek independent advice/ assistance (although it is impossible to say whether this reflects a greater litigiousness on the part of older people or the advice agencies' lack of appeal to younger age-groups).

Views on the efficacy of the assistance received from such sources were mixed, varying from unstinting praise ('they were so wonderful and understanding') to outright disparagement ('I might as well have gone to see a vet'). What claimants seemed to be seeking, however, was summed up by one respondent: 'I'm not silly, but even I have trouble with the way [the system works] . . . If you could get somewhere where you could sit down, have everything out . . . and say "I don't understand".'

The majority of respondents (55) had never resorted to appealing to a social security tribunal or related adjudicating authority, characteristically it would seem because they felt this would 'make no difference', because they were 'too frightened', or because they were 'not that bloody-minded'. None the less, a third of the sample – a relatively high proportion in relation to the claiming population as a whole – had at some stage (often several years ago) lodged an appeal or at least by some means sought a formal review of a determination. Three of these appeals were actually pending at the time of interview, and of the respondents whose appeals had been dealt with, a half had had their appeals superseded or withdrawn without a formal tribunal hearing. Views as to the efficacy of the appeals process (when expressed) were once again very mixed, but tended to have in common a sense of the distance between appellants and the tribunal (c.f. Dean 1991). Regardless of the degree of 'sympathy' which tribunals demonstrated to respondents, they were regarded as being 'under orders', or else 'they had a stronger hold, they had documents and poor little me didn't have all these documents. They were very sophisticated, but don't forget they were the government and they had all these things to say'.

Although the claimants we spoke to were not explicitly asked about the strategies which they might adopt in their personal dealings with benefit authorities, some (27 respondents) did mention the way they generally conducted themselves upon encountering a problem. Of these, the largest group (12) described how they would endeavour to use persuasion or argument (either face to face or over the telephone), while a handful (4 respondents) said they preferred to deal with such matters by writing letters. Only 6 respondents admitted using confrontational strategies (e.g. displays of anger or refusals to leave DSS premises) and 5 respondents claimed to deploy manipulative strategies (e.g. by giving partial or misleading information). Two respondents described a strategy (which is in all probability less consciously adopted by many claimants) of compliance of 'not making a fuss' or just 'giving them the right answers'.

The impression gained from discussing with claimants the grievances they have had with the social security system is that, while claimants often experience a need for help and may often wish to challenge decisions relating to their benefit entitlements, they are not by and large highly litigious or manipulative of the system.

Anger towards the system

To establish what it was that most angered or annoyed them about the social security system, the claimants in our sample were asked whether this might be 'the rules of the system, the way you are treated or just the amount of money you get'. Only three respondents definitely said they had never been angered or annoyed by the social security system, while the overwhelming majority of the sample (80 respondents) had felt some anger or annoyance towards it (about a quarter of these citing more than one reason for so doing). Of those expressing anger or annoyance, two-thirds (52 respondents in all) referred to the way that claimants are treated or to the attitude or inefficiency of official personnel; half this number referred to the rules of the system or the tightening of the rules and a similar number referred to the inadequacy of benefits.

The levels of dissatisfaction with the service are therefore high and tend to stem less from claimants' expectations with regard to benefit levels than from their expectations about the way in which they ought to be treated. Resentment at the treatment received at the hands of official personnel appeared, proportionately speaking, to be slightly higher amongst single parents (compared to non-employed benefit recipients); among members of the oldest age-group in the sample (compared to members of the younger age-groups); and among owner-occupiers (compared to council tenants): groups who possibly may feel that they are in some way more deserving of respect or better treatment (as one middle-aged single parent complained, 'I get as much respect as a teenager').

A study of the discursive content of our interviews helped to pin down what it was in the treatment which claimants receive that disturbs them. This revealed that several of the respondents who had not specifically cited the matter of their treatment as a cause for anger had none the less at some point in their interview complained about their treatment by the social security system. In all, over two-thirds (61) of our interview transcripts contained passages making or implying criticism of the treatment respondents had received. Of these, most (46) referred to the degrading, offensive or unsympathetic nature of the treatment they had, and only some (15) to the question of the inefficiency or incompetence of the DSS (or other benefit agency).

It should in fairness be emphasised that even among the respondents who were most critical of their treatment, many were at pains to point out that adverse treatment was not universal and that some officials treated them better than others (for example, 'they're not all gruff' and 'you meet one good one and then half a dozen bad ones'). However, uncertainty about the reception which claimants might receive can clearly heighten their general feelings of anxiety and vulnerability. One single parent described her initial experience in the following terms:

> I was questioned and it was very degrading. I had to tell them all my details about why I'd left my husband, the bruises and so on. I didn't want to tell them, it was a part of my life I'd rather forget. She [the DSS official] sat rubbing her hands with glee virtually, wanted to know all the gory details. Then I said to her, 'When will I get anything? I need something today. I haven't got any money', and I hadn't had any money for over a week. And she looked at me and said, 'It will be processed and you will get it when you get it.' It was as if she was going to give it to me out of her own pocket; that's the thing that really, really got my goat . . . and I came out shaking and very angry . . . Then I had to go back and I got another person who was really, really nice, very sympathetic. She said, 'You don't have to be in a particular group of people to be knocked about.' She was so nice and there was such a difference in the attitude.

Perceptions of fairness

Encouraged to think about the social security system as a whole, rather than in relation to any particular problem or difficulty which they might have happened to experience, the claimants in our sample were asked whether they thought the system was fair or unfair. Some respondents (18) were ambivalent on the matter or said they did not know or could not say, but of the respondents who gave definite replies (64), two-thirds said unequivocally that they found the system to be unfair and only a handful (7) said that they found it to be fair or 'fairish'. Of the remaining respondents, some said the system was fair to them but they recognised it was unfair to other claimants, and, conversely, a few claimants said the system was unfair to them but they recognised it was fair to other claimants. Younger respondents and non-employed respondents were proportionately rather more likely to regard the system as unfair than were older respondents and single parents respectively.

Respondents were not pressed to explain these answers, but 50 members of our sample did choose to elaborate upon the subject (women being somewhat keener to do so than men). Of these, the largest group (15 respondents) complained that the system is unfair as between different claimants: that is to say that it treats people differently, so that some people get more money than others or else people who should get benefit do not while people who should not get benefit do. Conversely, rather fewer respondents (6) complained that the system was unfair precisely because it treats everyone the same regardless of circumstances, and/or that it is insensitive to individual need. Other respondents (14) put the unfairness of the system down to the way in which claimants are treated (a recurring theme). Only 5 respondents (4 of them women) mentioned the inadequacy of benefits as the reason for the system's unfairness.

To investigate the nature of their experiences with the mechanisms of the claiming process, the claimants in our sample were also asked whether they had found the business of claiming easy or difficult. This apparently simple question none the less required respondents to make a distinction between how easy it might be to qualify for benefits and how easy it might be to complete the necessary forms and formalities. In fact, less than a third of the sample (23 respondents) said unequivocally that they found the claiming process easy or relatively straightforward, and getting on for half the sample (39 respondents) said unequivocally that they found the process difficult. Of the other respondents, some said they found the process easy but recognised it might be difficult for other claimants; a few said either that they had found the process difficult at first but that it had become easier or that it was difficult for some kinds of benefit and easy for others; a similar number said it was neither easy nor difficult, but annoying, tedious or 'ridiculous'; a handful of respondents (3) said it was easy provided you knew what you were doing or had someone to help you. The most common complaint was the length and confusing nature of the forms involved. Men were slightly more likely than women to say they found claiming easy. Single parents and young people were proportionately more likely to find it difficult than non-employed respondents and older people respectively.

The claimants in our sample were similarly asked how they managed on social security benefits – whether it was 'usually OK' or 'always hard'. Only around one-seventh of the sample (13 respondents) replied that managing was 'usually OK', or that it was 'OK' if one was frugal, careful or adaptable. Almost two-thirds of the sample (56 respondents) replied unequivocally that managing was 'always hard'. Of the remaining respondents, some respondents said that managing was 'sometimes OK', but sometimes hard; a few said that managing can be 'OK', but was usually hard; two respondents said that managing was 'OK' at first, but that it gets harder with the passage of time. An expression used by five respondents which characterised the hand-to-mouth existence described by most respondents was 'you're always robbing Peter to pay Paul': for many the business of getting along was a cause of continual anxiety and struggle.

Women were proportionately less likely than men (and single parents less likely than members of the non-employed group) to say that managing on social security benefits was 'OK', reflecting in all probability the fact that women are more likely than men to be involved in and therefore to be conscious of the problems of managing from day to day (c.f. Bradshaw and Holmes 1989) and/or that single parents' living standards are more constrained than those of other groups on social security.

The state and the citizen

We would conclude that the increasingly stringent, coercive and punitive nature of state intervention may strengthen claimants' inclination to view the state as adversary and may reduce the likelihood of their co-operation with the state.

Reference has just been made to the complaints expressed by respondents concerning the treatment they received from the social security system and/or the perceived unfairness of the system. It will also emerge later in this chapter that there is an extent to which a general sense of betrayal by the system may be associated with the willingness of some claimants to 'fiddle' the system to some degree. What may be more important than this is a more general threat that claimants' expectations of the state are so undermined as to engender a combative predisposition and/or to erode their 'faith' in citizenship. One claimant we spoke to said, 'these people make you feel they're trying to do you out of something', and another went so far as to say, 'there's no use having faith in the system . . . You can't depend on it, you've got to depend on yourself.'

It is not contended that all claimants in our sample took an entirely negative view of the state: several expressed gratitude for the benefits they received or would acknowledge, for example, that 'they [DSS] have been ever so good'. However, such respondents would invariably add remarks which belied their 'faith' in the state (such as, 'I must have been one of the lucky ones'), or else they would qualify their observations with remarks about the inadequacy of benefits or the degrading nature of the experience. Gratitude was always tinged with resentment. State benefits were seen as a form of largess with which the recipient is supposed to feel uncomfortable, and that sense of discomfort was often compounded by the nature of the treatment claimants receive: 'sometimes they treat you just like a parcel, sort of like stamp you and you have to wait to go out.' Thus while claimants feel they ought to be grateful, the begrudging nature of the largess just makes them feel bad: 'it sets a lot of nasty feelings inside you . . . Instead of helping us [they] are making us feel like worms rather than have a bit of dignity.'

For other claimants, the begrudging nature of the government's largess was seen as explicitly punitive. One respondent expressed the view that 'people in prison have as good a time', and another, who had also compared the social security system to the prison system, said:

> What's the fucking point in making an effort . . . to take part in a world which is out to destroy every effort I make, just to be stupid about it, be mean-minded and think only about money . . . they

should make people feel clean, make them feel happy . . . I know the world doesn't owe me a living . . . but I would at least like to see an amount of respect . . . from the people in power. You don't get it. It doesn't matter how much fucking people ponce off the state, or whatever . . . if you don't respect them as individuals, you'll never get them to change . . . I don't feel I've got a right to [benefit]. I feel it's given begrudgingly . . . if I ever make it back to being independent again, there'll be this constant memory, the fact that, while I was down, these bastards I'm working with begrudged me every penny they gave me.

Although few respondents expressed themselves with such vehemence, several spoke of being 'beaten' or 'taken over' by the system or else remarked in various ways upon the disparity of power between claimant and state:

The odds are stacked against me if I want to take them on . . . that's an unfairness. If I write to them they may or may not choose to acknowledge receipt of my letter . . . it's actually [a] conflict . . . that's really how I perceive it . . . these people aren't my friends, they are not here to help me.

It is of course difficult to say to what extent such feelings of discomfort, anger or impotence have long been endemic to the receipt of social security benefits or to what extent they may have been exacerbated by recent changes. However, some claimants clearly were conscious of recent changes. One unemployed woman, who indeed felt 'grateful' for the benefit she received (and had even contemplated writing to her local DSS office to thank them for their assistance), none the less felt 'paranoid' about the introduction of the 'actively seeking work' test and the way 'they're so down your throat now'. Another respondent commented that the new regime 'doesn't motivate you, it just makes you angry'. Several respondents were conscious of the redoubled preoccupation in recent years with the detection of fraud and abuse and complained about never being believed when they explained things at the DSS. One respondent, an Iraqi Kurdish refugee who following his wife's death had been claiming income support as a single parent, was particularly alarmed to have been interrogated on suspicion of having undeclared earnings from occasional part-time mini-cab driving, an experience which unhappily reminded him of the kind of surveillance exercised upon its citizens by the Iraqi government. Similarly, some respondents were intimidated by the redesigned social security claim forms which, because of their length and repetitive nature, seemed to respondents to be intended to catch them out or trip them up.

The sense of vulnerability which claimants can feel was summed up by one single parent:

> You put a foot wrong and they can prosecute you, you know . . . and you also feel your privacy being invaded, you know. You have to tell them everything . . . they really know a lot about you.

And one cynically perceptive claimant put it thus:

> the point I'm making is that they're taking the aggression to the people . . . they make sure you know what your status is if you're going up the social security . . . they make sure they score a point or demoralise you in some way. I might think that personally the people who are doing it are not aware of what they're doing . . . they're bloody just as caged as I am; a different cage, but just as caged as I am, you know. My freedom is relative to their freedom, but I don't think much of their freedom either.

If nothing else, it cannot be said that such widespread and often deep-seated feelings of resentment and mistrust are conducive to 'good citizenship'.

Participation, active citizenship and popular imagery

In Chapter 3 it was also suggested that the general direction of social security reform in the 1980s was such as increasingly to distance or isolate social security claimants from the wider community. This is partly because the relative reductions in living standards for social security claimants may tend to exclude them from certain forms of social participation, and partly because many of the reforms have been informed by and allowed to fuel popular fears and prejudices regarding social security claimants and the 'burden' they represent.

Social isolation and social engagement

In order to see to what extent the claimants in our sample were engaged with or excluded from 1) contact with family and friends,

2) social and recreational pursuits, and 3) community activity, respondents were asked whether they got 'out and about' much and what they did with their time. We sought to establish how regularly respondents had contact with some chosen circle of family and friends; whether respondents were involved in some reasonably regular, organised social, sporting, leisure or entertainment activity; and whether respondents had some reasonably regular involvement with a community, voluntary, charity, political or religious group (on a formal or informal basis).

Only 6 members of the sample were involved in all three forms of social participation. The largest group (27 people) reported contact with family and friends only, and the next largest (17 people) were entirely isolated from any social engagement with family, friends, recreational or community activity. Two groups (each of 14 people) reported both contact with family and friends and involvement in *either* recreational *or* community activity respectively, and just 5 respondents reported involvement in recreational and/or community activity but lacked contact with family and friends.

The nature of the data permits only rather broad conclusions to be drawn, but there is some justification from our evidence for suggesting that single parents and older claimants were proportionately rather more likely than members of the non-employed group and younger claimants respectively to be relatively socially isolated.

Getting on for two-thirds of the sample (55 respondents) (including 5 of the 6 respondents adjudged to have been the most 'socially engaged') said that they would like to have more of a social life and attributed the constraint on their participation to lack of income and/or to being on social security benefit(s). Of the remaining respondents, some (14 respondents, 9 of them over 40 years of age) said they were not bothered or were happy as they were with the extent of their social involvement; a few respondents said they would like to have more of a social life, but attributed the constraint upon their participation to other factors (such as health problems or caring responsibilities); just one respondent (a single parent who was undergoing training in counselling) said that being on social security had provided her with opportunities to do things she would not otherwise have been able to do.

A study of the discursive content of our interviews helped to determine the primary cause or nature of the relative social isolation experienced by some claimants. This revealed 49 instances in which respondents could be observed to have admitted some actual feeling of social isolation. Of these respondents, almost half (22) had indicated that their isolation was due primarily to financial or practical considerations and/or to some physical separation from family or friends; slightly fewer respondents (19) indicated that they suffered some sense of social inhibition, arising through feelings of exclusion or embarrassment or an inability to reciprocate (for example, in terms of entertaining at home, buying coffees or drinks, etc.); a few respondents (8) admitted simply to being 'shy' or not especially gregarious.

The picture which emerges is that, while social security claimants' opportunities for social participation are constrained, many do sustain some degree of participation and most aspire to achieve more. There was little evidence of respondents being resigned to low levels of participation. Only two of the respondents who fell into the most severe 'social isolation' category declared themselves to be 'not bothered' by this: one was a middle-aged Bangladeshi man who had recently been made redundant from a very low-paid job and was clearly in desperate straits trying to maintain his wife and four children; the other was a middle-aged woman, whose husband had recently left her, and who (though registered as unemployed) supported a 17-year-old son (who had refused to go on a YTS and had no job or income) and cared for her disabled mother-in-law (who lived near by). Both these respondents were struggling to survive and, in spite of their modest expectations, neither could be described as reclusive or apathetic.

Political participation

The claimants in our sample were also asked whether they usually voted in parliamentary and local elections. Of the respondents who replied, 63 per cent (50 out of 80) said that they always or usually voted, indicating a relatively high level of political participation, although a lower level than that in the general population (the turnout in the 1987 general election was around 82 per cent). This finding is consistent with those of other studies (see, for example, Heath 1991), but what our investigation also showed was that, of those who said they always or usually voted, one fifth

indicated that they at present or had recently had some formal
political allegiance or involvement in political (including non-party
political) activity or campaigning (such as tenants', residents' or
women's movement campaigns). Interestingly, seven of the respondents who seldom or never voted also indicated some degree
of political or campaigning activity. Men and women were equally
likely to say they regularly voted, but although the numbers involved are small, the data indicates that men were proportionately
more likely than women to be in some way politically active. The
younger age-groups were proportionately less likely than the
oldest age-group to vote or to be in any way politically active.

It was easy to see how some respondents had been excluded from
political participation by reason, not of apathy, but of the social
isolation factors described above. Thus one of the claimants we
interviewed, a single parent and strong Labour Party supporter,
explained:

> every time you wanted to go to a meeting it was in this pub or that
> pub . . . a lot of people would have lots more money, and I knew if I
> went in a pub, even an orange juice and lemonade costs over a
> pound . . . and you have to weigh it up. And then also it's the clothes
> part of it, if you don't go out you don't need any.

Another respondent, a former Young Conservative local chair-
person now recovering from tranquilliser addiction, said:

> it's very difficult to go along there [the local Conservative Associa-
> tion] and say, 'I've had a sort of nervous breakdown or whatever
> and I'm living on social security, but I'd like to support you and I'm
> sorry I can't buy you a drink because I can't afford it.'

Claimants and the wider community

Our research also sought to establish to what extent the immediate
social circle of each of the claimants in our sample was composed
of other social security recipients. Respondents were therefore
asked whether many or any of the friends and family they had
most to do with were also getting some sort of social security
benefit. Only a quarter of the sample (21 respondents) indicated
that their immediate circle was composed mainly of (or included
many) other social security benefit recipients, while getting on for

half the sample (37 respondents) indicated that their circle of friends and family was composed mainly of (or included many) non-social security recipients. Other respondents gave more ambiguous replies, indicating either that their immediate circle included a mixture of social security recipients and other persons or else that their social circle was limited and/or that they were unaware of whether or not the people they had most to do with were on social security.

Clearly, most respondents could not be said to be enmeshed in a claiming culture. The respondents, however, who did mix more with other social security claimants were proportionately more likely to be members of the non-employed group than to be single parents. Predictably, perhaps, respondents from a professional/managerial or a clerical/retail/catering occupational background were proportionately less likely to be numbered among this small group than were respondents from manual occupational backgrounds, although respondents from skilled manual backgrounds appeared more likely to be included than those from semi- or unskilled manual backgrounds.

The claimants in our sample were encouraged to talk about their perceptions and images of themselves as claimants and of other people. Respondents were first of all asked how they felt about the fact that some people claim that the recipients of social security benefits are all 'scroungers' and 'layabouts'. Less than a quarter of the sample (18 respondents) said that they were not bothered by this or were by and large dismissive about it. Twice as many respondents (36) were angered, distressed or annoyed by this characterisation of social security claimants. A further quarter of the respondents were clearly disturbed, indignant or upset at being personally identified in this manner, but were not inclined to defend claimants as a whole, feeling that some social security claimants are indeed 'scroungers' and 'layabouts'. Relatively few respondents (10) felt that such imagery was justified and that being in receipt of benefits did mean there was a sense in which they were perhaps 'scroungers' and 'layabouts'. Two claimants gave contradictory replies, reacting at one moment with resentment, but claiming at another that they were not really bothered about it – evidence perhaps that other respondents who had been dismissive of this kind of allegation were merely being defensive and were concealing an underlying discomfort.

Men were proportionately more likely to appear dismissive, women to express concern. Younger claimants were proportionately less tolerant than older claimants of this kind of popular stereotyping. Unsurprisingly, respondents who had said their immediate social circle consisted mainly of or included many other social security claimants were proportionately more likely than other respondents to be angered by popular stereotypes, presumably because their experience was more likely to reveal such stereotypes to be unjustified. However, respondents from manual occupational backgrounds were proportionately less likely than those from non-manual occupational backgrounds, and council tenants were proportionately less likely than owner-occupiers, to express anger or resentment, possibly because members of these groups are more likely to have come to feel that they are in some way less 'deserving' and that such attacks upon them must be tolerated.

Leading on from this issue, the claimants in our sample were asked to sum up how they would feel or how they felt about having to live on social security benefits for a long period of time. Almost two-thirds of the sample (54 respondents) indicated negative or uncomfortable feelings about such a prospect. Some respondents (15) indicated neutral feelings or feelings of resignation, and a few (6) indicated mixed or ambivalent feelings. Only 4 respondents felt positive or comfortable about the long-term receipt of social security benefits. All of these had been among that group of respondents who had expressed anger at the popular stereotype of the social security claimant as a 'scrounger' or 'layabout': they each (for different reasons) had cause to feel they were entitled to what they received and resented assertions to the contrary. Conversely, almost all the respondents who had claimed to be unperturbed by prejudicial popular stereotyping (15 out of the 16 so responding) said they felt or would feel uncomfortable or ambivalent about having to live on benefits for a long time: their apparent indifference to the strictures of others was not reflected in strong or positive feelings about their entitlement to benefits. Either way, there is little evidence in the current climate of opinion that the benefits of welfare citizenship bring happiness (let alone complacency) to their recipients.

Studying the discursive content of our interviews helped to identify the reasons for respondents' negative or uncomfortable feelings towards the long-term receipt of social security benefits. In some three-quarters of the interviews we conducted (64), respondents had indicated or expressed some unease related to long-term claiming (even though some of those respondents may not have referred directly to such feelings when answering the question mentioned above). Of the respondents concerned, some (18) referred with pragmatism to the financial or material discomforts of living on social security, but more than half of the entire sample (47 respondents) referred to reasons of principle, to moral factors or questions of self-esteem, saying, for example, 'it's not a nice way to live' or 'I don't want my children growing up thinking this is a natural way to live'.

The claimants in our sample were also directly asked how they felt about other social security claimants, and particularly long-term social security claimants. As in the Social Attitudes Survey (see Table 3.3), somewhat fewer than half the sample (38 respondents) indicated feelings towards other claimants which might be described as positive, sympathetic or tolerant (but see p. 136 below). Of the remaining respondents, some (23) gave answers in which they discriminated between deserving and undeserving groups of claimants; others (15) were ambivalent or even indifferent towards other claimants (but see pp. 121 and 146 below); and 6 indicated feelings which were generally negative, punitive or intolerant. Predictably, those respondents who had said their immediate social circle consisted mainly of or included many other social security recipients were proportionately more likely than other groups to express positive, sympathetic or tolerant views. But, once again, it is suggested by the data that council tenants were proportionately less likely than owner-occupiers, and respondents from lower occupational class backgrounds were proportionately less likely than those from a professional/managerial background, to be positive, sympathetic or tolerant towards other claimants: possibly those groups in society which are made to feel less deserving are less inclined to a liberal or charitable view of their fellows. Certainly, there is little evidence here of a general sense of solidarity among social security recipients.

Fiddling the system

A different insight into the potentially corrosive effects of the claiming experience was precipitated when the claimants in our sample were asked about those changes to the social security system which were concerned with clamping down on fraud and abuse. Respondents were initially asked whether they thought there was a lot of social security 'fiddling' going on: that is to say whether or not significant numbers of claimants were claiming benefits to which they were not entitled (for example, by concealing the presence of a live-in partner or earnings from illicit employment or by claiming from false addresses, and so on). Of the respondents for whom replies were recorded (79), a majority (40) believed there was a lot of 'fiddling' going on, although such views were based entirely upon anecdotal evidence and upon impressions received through the press and broadcasting media. A further third of these respondents (25) believed there was some or 'quite a bit' of 'fiddling' going on; 6 respondents had the impression that there is less 'fiddling' now than before; only 8 respondents believed there is very little 'fiddling' or that it is not a big or a significant problem. The discursive interview sample appeared to believe that there is substantially more benefit fraud than the Social Attitudes Survey respondents were prepared to imply in the circumstances of a structured interview (see Chapter 3).

The claimants in our sample were then asked, 'if you knew you could get away with it, would you "fiddle" the system to get extra benefit?' Of those responding (79), just over a half (42) said yes (and one gave a contradictory reply by saying no when he had already admitted to having undeclared earnings). Just under a half (36) said no, but of these, less than half (16) appeared to be saying no on principle: other respondents (10) said no on purely pragmatic grounds, saying that 'fiddling' the system was too difficult or it 'wasn't worth it'; some respondents (8) said no because they would be too frightened or anxious about getting caught; 2 respondents admitted they had claimed fraudulently in the past, but said they would not do so again in the future.

In interpreting this finding, it must firstly be emphasised that of the respondents who said they would 'fiddle' the system, most were replying purely hypothetically: they were saying they would do so if they knew they could get away with it (c.f. Johnston 1988). The likelihood of these respondents actually seeking to defraud the system is probably very slight. Only one-sixth of the sample (15 respondents) acknowledged that they were presently 'fiddling' the system or had done so at some time in the past. Secondly, this should be interpreted in the light of the previous finding, namely that most of these claimants subscribed to the popular belief that fraud and abuse in the social security system is already widespread: governmental concern to highlight the issue in public debate may in fact be self-defeating.

Willingness to 'fiddle' the social security system, while clearly correlating with a belief in the extent to which other claimants are already doing so, also correlates with two other factors: views on the 'fairness' of the system (see p. 106 above) and views on the recent changes to the social security system (to be considered in Chapter 5). Virtually all (all but one) of the respondents who expressed a willingness to 'fiddle' the system either regarded the social security system as in some way less than 'fair', or were resentful of the cuts in welfare benefits during recent years, or both. (The respondent not to fit this pattern was in any event among those who believed a lot of other claimants were 'fiddling'. This was in fact a middle-aged separated single parent with a 14-year-old son; she bitterly resented the necessity to 'ponce' off her grown-up daughter when money ran short, but would undoubtedly have been far too timorous to risk social security fraud as a means to independence.) It would seem, therefore, that the relatively high incidence of a willingness to 'fiddle' the system may primarily be a reflection of claimants' adverse experiences or frustrations with that system. This would seem to be confirmed by cross-tabulating answers to this question with those from the earlier question about the causes of respondents' anger with the system: virtually all (all but one) of the respondents who expressed a willingness to 'fiddle' the system had also given reasons for having been angry about that system.

In practice, it was a much smaller number of respondents who were or had ever been involved in any sort of 'fiddling'. Five respondents, as already indicated, held undeclared part-time jobs. Of the other respondents who reported past and present misde-meanours, some were single parents who had had a live-in partner for intermittent periods. Another respondent, suffering from mul-tiple sclerosis, related how he had slightly exaggerated his condition on the day he had been medically examined in order to qualify for mobility allowance: however, he did not really regard this as 'fid-dling' because he felt he was morally entitled to the additional bene-fit. A few respondents appeared to be engaging in pastimes or

'hobbies' not amounting to employment which none the less generated supplementary income or goods in kind which ought strictly
speaking to have been declared to the DSS (although in most instances it would probably not have materially affected entitlement).
These instances ranged from a claimant whose husband bred and
sold budgerigars, to a man who claimed to have a systematic income
from a meticulously researched system of horse-race betting. More
usually, however, such activities were restricted to petty trading
through the running of mail order catalogues or in the buying and
selling of second-hand clothing and household goods at jumble sales
and boot fairs; activities which yielded very modest returns.

As has already been made clear, it is not contended that all
respondents had adverse experiences with the social security system, and as one respondent, who felt reasonably satisfied with the
service she had so far received and who said she would not fiddle
the system, put it, 'if they would be fair to me, I don't think I could
do that to them'. Conversely, however, there were respondents
who believed, for example, that the social security system 'has
been abused by this present government', that 'the government
has lost faith with the workers' or that 'you can't be too honest'
(i.e. because the system itself does not treat people honestly). It is
of course impossible with any degree of accuracy to estimate the
extent of fraud and abuse in the social security system. Our
research indicates that, in the day-to-day business of survival, a
modest number of technically fraudulent claims may be going un-
detected. More importantly, the findings suggest that the gap between claimants' expectations of the social security system and
their experience of it is significantly greater than the gap between
the state's requirements of claimants and claimants' compliance
with those requirements.

Coping with public contempt

The climate of opprobrium to which social security claimants are
themselves increasingly subject may therefore create tensions or
contradictions with their own privatist/exclusivist preoccupations,
resulting in resentment, mutual suspicion, nihilism or despair.

Attention has already been drawn to the sheer diversity of claimants' reactions to the claiming experience and to the prevalence

among them of often quite punitive attitudes towards other social security claimants, reflecting their endorsement of popular resentment towards people in the very position in which respondents found themselves. Some respondents dealt with their dilemma by resorting to a blinkered, isolationist position, acknowledging that in their view some claimants were 'scroungers', 'fiddlers' or 'wasters', but insisting, 'it's up to them', 'that's their business' or 'that's their problem'. As one single parent put it, 'I don't know anything about them [other social security claimants]. Why they're on it is down to them . . . I don't feel anything towards them and I wouldn't want anybody to feel anything towards me because I'm on it.' Claimants who spoke in this vein would sometimes go further and say such things as, 'if they can get away with it, good luck to them'. But closely associated with this *laissez-faire* attitude of not caring what other people do was a nagging suspicion, fuelled partly by confusion and uncertainty over benefit entitlements (see Chapter 5) and partly by a general belief that malpractice or 'fiddling' is widespread, that other claimants in similar circumstances to the respondents might be receiving more in benefits than they were themselves. In such instances, a posture of indifference could readily turn to one of resentment: resentment, for example, towards certain 'other' claimants who 'give us a bad name', or who perhaps 'don't deserve it'. For some respondents this resentment could reach such proportions that it distorted their views, not just of other claimants, but of the probity of the social security system itself:

> I have been given the name by DHSS of a scrounger and a bum . . . I don't think I'm a bum, but there's an awful lot who are . . . they've had the time to sit down and find the ways in and the ways out and claim for this and claim for that. A fairly ignorant person like me comes along who's suddenly put in a bad position, thinks fair play will be had. That's not the case . . . if you're a fairly honest sort of person, then you get nothing.

It was difficult if not impossible for claimants in our sample to shrug off the negative imagery associated with their claimant status, and, of those who claimed to have done so, one admitted he found this 'sinister' in itself. Another haltingly articulate respondent recognised what he himself described as a 'self-fulfilling prophecy':

> there is a kind of sullen type of almost what you call passive resistance, kind of thing. 'Well, if we are scroungers,' (this is the most dangerous thing), 'well we're a load of bloody dossers anyway . . .

well who cares, we might as well sodding well act like ones anyway'
. . . it's a kind of sullen type of indignation.

Respondents were often very conscious of the image which the outside world expected of them; of what 'looking the part' might or might not entail:

You always think you have to go there looking pathetic, if you have to go and see them [at DSS] . . . Everybody's got different opinions of how you should behave and . . . I didn't tell anybody around here of my position, because they say 'she shouldn't have that because she's on social security' . . . so, if you're in a weak mood you do feel guilty, you feel as though you've got to look the part. Why should you have to look the part? Why should you not have a takeaway meal now and again like normal people?

For other claimants, it was not a question of 'looking the part' but of feeling diminished by the experience of claiming benefits. Respondents would say such things as, 'I'm a disgrace'; 'it makes you feel low'; 'all your sense of worth just goes'; 'you're lumped into a category'. Three respondents were even reduced to tears in the course of their interviews when describing such feelings. Even those few respondents who ostensibly rejected all negative imagery were clearly affected by a threat to, or a need to defend, their own individuality or integrity; by a need to distance themselves from those 'others' whom they refrained on principle from judging. As a single parent, who was also a local government councillor, stoically explained:

Perhaps some of them get into the rut where it's the normal thing to do, it becomes a way of life, but I think I fight against that and each time I go it reminds me of the position I'm in . . . There is no way that I ever think I am better than those other people, that I shouldn't be here sort of thing. As far as I'm concerned, we are all equal . . . perhaps it keeps me in my place a bit.

Conclusion

The overall conclusion to emerge from our investigation is that any social security policy based on the notion of 'dependency culture' is likely to be counterproductive: first, because the implication that claimants are 'culturally' separated from the rest of society is inaccurate and unhelpful; secondly, because the notion obscures rather than assists our understanding of dependency and, in particular, the nature and consequences of state dependency.

People in contemporary Britain tend to follow a value-orientation in which material dependency upon the wage relation is seen as natural and necessary to personal identity; emotional dependency within the family is seen as natural and necessary to self-fulfilment; state dependency is seen as perhaps less than natural, but represents an important guarantee of last resort. As explained in Chapter 3, however, patterns of dependency upon paid employment, within the family and upon the state are being reconstituted as a result of processes of social and economic change. These shifts generate qualitative changes in the significance of the wage relation and of the family and added importance for the role of the state. Such changes inevitably place strains upon people's expectations as workers, as members of families and as citizens.

Recent social security reforms have been informed in part at least by the aim of revalorising dependency upon employers and families by problematising dependency on the state. The effect is not to reduce state dependency, but to compound the strains upon the expectations of social security claimants. Policy changes are working 'against the grain' of changes in social attitudes, as our discussion of Social Attitudes Survey data in Chapter 3 has shown (c.f. Coote, Harman and Hewitt 1990; Taylor-Gooby 1990). By and large, claimants do not need encouragement to work and indeed their ideals and expectations may already be badly out of line with their actual employment prospects. Claimants do not wish to seek material assistance from their families because this will tend to undermine the value which they have come to place upon family relationships. Claimants do not need to be discouraged from claiming state benefits, so new obstacles to the establishment of benefit rights may undermine claimants' faith in the guarantees (and perhaps therefore the obligations) of citizenship.

CHAPTER 5

DEPENDENCY OR CAPTIVITY?

We're all sorts of people; a cross-section of all society; we're all thrown together in the same situation . . . [but] . . . we're not on a track of our own, we're all off the track, all derailed and in a siding.

This perceptive and despairing comment was made by one of the long-term social security claimants interviewed in the course of the authors' research. It is a comment which, more than any other, reaches to the heart of what this book has to say.

In Chapter 4 we outlined the essentials of our recent research findings. We have argued that social security claimants are not part of an underclass characterised by a distinctive dependency culture, but that such claimants subscribe by and large to mainstream norms, values and lifeways. We have further suggested that reforms to the British social security system introduced in the 1980s were in many ways counterproductive. Certainly they have not reduced state dependency and they have worked against the grain of social change and popular expectations. But there is more to it than that.

The 'failure' of the social security reforms to reduce state dependency may not be the result (as even some claimants have told us) of 'inefficiency' or bad implementation: indeed, in one sense the reforms may not have failed at all. It could be argued that the government has succeeded in constituting state dependency as uniquely problematic and in refining the disciplinary nature of the claiming experience. It has done so by diminishing rights to certain benefits, by increasing the surveillance of claimants, by bringing new pressures to bear and by promoting a climate of heightened mutual suspicion. The social security system does not foster a dependency culture, but it constructs, isolates and supervises a heterogeneous population of reluctant dependants.

It is tempting to suggest that, while there is no 'dependency culture', there is perhaps a 'captivity culture'. This, however, would be to miss the point. What we are indicating is not in essence a cultural phenomenon at all, but a palpable disciplinary effect of the social security system. The analogy used by our anonymous respondent is a powerful one and strikingly apt: social security claimants do not travel together on a track of their own, they have been derailed from the main track and pushed out of the cultural mainstream; they are not running upon an independent, state-subsidised branch line, they are being retained in varying states of dereliction in isolated sidings.

In this chapter we shall take another look at the evidence from our own research in order to see, first of all, how the issues of dependency and poverty were discursively constituted for the claimants in our sample. Second, we shall consider whether claimants do or are able to act as competent subjects or whether they are manipulated or 'constructed' as passive objects. Third, we shall re-examine what conformity with mainstream norms, values and lifeways might mean for those who are dependent on the state.

The discourses of dependency and poverty

The word 'dependency', crucial to our investigation, was inconsistently used and understood by the social security claimants who took part in our research. To the extent that the concept of dependency is notoriously slippery (see for example Lister 1991) this is hardly surprising, but the range and breadth of the meanings which respondents seemed to attach to it are important. Broadly speaking, there were five senses in which the word was used or received.

First, dependency is sometimes equated with *addiction*: respondents spoke, for example, of the anxious wait for their Giro cheques to arrive in the post or their reluctance or sense of panic if required to part with their order books; 'you've got to have it, you know what I mean?' or 'you kind of get hooked with it'.

Second, some respondents sometimes equated dependency and *indebtedness*: they spoke in terms of whether or not they should feel obligated or 'beholden' to the state or to their partners, families or employers or whether any of these agencies could be 'trusted'; dependency meant that 'you're not free to do what you want' or was something to which you 'succumbed' if you could not 'depend on yourself'.

Third, dependency is linked to *poverty*: respondents spoke in terms of the constraints of 'not having enough money', of lacking the personal autonomy which having an adequate income would provide.

Fourth, dependency is sometimes equated with *the necessity of subsistence*: respondents spoke in terms of hierarchies of dependency or of preferred forms of dependency; because 'you've got to be dependent on someone' or 'someone's got to subsidise you' dependency is something inevitable; but there might none the less be something 'not quite right' about depending on the state, or else 'when you're an employer-dependant rather than a government-dependant . . . you've got a lot more, you're able to do a lot more', or again women might sooner depend on the state than on a man or vice versa.

Finally, some respondents spoke of being 'trapped', 'caged', 'caught in a vicious circle', or they said that in some ill-defined way their attempts to get off benefits were frustrated by the system itself. They hinted at a fifth meaning of 'dependency'; the dependency of the *captive upon his/her captor*.

While the meanings of the word 'dependency' are inevitably elusive, claimants of course used other words with concrete meanings but capable of metaphorical application in order to address the issue of dependency. Characteristically, respondents often addressed the question of whose 'pocket' they should be dependent upon. Respondents would, for example, protest against the unjustifiable sense of indebtedness forced upon them by social security officials acting 'as if the money was coming out of their own pockets' (see, for instance, p. 106 above). One single parent, justifying her 'dependency' on the government and her reluctance to seek help from her family, said, 'Once you're not earning a wage you can never be totally independent, because if you're not going to depend on the government, then it means you're digging into someone else's pocket.' Symbolising as it does the individual possession of money, this use of the word 'pocket' is a powerful indicator of the way in which dependency is perceived.

'Poverty' too is a less abstract word than 'dependency', and one much more at the centre of political and popular discourse. The claimants in our sample were asked about their views on poverty, on whether poverty exists and, if so, 'who are the poor?' Very few respondents (just 4) claimed that poverty did not exist, while the largest group (29 people) applied the term to anybody on social security benefits, including themselves. Intermediate opinions fell into three categories: a small group (9 people) adopted a punitive view of poverty, attributing it to the behaviour of poor people, their bad management or fecklessness; a much larger group (25 people) applied the term to residual categories, such as the roofless or destitute; while another group (14 people) identified wider categories, such as the elderly or low-paid people with large families, as poor – but did not include themselves.

The replies again demonstrate the heterogeneity of our sample, two-thirds of whom, in spite of their dependence on social security benefits, did not necessarily consider themselves to be poor. Men were proportionately rather more likely than women to give replies towards the punitive and exclusive end of the continuum. Older age-groups were proportionately more likely than younger age-groups and single parents were more likely than non-employed respondents to count themselves as poor. Although there was little pattern to the replies when cross-tabulated by occupational class background, it did emerge that owner-occupiers were proportionately much less likely than council tenants to consider themselves poor and more likely to blame poverty on the behaviour of the poor. It is not surprising that long-term claimants were proportionately more likely than short-term claimants to consider themselves poor, but interestingly, it was medium-term claimants who were proportionately the most likely to consider themselves to be poor, suggesting perhaps a tendency for claimants to readjust their perceptions of themselves over time.

In a similar way the claimants in our sample were asked directly whether the money they were receiving from the government made them feel dependent, or whether there was any sense in which it gave them independence. Understandably, a few respondents had difficulty understanding this question, but of the 77 respondents who clearly did understand and made a coherent response, over half (45) indicated that they felt they were dependent on the government. Those who felt dependent in this way were just about equally divided between those who felt unequivocally dependent (replying, for example, 'oh yes, I am a bum!'), and those who were more equivocal, in so far as they recognised a sense in which benefits gave or could give them independence but felt more dependent than independent (replying, typically, 'they don't give you enough to make you independent, do they'). Some respondents (12) were completely ambivalent on the issue and only a quarter of those responding to this question (20 respondents) indicated that they had a sense of independence: of these, two-fifths (just 8 respondents) felt unequivocally independent (justifying this, characteristically, with reference to the taxes and national insurance contributions which they or their forebears had paid), while three-fifths recognised a sense in which benefits made or could make them dependent but felt more independent than dependent.

Cross-tabulations of the above findings revealed trends which were more subtle than decisive. On the whole, women were more likely than men to feel dependent and the sense of dependency appeared to increase with the age of the respondent. Respondents from professional/managerial and skilled manual occupational backgrounds were proportionately more likely than those from clerical/retail/catering and unskilled manual occupational backgrounds to feel dependent (possibly because the former groups had in the past placed a more particular value upon their skills as their means to 'independence').

In discussing this question, claimants were often able to see that social security benefits might act as a protection against other forms of dependency or exploitation, but for most there remained a pervasive sense in which the nature of the social security system, the manner of its administration and the parsimony of its benefits rendered them at least partially dependent. In the course of the interviews, several respondents (21 in all) spoke quite explicitly of a sense in which they were captives of the social security system. Of these, a few (9) said they had become lethargic or somehow inured to or comfortable with life on benefits, or else they recognised this as a danger which militated against their coming off benefits. Other respondents (4) described how they had become so busy, preoccupied with or exhausted by the mechanics and rhythms of the claiming process, or else their own self-motivation was so stifled by the requirements of the system, that they felt it hard to break out of the cycle. Other respondents again (4) explained how they had become afraid of the insecurity and uncertainty of the labour-market and in many ways preferred the predictability of claiming benefits (in spite of their inadequacy). Finally, some respondents (7) spoke explicitly about how they felt 'trapped', 'caged' or 'caught in a vicious circle', or else they sought to explain how perverse the social security system seemed, because it somehow frustrated their attempts to get off benefits. This is a theme to which we shall shortly return.

Although single parents appeared to be proportionately rather more likely than non-employed respondents to have felt dependent on the government, a few (22) of the women taking part (all but two of them single parents) were asked whether they would prefer dependency on the state to dependency on a man. The findings were broadly consistent with those of other research (c.f. Graham 1987) in so far as a majority of the women (12) agreed they would prefer dependency on the state. None the less, 9 of these women said they would prefer dependency on a man and one said that she would only wish to be dependent on the state to the extent that it should enforce and supplement the maintenance due from her ex-partner.

Clues to some of the more palpable ways in which the social security system enforces state dependency were provided by a group of respondents (22, of whom 9 were non-employed and 13 single parents) who highlighted instances of the system's propensity for counterproductive deterrence. Of these, 4 respondents mentioned that the hassle of the initial claiming process (particularly, for example, their perception of the voluntary unemployment disqualification rule or the rules governing the payment of mortgage interest during the initial weeks of an income support claim) deterred them from taking temporary or insecure employment (or else encouraged them to do so without declaring it) because of the difficulty of getting back on to benefit. Similarly, another group of respondents (20) mentioned that the low level of the income support earnings disregard and the 'hassle' involved in declaring (often unpredictably fluctuating) part-time earnings discouraged the respondents from taking part-time work, or tempted them to do so without declaring it. (Two respondents had mentioned both these possibilities.)

These are specific instances of economically rational behaviour on the part of social security claimants in response to rules not necessarily intended to have such consequences (c.f. McLaughlin, Miller and Cooke 1989). Such instances might be taken to vindicate the fears of right-wing commentators such as Charles Murray (1984). On the other hand, they reflect the often contradictory objectives which social security policies attempt to fulfil (see Dean 1991). The point to be grasped, however, is that social security claimants are not necessarily constituted as competent and rational economic actors and that the consequences of state interventions are not necessarily intelligible in terms of stated policy objectives.

Competent subjects or manipulated objects?

The discursive material from our interviews with social security claimants enabled us to interpret the 'competence' of the respondents who took part as citizens of the welfare state and their capacity to assess the way in which they were treated by the system upon which they depended.

Knowing the score

First of all, an overall assessment was made, based on the discursive content of each interview, as to the extent of each respondent's knowledge and awareness of, or their 'competence' with, the social security system. More than a quarter of the sample (24 respondents) were evidently confused or uncertain about their entitlement; just over a third of the sample (30 respondents) appeared confident about their entitlement but none the less exhibited significant confusions or expressed materially mistaken beliefs about the rules and/or functioning of the social security system; a similar number (that is to say, only 31 respondents) appeared generally knowledgeable about their own entitlement or at least betrayed no evidence to the contrary. More subtle inferences could be drawn from an examination of the claimants' use of language and, in particular, the different meanings which respondents appeared to attribute (sometimes even within the course of the same interview) to words such as 'dole' (and, as we have already seen, 'dependency').

The word 'dole' was used by respondents variously to refer to contributory unemployment benefit; to means-tested income support (or supplementary benefit) where paid to the registered unemployed; to income support (or supplementary benefit) when paid to anybody not of pensionable age; and to any sort of social security benefit administered by the DSS, whether contributory or means-tested. 'Dole' was a word of pejorative effect rather than specific definition. Similarly, the words 'social security' (or simply 'social') were used just as inconsistently to refer to any of the same things and with the same pejorative connotation.

This non-specificity of language seems inextricably linked to the widespread confusion and uncertainty which respondents felt or exhibited about their entitlement to benefit. Respondents would frequently stumble or hesitate over the names of the specific benefits they received or had claimed. Although it had been 12 years since family allowance was reformed to become child benefit, respondents frequently referred to child benefit as 'family allowance', 'child allowance' or, for example, child or family 'thingummy'. In itself, none of this is surprising in so far as it reflects the partially informed nature of popular discourse (and the low priority given to the technicalities of social security provision in the press and broadcasting media). It is significant precisely because there is no evidence that a more informed or specialised discourse or vocabulary has developed among social security recipients themselves. A 'street-wise' sub-culture, if such existed, would surely have generated a language that was more consistent or accurate upon matters of common concern.

The claimants in our sample were asked directly whether they had any views about the recent changes to the social security system or 'hunches' about the direction in which it was changing. No replies at all were obtained from some (10) respondents and almost a quarter of the sample (20 respondents) said they did not know (women being rather less likely than men to express an opinion). Of the 55 respondents who expressed a view, four-fifths (44 respondents) held negative opinions: around one third (18) had experienced recent changes as a deterioration of the system or regarded recent reforms as flawed or counterproductive; around one quarter (14) were clearly aware of a trend towards the residualisation of the welfare state, often extending their remarks to talk about health and education and expressing disapproval of what was happening; the remaining respondents with negative opinions (12) subscribed to a simplistic conspiracy theory and believed the government intended to phase out or abolish the social security system. Only 6 respondents expressed positive opinions: 3 had experienced recent changes as an improvement; 3 were aware of a trend to welfare residualisation and approved of this. Another 3 respondents were aware of a trend to residualisation, but expressed neither approval nor disapproval, and another 2 respondents subscribed to a simplistic crisis theory and believed that current social/economic trends were overloading or overburdening the system. Thus, although the views put forward were by and large critical, they were not by any means unanimous. Claimants' experiences of the social security system do not seem to have made them any more informed as commentators upon the development of that system than any other section of the community.

Of the claimants to whom we spoke who had been most communicative, some 22 talked about the changes in their political attitudes which had resulted from their experience of claiming social security benefits. These remarks fell into four general categories: some respondents (8) said they had become more politically aware and/or more consciously critical or mistrusting of the government; a similar number of respondents (9) admitted they had once supported the Thatcher government and/or the principles of Thatcherism, but had become disenchanted; other respondents (3) expressed personal animosity or even violent intentions towards specific members of the Conservative Party or government; just 2 respondents voiced expressly anarchic or extremist sentiments (one of whom is referred to at p. 92 above, the other being a young man with a history of psychiatric illness who had evidently been much influenced by his recent attendance at a meeting of the Socialist Workers' Party). Taken, however, with the evidence set out in Chapter 4, it is difficult to conclude that for most claimants the ordeal of claiming is an especially politicising experience. Much of the evidence from our research suggests, to the contrary, that for many claimants the claiming experience has a countervailing and perhaps more powerful depoliticising tendency.

Respondents occasionally indicated that their experience of claiming benefits had changed their views in other ways, but relatively f;w respondents (16) talked about this. Some (5) reported that they had begun to feel more sympathetic towards other claimants; others (4) that they had begun to feel more justified about their own situation and/or more aware of the advantages of the welfare state; some (6) went so far as to say either that they had begun to feel liberated from formerly held prejudices and moral constraints, or that they feared such constraints were in danger of being eroded; 3 respondents acknowledged that they had simply become more passive as a result of their claiming experience, more accepting of DSS authority and less inclined to question or study the workings of the system; one respondent indicated that she felt less 'at peace' with herself and with the welfare state. Thus, while there was some evidence that the claiming experience may unsettle the views which claimants previously held, there was no clear indication of any *particular* kind of conscious reorientation.

Displaced cargoes

The essence of the railway analogy with which this chapter started out is that railway rolling stock, unlike the anthropomorphised Thomas the Tank Engine of children's fiction, has no autonomy: it must be externally manipulated, complete with its cargo, from track to track, and it is ultimately as dependent on external assistance whether it be on the main track or stuck in a siding. When active citizens are 'derailed' to become social security claimants, it is of course a significant experience, but they come complete with an already loaded cultural 'cargo' of received expectations and prejudices. Part of our argument in Chapter 4 was that the discomfort and dislocation which claimants, as real human beings, experience arises, not ultimately from any increase in dependence, but from the tensions generated by their displaced 'cargo' of expectations and prejudices: tensions between their expectations of the state and the treatment they actually receive from the system, and tensions between their prejudices about state dependency and their need to receive state benefits.

Claiming benefits is an inherently individuating process by which each claimant is constituted as a 'case' (see Dean 1991). It was quite striking that as many as 12 of the 85 claimants to whom we spoke were at pains in the course of their interviews to portray their own 'case' as in some way unique or unusual, saying such things as 'you might not come up against many cases like mine' or 'I'm not your typical unemployed person'. Indeed, some of these respondents clearly attributed their difficulties with the social security system to the perceived uniqueness of their 'case', because for example 'they [the DSS adjudicating authorities] had never come across someone in my situation before', or 'a person in my position [a widower with three children] . . . does not exist in a category and therefore there was nothing they could do to help'. Far from being drawn into a community of benefit recipients, these claimants had been made to feel different; far from losing their individual identities, their identities had been isolated and underlined.

In order to discover more about the way that the claimants experienced their relationship to the state, the transcripts from our interviews were studied for certain key words. These were all words which had carefully not been introduced into conversation by the interviewer but which had been introduced by respondents. The key words chosen were selected on the basis of their relevance to the themes under analysis and because they emerged during the interviews with some regularity. Some 35 respondents were identified as having definitely used one or more of the words so selected in the specific sense of describing their experience of claiming benefits.

The most popular word used was 'degrading' (or 'degraded') used by 16 respondents; 9 respondents spoke of their sense of 'guilt' or of feeling 'guilty'; 8 respondents spoke of 'embarrassment' or feeling 'embarrassed'; 4 respondents spoke of 'humiliation' or feeling 'humiliated'. Five respondents used the word 'sponge' (or 'sponging') and 2 the word 'ponce' or 'poncing' in relation to their claims for benefit. Six respondents used other words such as 'demeaning', 'demoralising', 'distressing' and 'ashamed'.

On the whole, women were rather more likely than men to use these key words but, for example, while women were proportionately more likely than men to speak of feeling 'degraded', men were proportionately more likely than women to speak of feeling 'guilty', suggesting subtle differences in the meaning of the claiming experience which we shall explore further in Chapter 6.

Such discourse is not conditioned by the claiming experience itself, but by the expectations and prejudices with which claimants come to that experience. Our interview transcripts were trawled for certain key self-attributes. A range of significant personal attributes were identified as having been claimed or valorised by some 33 of the respondents in the course of their interviews. The most popular attribute claimed by 14 respondents was an aversion to idleness or a desire to 'keep busy' or 'work hard'. Ten respondents were anxious to identify or to distinguish themselves as 'genuine' cases; 12 respondents were at pains to emphasis the value they placed on cleanliness or hygiene; 3 respondents referred to their temperance or sobriety. At the level of discourse, therefore, many claimants were struggling, not just to 'act a part' (see Chapter 4), but to sustain a self-image which they felt to be under threat.

Closely connected with such anxieties were anxieties about the health or dietary problems which might be associated with living on social security benefits or on low incomes. It was quite significant that, in the course of talking about their current lifestyles, 15 respondents voiced entirely unsolicited expressions of concern about their own or their children's diet or state of health. While some unemployed respondents referred to their susceptibility to colds or to depressive symptoms, some single parents felt badly that they were having to feed 'junk food' to their children (c.f. National Children's Home 1991):

> Every time you open or see a magazine, or see a commercial on the television . . . it's all about the new healthy lifestyle, it's all about eating the right diet, which I'm quite aware of what the right diet is, but you can't possibly keep to it.

The pressures upon claimants stem not just from the social security system but from expectations and prejudices continually reinforced from the outside world and especially the press and broadcasting media. In the course of talking about lifestyles and participation, most of the claimants we spoke to were asked whether they took a daily newspaper. Of the 72 respondents who replied, 34 said they usually or regularly bought newspapers; 10 respondents said they sometimes bought newspapers or else had access to somebody else's; 17 respondents said they did not buy newspapers because they could not be bothered with them; and only 11 respondents said they never or seldom bought newspapers because they could not afford them. While perhaps relatively socially isolated, claimants were not necessarily culturally insulated.

To explore cultural links with the mass of the population further, a trawl through the interview transcripts was made in search of certain key images. The images sought related to stereotypes where these had been deployed pejoratively by respondents in relation to other people. Thirty-four respondents were identified as having deployed such stereotypes, including a third (12 out of 38) of the respondents who had expressed generally sympathetic, positive or tolerant views towards other social security claimants (see p. 117 above). The most popular image to preoccupy respondents (used by 12 respondents) was that of the social security claimant who spends his – and the stereotype is characteristically male – money on drink or in the pub: the image of the 'alehouse loafer' appears to have endured since Victorian times. Nine respondents referred unsympathetically to a related but different stereotype – the dosser/tramp/wino/down-and-out/alcoholic or addict; 8 respondents referred in similar vein to families with 'too many' children; 7 respondents referred in derogatory terms to 'young people' or 'young layabouts'; 7 respondents referred to 'people from abroad' or to 'blacks' (interestingly, 2 of the black people interviewed – both British born – referred with resentment to people who arrive from abroad and receive social security benefits). Four respondents deployed other sorts of stereotypes, such as 'rough' families, 'problem' families or 'gypsies'.

The very language of the claimants we spoke to tended in many instances to reinforce the picture provided by their substantive answers and statements. The sample, though not strictly representative, included a full range of typical social security claimants of working age. They formed a heterogeneous group who subscribed by and large to mainstream cultural values, who often manifested the sort of popular prejudices and punitive attitudes to be found throughout the population, and were predominantly uncomfortable with if not actually resentful of their status as social security claimants.

However, in seeking to map out a more or less coherent picture from claimants' diverse reactions to their claiming experiences, it is essential to appreciate that those reactions did not in themselves present a coherent discourse. Indeed there were some quite revealing instances of contradictory discourses within transcripts relating to the same interviews; instances which classically illustrate the ways in which every day 'common sense' is capable of accommodating conflicts between general ideas and situated judgements; between popular and personal perceptions (see Hall *et al*. 1978: 150–6). For example, one respondent who had worked overseas as a civil engineer at one point patriotically insisted that Britain has the best social security system in the world (in spite of his complaint that it had failed him lamentably), but subsequently spoke most cogently of the community-based social welfare arrangements which he had observed in African tribal society as being 'far better than ours'. Other respondents, having said that their own benefit levels ought to be increased and described how difficult it was for them to find or to undertake paid employment, none the less went on to say that it would be a 'good thing' if the social security system was phased out so as to force people to fend for themselves or to find work.

Axes of conformity

In Chapter 4 we sought to characterise the mainstream orientations to which social security claimants, in common with most contemporary British people, would seem by and large to subscribe in terms of their norms, values and lifeways. Observing and characterising those orientations, however, tells us little about what conformity or non-conformity might mean so far as social security claimants are concerned. Because they are constrained by the status of claimant, they cannot express conformity in the same way as others do. Conformity may be adjudged with reference to claimants' orientation along the following three axes:

1. The *isolation v. participation* axis, upon which those who are excluded from mainstream social activity are likely to be constructed as 'menials', 'outcasts' or 'rebels'. Menials (who accept their 'lowly' social status) and outcasts (whom force of circumstance have excluded) may none the less retain an essentially socially conformist orientation, retaining their desire or propensity for participation. Only rebels, by turning their backs on conformity and constructing alternative forms of social participation, may properly be regarded as part of an alternative or counter-culture.

2. The *incentive v. disincentive* axis, upon which a conformist orientation values security (financial and emotional) above consumption and may tolerate deprivation in preference to anxiety,
   whereas a non-conformist orientation would value consumption
   above security and would tolerate anxiety in preference to
   deprivation.
3. The *impotence v. adaptation* axis, upon which a conformist orientation is likely to imply passivity, ignorance and an acceptance of
   'dependency', whereas a non-conformist orientation is likely to
   imply resistance, anarchy and a struggle for 'independence'.

The evidence is that, while not all the claimants to whom we
spoke conformed upon every axis, the above model is sustainable:
most claimants conformed to some degree upon each axis and no
respondents conformed upon none of the axes. What is more, non-
conformity, where it was evident, did not adhere to any discernible
pattern and was generally intelligible in terms of diverse variations
upon mainstream orientations, rather than consistent manifesta-
tions of any distinctively different orientation.

Isolation v. participation

Considering first the posited isolation v. participation axis, we have
already in Chapter 4 discussed the tendency for claimants to be
subject to some degree of social exclusion or isolation, but for
many still to sustain a level of social participation in terms of
contact with family and friends, involvement in social and recreational pursuits and/or community activity. Some claimants could
not be said to be especially socially isolated, but for those for
whom social isolation was evident or was problematic, exclusion
would seem to have arisen more through respondents' social construction as 'menials' and 'outcasts' than as 'rebels'.

Those who might be regarded as having been constituted as
'menials' were characteristically self-effacing or self-deprecatory
or gave the impression that they were resigned, not necessarily to
state dependency, but to standards of living and social participation which they themselves portrayed as relatively modest. Those
who adopted the role of 'outcasts' were characteristically aggrieved by their present situation and gave the impression that

they aspired, not necessarily to independent prosperity, but to higher standards of living and social participation.

At most, only five respondents might have been said to be socially constituted as 'rebels' and, in quite different ways, to have embraced alternative forms of social participation. The first of these respondents (already mentioned on p. 112 above) was using the opportunity provided by being on social security to pursue activities from which she felt she would otherwise have been debarred, although her long-term ambition (to become a trained counsellor) was eminently socially respectable and she remained very conscious that when on social security benefits 'you are not totally free'. The second (already mentioned on p. 132) was an angry young man with a history of clinical depression who, in spite of being particularly unrepentant about an ostensibly rebellious lifestyle, said he wanted to be 'more stable' and clearly felt betrayed in his expectations that the state should either provide a lasting and effective remedy for the causes of his 'instability', or at least provide for him more adequately on a financial basis. The third (already referred to on p. 92) claimed explicitly to be part of a 'sub-culture' of social security claimants, yet this assertion seemed not at all consistent with his account of the personal pain involved in sustaining an alternative lifestyle, or with his estimation of the limited capacities of other social security claimants to sustain an autonomous 'streetwise' sub-culture. The fourth was an unemployed labourer whose life revolved around amateur rock music and his ambition to play full-time; thus while his lifestyle was arguably unconventional his aspirations were perfectly intelligible in relation to mainstream values. The fifth such respondent was a single unemployed man, a Liverpudlian of Catholic/Irish extraction, with a free-wheeling but far from extravagant lifestyle: while not socially conformist, he might best be described as a petty capitalist adventurer for whom state dependency was not a permanent or decisive element of existence, but merely an intermittent experience between highly diverse spells of employment.

Incentive v. disincentive

Turning now to the incentive v. disincentive axis, the evidence suggested that by and large claimants felt more anxious than deprived and were motivated more by a desire for security than by a desire for consumption.

Most claimants expressed some sense of anxiety about their financial circumstances. Claimants were preoccupied with 'managing', troubled by the bills they faced or in a state of 'constant worry'. Some claimants spoke about the sense of insecurity from which they suffered. As two single parents respectively put it, 'it's largely to do with uncertainty – insecurity, yes, that's the core of it'; and 'I feel insecure at the moment because of the way this government behaves.' One 32-year-old unemployed man, who had recently been forced to return to live with his parents, said, 'unemployment can be very hard work . . . when you run out of money you really need to go and find something to eat and that's not fun, there's people who'd sooner be smashing up rocks with a sledgehammer than doing that.'

Fear of not being able to manage and frustration with hand-to-mouth living clearly tempered, but did not necessarily extinguish, claimants' aspirations to higher levels of material consumption. Even those who hankered after greater spending power would tend to put questions of security for themselves or their families first: 'as long as the mortgage is paid and thc kids have got food, that's what really counts – all the while we've got a roof over our heads we've got a chance'. Claimants would insist that they did not seek to live 'in the lap of luxury', they simply wanted to live 'without having to struggle'. The struggle to survive was bewildering for some respondents: 'they think that I can buy food, pay the bills and buy our clothes as well, which doesn't work and I must look stupid, you know, to people in the dole place'; and 'I thought . . . is everyone supposed to manage on this sort of money, I mean, am I such a spendthrift?'

A few claimants did not express such views, in some instances because they received occupational pensions or fairly substantial help from their families to supplement their state benefits, in other instances because of the particular pride they took in being able (or being seen) to manage on a low income. However, even those who claimed they could manage would often betray underlying anxieties, especially on the subject of borrowing. Respondents would admit having reluctantly to borrow money from friends or family or else would express their horror of borrowing and the lengths to which they would go to avoid it.

Only four of the claimants in our sample (all men) might be said to have exhibited no sense of anxiety over their reduced financial circumstances. The first of these was the free-wheeling Liverpudlian referred to above, who said that although he 'used to be a worrier', he now adopted a different outlook and that his needs were modest in any event: 'as long as I've got a cigarette that'll do me. Many a time I've just lived on toast and tea, just to get by. It's not too bad.' The second was a single unemployed man who had recently sustained head injuries in a 'mugging' and who, claiming to be suffering from brain damage, displayed no anxiety about his straitened circumstances, only anger at the inefficiency and parsimony of the social security system, and an ambition to be 'independent and wealthy' – as a result, it would seem, of the compensation he believed he should eventually obtain from the Criminal Injuries Compensation Board. The third was an unemployed man with a young family who, in spite of having been an active pro-Thatcherite member of his local Conservative Association, seemed remarkably relaxed about his situation, justifying his right to income support with reference to a somewhat liberal interpretation of the insurance principle, but resigning himself to the restraints of the system:

> It's hard [i.e. managing on benefit], yes. It would be no good if we all went about moaning – what's the point, you've got to learn to put up with it. In a sense, if you take a low-paid job, you've got to . . . in the end something crops up and you do it.

The fourth such respondent was an unemployed man with a wife and five children living in an overcrowded third-floor council flat, who, while admitting that managing was a struggle, said he was 'comfy for the time being' and 'can't really complain', because his overriding preoccupation was with getting a tenancy transfer to a more suitable flat. He was evidently convinced that, once his family was settled in better accommodation, he would be able to get a job and provide for them in a more fitting manner.

Impotence v. adaptation

Finally, turning to the impotence v. adaptation axis, the evidence showed that, in terms of their failure to adapt and (for most) their very sense of dependency upon the state, respondents were more manipulated by than manipulative of the social security system. For some three-quarters of the sample, there could be little doubt that they were more impotent than adapted to their situation as social security claimants. Of the remaining respondents, while they had to a degree adapted themselves to life on benefits, they exhibited none the less a sense of powerlessness or unhappiness or both.

Several of the claimants who had ostensibly adjusted and were reconciled at least to a period of state dependency would still betray a sense in which they found the social security system mysterious or confusing: 'when we got to the new system [income support] I'd given up because I want to get off it, I haven't even found out how this new system works'; and 'everybody seems to be getting more money than what I have, I don't understand it though'. One single parent, defeated by the complexity of her problems with her income support entitlement, declared, 'I feel so totally controlled by this muddle.'

Alternatively, as indicated above, respondents who were ostensibly competent in dealing with their claims to benefit would often demonstrate a lack of 'street wisdom' and, in particular, some uncertainty about the powers which state officialdom could actually wield. For example, a former civil engineer who had been out of work for eight years (in which time he had had to care for his wife during a serious illness) confidently claimed that he had 'fought to maintain [my house and home] rightly or wrongly using this system', but in spite of his litigious disposition he admitted he had found the system 'like the Mafia – you couldn't find out anything': in the course of the interview it emerged there were still things about his own and his wife's entitlements which he did not fully understand. Another respondent, a partially disabled gay man, had assumed a self-appointed role in attempting to 'rehabilitate' male prostitutes and claimed in the process to have acquired considerable knowledge of the social security system: he had himself evidently adapted to a frugal life on benefits, yet he espoused some rather extraordinary claims regarding the imagined discretionary powers of social security officials and a sense of paranoia about the allegedly capricious way in which such powers could be exercised.

Several of the claimants who spoke of adjusting to life as claimants would express a sense of guilt, defeat or despair. One respondent, unemployed for six years and now approaching pensionable age, described how he would eke out his razor blades to get sixty shaves from each blade and how he and his wife survived on 'bubble and squeak' and cheap sausages: he ended his interview in tears, saying,

> Cor, dear oh dear . . . we can always make something up if we ain't got nothing, we can always make something to eat. If it wasn't for this money [income support] I don't know what we'd do. I feel guilty sometimes taking it . . . because it don't seem right. I'm a healthy man, there's still work in me and I should be working for my own keep, my own home. Why should I have to take it off the government, but it's just people won't give me a job.

Another, much younger, single unemployed man described his strategy:

> I'm not totally attracted [to living on benefits] for the rest of my life, but . . . there comes a point . . . where one does in fact put in a lot of detailed planning into permanent existence, because . . . you can't rule it out, jobs don't turn up tomorrow . . . You have to rely on . . . what you might call habits and rituals. You've got to look at what's really important, what you can't do without . . . [I]f you're going to survive . . . you have to put a lot of concentration one way or another into the business . . . of making certain one knows where one's going to be most of the day or any part of the day . . . [I]t's not some point of eternal rest . . . it can be very stressful.

Other claimants made the point that they could not 'relax' while they were dependent on benefits, that they felt insecure, vulnerable or somehow 'ground down'.

One particular claimant to whom we spoke, a black single man in his late twenties who had been in and out of unemployment since leaving school, exhibited feelings of both powerlessness and unhappiness. Superficially, he was very 'laid back' about his situation, but the views he expressed were full of extraordinary contradictions: anger at his treatment by social security officials and his vulnerability to exploitation by low-paying employers; but condemnation of other social security claimants and his own failings. While in one breath he would say, 'I can't really complain, because to me it's free money', in the next he'd say, 'I hate the social security system: they shouldn't even have the system for me personally, because I've been on it so long.' Faced with such conflicts in his own mind, he frankly concluded, 'I can't make head or tail of what's going on in my life.'

Modernity, dependency and captivity

The tensions and contradictions experienced by social security claimants along these axes of conformity may simply reflect the tensions and contradictions which some writers attribute to the lately shifting conditions of 'modernity' (or, alternatively, the emergence of an incipient 'post-modernity'). Fiona Williams has recently suggested that, far from supervising our lives 'from cradle to grave', the welfare state now pushes its subjects 'from pillar to post' (1991: 3).

The notion of 'modernity' has been used by some sociologists to sum up the essence of the society which emerged as mass production techniques and the mass market began to shape our economic arrangements, and administrative techniques and bureaucratic government began to shape our individual lives. However, the nature of modernity may itself be changing (or being superseded) through the consequences of its own logic, the impact of information technologies and mass communications media, and the emergence of cultural influences which can be simultaneously globalised and dispersed.

The left-wing Fabian (and inherently modernist) conception of the welfare state sought to promote the social participation of subjects through the provision of rights and benefits. At the same time, however, modernity itself involves the separation of the technical systems by which such rights are administered from the lifeworld which gives meaning to social participation and in which the well-springs of behaviour are located (see Habermas 1987). Modernity has been changing the very nature and meaning of social participation through a process which Giddens (1990) describes as 'the transformation of intimacy'. We have already seen that the claimants in our sample tended to value the family for the intimacy of its relationships rather than as an institution for material support. Furthermore, while claimants may be excluded from certain aspects of social life beyond the family, their orientations are essentially 'privatist' in nature and the activities from which they are excluded may be conceived by and large as recreational or 'leisure' pursuits, involving economic consumption as much as social participation.

The essence of modernity is that, through the development of mass markets and rights guaranteed by bureaucratic government, it has increasingly overcome dependency on personal ties and, as Giddens puts it, 'the opposite of "friend" is no longer "enemy" or even "stranger"; rather it is "acquaintance", "colleague", or "someone I don't know" ' (*ibid.*: 119). The participation and solidarity which modernist supporters of welfare sought to promote has failed to materialise, not just because the administrative system of state welfare has been inadequate, but also because of the lately countervailing tendency of modernity itself to foster diversity and relative isolation, as people become more highly individuated yet more uniformly culturally inscribed.

In contrast, the right-wing neo-liberal (but equally modernist) conception of the welfare state has sought to adapt welfare regimes in order to provide economic incentives and disincentives which might impel rational subjects to seek employment or rely more upon their families. At the same time, however, modernity has been driven not only by the imperatives of capitalist accumulation, but also by the imperatives of what Giddens (1990) describes as 'abstract systems'; by the symbolic forms and technical expertise necessary for the perpetuation of social relations across increasingly indefinite spans of time and space. And indeed we have seen that the claimants in our sample tended to value ontological security above uncertain prospects of increased affluence. The rationality demanded for survival in the context of a world increasingly dominated by abstract systems is not necessarily consistent with simple economic rationality. The incentives and disincentives which modernist detractors of state welfare sought to promote have been ineffectual, not because they have inflicted no pain, but because of the lately countervailing tendency of modernity to foster environments of trust and risk in which the construction and maintenance of individual identity is at least as necessary as the pursuit of physical comfort. Whether or not people respond to such incentives, they experience the reduction of their motives to a simple response to carrot or stick as an assault upon their individuality.

In this section we have sought to demonstrate that the claimants in our sample were by and large more impotent than adapted to life on social security benefits. Caught between the administrative power of the state, the weight of adverse popular opinion and their own struggle for individual identity, many actually expressed a sense of powerlessness or of sometimes quite profound unhappiness. The disciplinary nature of the claiming experience was illustrated, as we have shown, by the way some claimants blamed themselves for their uneasy predicament. Others, however, were able to articulate ways in which they blamed the system for their powerlessness and/or unhappiness. They spoke in terms evocative of the relationship between captive and captor.

As indicated above (p. 126), several respondents spoke of being 'trapped' or 'caged' by the social security system:

> I can survive, but it's not surviving on the sort of thing you'd like to survive on . . . you've got to cut it down, you've got to stop there and you are kept there. It seems as if you were suspicious, as if you were captive and there's no way you can get out of that captivity. This is how it seems. You are in a ring and no matter what you do, the wall is too high, you can't jump over it, you can't climb over the top. This is how it seems to me.

Different respondents made various attempts at pinning down the nature of their captivity within the system, some of them responding in fairly conventional terms to the effects of the poverty or disincentive trap (see p. 93). One respondent, conscious of the wage he would have to command to escape from benefit dependency, said, 'It's a bit of a gilded trap really.' Another doggedly pro-Thatcherite respondent put it this way:

> You know, Norman Tebbit [a former Conservative Secretary of State for Employment] was right, they ought to get on their bikes . . . but what he doesn't know is how inefficient, how wrong and inefficient the system is. It does not work. It is not cost-effective . . . it achieves the opposite of what it set out to do . . . it seems to create a permanent underclass . . . I have been thrown into this underclass by events outside my control. Now I am there, the very system that is trying to get me out is . . . keeping me there permanently.

However, perhaps the most revealing insight came from the respondent already quoted at the beginning of this chapter. He was replying to the question, 'So how do you feel about other people who live on social security benefits?':

> I don't give a toss about them . . . Well, it bothers me. I mean, I'm sorry for them . . . I feel empty for them, do you understand me, but I can't do anything for them if I'm dead . . . I can only do something if I'm alive and well and functioning creatively and, actually, I can't do it as long as I spend every spare minute just surviving. So I shut them out in that sense . . . I do care about my neighbour who's in

the same boat, but I feel like [I'm one of] a little army of people, always in the same boat, not actually responsible for ourselves and we're not even friends. This is the problem about it. We're all sorts of people; a cross-section of all society; we're all thrown together in the same situation . . . [but] . . . we're not on a track of our own, we're all off the track, all derailed and in a siding.

Conclusion

These last two quotations stand in opposition to each other. The one subscribes to the notion of underclass and the perverse failure of the social security system to stamp out dependency. The other subtly alludes to the success which the social security system has in isolating claimants and sustaining a particular kind of dependency.

When we dismissed the notion of underclass in Chapter 2, we drew indirectly upon the work of Michel Foucault to argue that the persistence of poverty in western societies need not imply the failure of social security and relief systems. On the contrary, such systems may be understood as succeeding extremely well in producing state dependency as a specific type, a politically or economically less dangerous form, of poverty; they succeed in constructing benefit recipients in an apparently marginal, but in fact centrally supervised, milieu (see Foucault 1977: 277; Dean 1991: Ch. 4).

We believe that the evidence from our own research, as outlined in these last two chapters, lends significant support to this argument. We have demonstrated first, not the existence of a distinctive dependency culture, but the centrality of the mainstream cultural milieu in illuminating the contradictions experienced by social security claimants; it is the mainstream milieu which provides the handles or the levers with which discipline may be exercised. Secondly, we have demonstrated that even when one considers those claimants who appear at first glance as exceptions to the general rules implied by mainstream orientation, none of these 'hard cases' can intelligibly be understood to have escaped entirely the intersecting 'axes of conformity' which we crudely modelled for the purposes of this limited study.

We may indeed conclude that the social security reforms wrought by the Thatcher governments of the 1980s were crassly insensitive to the nature of social change, popular expectations and the objective needs of claimants. However, at another level we might conclude that such reforms constituted none the less an element of one of Foucault's 'great anonymous, almost unspoken strategies' (1976: 95). To the extent that the reforms were undeniably directed to the administrative manipulations of the conditions of life of state benefit recipients, they sustained state dependency as a uniquely visible form of dependency.

It is the very visibility of this form of dependency which occludes and indirectly thereby reshapes all other forms of dependency. Just as the captivity of the convict and the symbolic trappings of the penal system define and underwrite certain fetishised conceptions of freedom, so the captivity of the claimant and the symbolic trappings of the social security system define and underwrite certain fetishised conceptions of independence. The issue at the heart of social security reform is not dependency and the dependency culture, but power and the technology of power over life. This is the question which will be addressed in our final chapter.

CHAPTER 6

DEPENDENCY AND POWER

In the 1940s and even the 50s and 60s the dominant thinkers and politicians had a vision, revealed by the laws and institutions they set up, of a huge, benevolent, all embracing, all providing state, which saw its duty of 'protecting and promoting the welfare of its citizens', as requiring it to take ever greater control over their individual lives . . . The shape and pattern therefore of the welfare measures enacted in those years too often had the effect of increasing people's dependence on the state and its attendant bureaucrats, and reducing the power and control they might have hoped to gain over their own lives. We [the Conservative government] have a different vision of what it means to 'protect and promote economic and social welfare' in this country. We believe that dependence in the long run decreases human happiness and reduces human freedom . . . Therefore the next step forward . . . is away from dependence towards independence. (Moore 1987: 3–4)

This statement, by the then Secretary of State for Social Services, was explicitly intended to begin a process of which the first and most important part was 'to change the climate of opinion' (*ibid.*: 6). What is striking about the statement is not its somewhat tautological reinterpretation of the history of the welfare state so much as the relationship which is posited between dependency and power. The paradigm implicit in Moore's statement is that power is inversely related to dependency; that the means to power is independence.

The purpose of this final chapter is not necessarily to defend the post-war welfare state against its detractors from the New Right, but to develop a less simplistic and more useful paradigm. It will be argued that dependency, whether it be upon the market, the family or the state, is the universal condition of all social beings, and that it represents a central axis for the exercise of power throughout the whole of our social fabric.

At the level of discourse, 'dependency' tends to be regarded quite universally as if it is some undesirable aspect of the human condition. It is regarded as a pathological feature of or within western culture, as something to be avoided where possible. At the very least, certain forms of dependency are regarded as less natural, less 'healthy' or less satisfying than others. The existence and central significance of dependency is denied or else it is conceptualised in a fetishised form. Our argument is that the ideological, theoretical and discursive contortions which have focused upon 'dependency' have in the process turned state welfare dependency in particular into something that is uniquely problematic.

In one sense, there is nothing inherently problematic about dependency, but in another it represents one of the main axes of the 'bio-political dimension' (Foucault 1976; Donzelot 1979); an axis along which the technology of power over life is exercised. Such technology, like all technologies, will always be historically specific to the social relations of production and exchange. However, it is dependency not power that is universally inherent to the individual, even if it is specific socially constituted relations of dependency that furnish the 'levers' for the power to which individuals are subject. This is the context in which current preoccupations with state welfare dependency should be adjudged and understood. The retrenchment of the social security system sought by the New Right in the course of the 1980s, while ostensibly aimed at reducing the politico-juridical power of the state, was unquestionably directed to the administrative manipulation of the conditions of life of welfare state recipients: by making welfare state dependency a uniquely visible form of dependency, it did not diminish but enhanced state power.

Dependency as failure

It was argued in Chapter 2 that the pejorative notion of 'dependency' that has lately been used to characterise a symbolic 'underclass' is based upon socially constituted definitions of failure. In his above-mentioned statement, the new 'climate of opinion' which Moore sought to create is one in which state welfare dependency is to be regarded as synonymous with failure. He contrasts 'the sheer delight of personal achievement' with the 'sullen apathy of dependence' (Moore 1987: 7). In describing the development of the post-war welfare state as an 'aberrant path toward ever more dependence on an ever more powerful state' (*ibid.*) he attempts to read off the intentions of post-war legislators from the intrusive and coercive effects of the professionalism and bureaucracy in which many social policy interventions have been enmeshed. In calling for a return to the ideals of 'self-help' once espoused by Victorian philanthropy he is oblivious to the intrusive and coercive nature of that philanthropy and to the continuity of development of the disciplinary techniques which have, from the fifteenth century onwards, been associated with measures for the relief of poverty (Dean 1991: Ch. 3). His view is informed by a robustly bourgeois (and patriarchal) individualism in which individuals should be 'helped to be independent, to use their talents to take care of themselves and their families, and to achieve things on their own' (Moore 1987: 4).

This view of dependency as powerlessness is consistent with the thinking of 'anti-collectivists' such as Hayek and Friedman and with an ontological concept of freedom as a natural right (George and Wilding 1985: Ch. 2). In the anti-collectivist tradition, freedom and power are formal and abstract; they are not social phenomena generated through human actions and relationships, but mysterious latent qualities vested in the individual. The Hegelian/Marxist tradition offers an alternative perspective upon freedom and power. Hegel suggested that, although it is the master who exercises power over the slave, the master thereby achieves a state of dependent consciousness (consciousness only 'for itself'), whereas it is the slave who achieves true self-conscious independence (consciousness 'in itself') through labour performed for the master (1966). Such a premise might imply that when the slave is at last made his/her own master (transformed into a formally 'free' labourer) she/he stands not to gain but to lose a self-conscious independence. In appropriating and criticising Hegel's philosophy, Marx was eventually to claim that the autonomy of individuals is not so much a condition precedent of a free market and a productive wage-labour system as an illusion necessarily created by those social relations of production and exchange which are historically specific to capitalism (1970). Human beings are estranged, Marx argues, not from their idealised objective selves (in Hegel's sense), but from the material product of their labour; capitalist social relations guarantee not individual autonomy, but class power.

Power, we shall argue here, is not inherent but largely external to the individual, being vested, if not directly or exclusively in classes, then in social structures. Where power does vest in individuals it is not by virtue of their own 'achievement', but through the dependency of others upon them. Thus employers wield power over their employees; 'breadwinners' have power within the households which they support; and social security officials exercise power in relation to claimants. It is nonsense to suppose that successful entrepreneurs, patriarchal providers or social security managers are in themselves 'independent': as individuals they too remain strictly dependent upon the services of others to obtain food, clothing, shelter, health and personal care, companionship and emotional support. It is precisely because individuals are mutually interdependent that relations of power are constituted at the social level, including especially the power that is mediated through the roles which individuals fulfil within such structures as the wage relation, the family and the welfare state.

From the New Right's 'anti-collectivist' perspective, dependency is quite logically a failure of individual autonomy. However, certain forms of dependency (i.e. dependence upon the wage relation and within the family) do indeed appear as 'natural' conditions of the social relations of production and reproduction, and only one form of dependency (i.e. state welfare dependency) remains visible. State welfare dependency may in reality result from a failure of some other dependency relation (such as dismissal from employment or the desertion of a marital partner), but uniquely it is state welfare dependency which is taken as evidence of failure at the level of personal achievement.

We have seen that the assault by Moore and the Thatcher governments upon the 'benefit culture' of welfare state dependency borrowed directly from American critiques of state welfare, in particular, the views of ultra-conservative American political scientist Charles Murray (see Chapter 2 above and Levy 1988). The notion of 'benefit culture' and the contrived theory of its historical development serve primarily to reinforce the far more self-evident cultural traditions of respect for work and for the family; traditions which the architects of the modern welfare state, far from eschewing, had aimed to preserve and strengthen. If the prescriptions offered in the 1942 Beveridge Report were at odds with those more recently tendered by the New Right, the discursive justifications were almost identical:

> The State in organising security should not stifle incentive, opportunity, responsibility; in establishing a national minimum, it should leave room and encouragement for voluntary action by each individual to provide more than the minimum for himself [sic] and his family. (Beveridge 1942: para. 9)

Economic and social changes have undermined the legitimacy of the technical assumptions and patriarchal prejudices upon which Beveridge's grand design was based (see Chapter 1 above; Mishra 1984; Parker 1989), but what the evidence in this book and that of other recent research has demonstrated is that certain essential cultural values reflected in the post-war welfare consensus are not really in jeopardy. For example, recent research into the reasons for the low take-up of means-tested social security benefits has concluded that

> Explanations can be found in people's expectations, in the existence of choice, and crucially in the importance of being independent. An admission of being unable to manage is an admission of not being able to support yourself and hence *a failure to be independent*. Independence appears to be at the end of many chains of questioning, a fundamental and unquestioned value in this society. [emphasis added] (Davies and Ritchie 1988: 6)

We might deduce from this that the 'climate of opinion' which Moore was so anxious to foster is already much in evidence and that, from this point of view, the contentious social security reforms of the 1980s were largely a waste of time. However, precisely because they appealed to an *existing* climate of opinion, they reinforced the association between state dependency and failure and in fact served to enhance the disciplinary nature of the claiming experience.

Dependency, the wage relation and the commodity form

Marxist commentators contend that the illusion of individual autonomy and 'independence' is an essential component that is common
to the fetishised categories of the wage relation and the commodity
form. Independence is the necessary condition of the individual
subject, formally free to enter contractual relationships for the sale
of his/her labour and for the purchase or exchange of commodities
in the market-place. Thus social interdependency is denied; it is
conjured out of sight. Dependency is displaced by the categories of
'work', 'trade' or 'consumption', because ordinary people, as the
objects of capital's exploitative power, necessarily appear to themselves and each other as autonomous subjects (see Marx 1970 and,
for example, Pashukanis 1978; Holloway and Picciotto 1978).

Dependency fetishism

It may be argued that the relations of power existing between the
welfare state and the welfare recipient are themselves derived
from or constituted by the fetishised form of the wage relation.
The power that is vested in the state as provider assumes the same
form as the power wielded by capital (as employers) over 'free'
labour (as workers). The dull compulsion of wage labour is extended beyond the immediate sphere of the wage relation into the
sphere of state–citizen relations (Dean 1991).

Labour discipline in a direct and obvious sense has always been
a preoccupation of policy makers in the field of poor relief and
social security provision, but the reforms of the 1980s were characterised in policy terms by a very distinctive switch from equity
goals to efficiency goals, by a concern that high benefit rates are a
disincentive to labour-force participation (Barr and Coulter 1990).
These reforms were informed by a belief that

> a significant number of benefit claimants are not actively looking for
> work. Some are claiming benefits fraudulently while working at
> least part-time in the black [sic] economy. Others seem to have
> grown accustomed to living on benefit and have largely given up
> looking for work. (Department of Employment 1988: 55)

The evidence of this book and that of other researchers (e.g.
McLaughlin, Millar and Cooke 1989; Gallie and Vogler 1990;

Heath 1991; and for a useful overview see Morris 1991) demonstrates that benefit claimants are by and large highly motivated to work and that, in some respects, the recent reforms are counterproductive since they may in fact deter claimants from seeking part-time or temporary work or from declaring the earnings from such work. Yet we have also concluded (see Chapter 4) that the mainstream cultural orientation which social security claimants clearly share is one which values employment, not only for its financial rewards, but for the essential social identity and self-esteem which it brings (c.f. Deacon and Bradshaw 1983). The effect of pressures on claimants to 'price themselves into' low-paid jobs threatens to undermine the primary value which claimants place on paid employment, as 'work'. The disciplinary effects of the claiming experience therefore stem not 'externally' or overtly from the pressures applied by the social security system, but 'internally' or covertly from the conflict between the claimant's own cultural orientation (which values employment) and the nature of his/her experience (which devalues it).

While the wage relation is founded on the dependency of the employee upon the employer for the means of subsistence, the imagined purpose of seeking and taking a job for most claimants is to establish their 'independence'. Similarly, it is the fetishised commodity form which constitutes social needs as individual needs and the individual not only as a juridical subject and a 'consumer' but potentially as an object of intervention; as a 'client', a 'claimant' or a 'case'. Thus the power that is vested in the state as provider can again assume the same form as the power wielded by capital (as owners of the means of production) over labour (as mass consumers of essential produce: Dean 1991).

The power especially of the press, broadcasting and advertising media to define people's tastes and to determine what is and is not acceptable can be used to fashion the consumption roles of people at whatever stage of their life-cycles and whether or not they are in receipt of social security benefits. A key factor to the social security reforms of the 1980s was the general climate in which they were introduced. The 1980s began with the commissioning of the Rayner Report on the payment of benefits to unemployed people (Department of Employment/Department of Health and Social Security 1981), the appointment of over a thousand extra staff devoted to fraud investigation and the introduction of specialist claims control units (R. Smith 1985), all of which occurred in the context of a burgeoning press and media campaign against social security 'scroungers' (Golding and Middleton 1982). The 'folk devils' portrayed were the affluent 'poor'; social security claimants with profligate lifestyles; welfare dependants with unrestrained consumption patterns. The classic focus for the high point of the moral panic thus generated were so-called 'costa del dole' scandals and the images conjured up of seaside social security offices 'thick with subsidised cigarette smoke, the smell of alcohol paid for by the state and the smugly tanned faces of leeches feeding off the hard-working, ordinary, silent majority' (from the *Daily Mail*, quoted in Campbell 1984).

What our research has clearly shown is that, in conforming to mainstream values, the overwhelming majority of social security claimants are not motivated by a desire for high levels of consumption and creature comfort, but are on the contrary racked with anxiety as they struggle to manage on limited incomes. They value security before consumption. The identity embraced by the various social security claimants to whom we spoke (see Chapters 4 and 5) was by and large that of the responsible consumer, worried about how to pay his/her way. What is more, in spite of this, most claimants resisted the suggestion that they themselves were 'poor', while some in fact agonised over how or whether to 'look the part' of the social security claimant. It is not simply that the media portrayals of 'costa del dole' scroungers were wide of the mark, but that the entire climate of suspicion and opprobrium has under-written the place and the identity of social security claimants as consumers in the market-place; it has added a new anxiety to their struggle for survival; it has obscured the nature of state dependency with preoccupations about managing.

Such observations tell us something about the nature and the derivation of the mechanisms and techniques of power which are immanent within relations between the welfare state and the individual as claimant. However, standing as it does outside civil society, the form of the state remains ambiguous and contestable. The status of the welfare claimant as the apparently autonomous juridical subject remains equally ambiguous and contestable. It is the question of dependency which seems in many ways to provide a focus for the contradictions of state welfare. Within the discourse of the New Right, state welfare is an 'aberrant path' towards conditions of dependency which can and must be avoided (Moore 1987). Within the discourse of the Fabian left, state welfare is the means of collective provision for 'states of dependency' which for the vast majority of the population are unavoidable (Titmuss 1963). These conflicting stances share essentially the same fetishised notion of dependency – a notion which regards dependency as an abnormal condition, as a departure from some natural and desirable state of independence, as something which must be either eradicated or compensated.

Both right and left have prescriptions for removing or concealing dependency from within the workings of the welfare state. The path to welfare independence prescribed by the right (and many of the centre) usually involves a new emphasis on 'consumerism' and 'consumer choice'. An alternative path prescribed by some commentators of the left (and some from the centre) involves the restoration of individual autonomy through the introduction of measures such as a basic income guarantee or social dividend.

Consumerism

Of all the major welfare state programmes, the social security system is perhaps the least likely candidate for the application of a 'consumerist' approach since, with the important exception of insurance-based benefits, it is difficult to contrive a reciprocal/contractual element to state income maintenance schemes. Certainly, the Social Security Act 1986 portended a major shift towards the 'privatisation' of retirement pensions (see, for example, Papadakis and Taylor-Gooby 1987), but in other areas of provision, the impetus to consumerism has been restricted to the partial privatisation of sickness and maternity benefits administration through the introduction of statutory sick pay and statutory maternity pay (Dean 1989/90; Dean and Taylor-Gooby 1990). There are limits to which even the administration of cash benefits can be devolved to non-state institutions, such as insurance companies and employers, and more recently the government has instead been concerned with the establishment of a semi-autonomous benefits agency within the Department of Social Security, responsible for the administration of benefits including means-tested income support (see Social Security Benefits Agency 1991). While critics may dismiss such moves as cosmetic, the discursive justification for the reforms has centred on recasting benefit 'claimants' as the 'customers' of a service and on improvements, not to benefits or the rules of the system, but to the delivery and image of the service.

Support for consumerism has grown out of disillusionment with the paternalism of the post-war welfare state (Clode, Parker and Etherington 1987). Consumerism and the ideological emphasis upon freedom of choice represent a fundamental shift in values, the stimulus for which came from the libertarian philosophies of the New Right. It must be noted, however, that such values are finding resonances within the discourses of the left, which is tending increasingly to reject municipal solutions (see Labour Party 1989).

In practice, this apparent shift in values has been translated into various initiatives intended to empower welfare recipients as consumers. First, there have been attempts to re-establish fiscal links between supply and demand for welfare services through the introduction of mechanisms such as voucher and service credit schemes or their equivalents in terms of cash benefits (Bosanquet 1987). Second, there have been attempts to enhance the participation of consumers in the planning and provision of welfare services through the introduction of community health councils, the co-option of tenants on to local authority housing management committees, the appointment of parent governors in state schools, the creation of neighbourhood councils and neighbourhood forums, and the encouragement given to co-operatives and self-help groups (Cook 1987). Third, there have been attempts to clarify and to valorise the rights of consumers in relation to welfare services through increased emphasis on information services, appeals mechanisms, etc. and, for example, through the introduction of negotiable social worker–client contracts and advocacy services for patients in mental health institutions (Carey 1987).

There is little evidence that such innovations have in practice materially improved the quality of services, the degree of substantive choice available to 'consumers' or the power of welfare recipients. Consider, for example, the switch in the funding of residential care for the elderly from the direct subsidy of local authority homes to the provision of indirect subsidy through social security benefits (enabling elderly persons to 'buy' places in private homes): the liberty which such funding arrangements sup-posedly bestow may be of limited value if the level of the cash benefit/service credit is insufficient to buy anything other than the lowest standard of care or if the elderly person might choose domiciliary rather than residential care. Similarly, the participation of consumer representatives upon decision-making bodies usually involves no real transfer of power over matters such as resource allocation and, by giving rights of audience to those 'consumers' who are most articulate (or who have the sharpest elbows), the process can compound conflicts of interest between consumers to the disadvantage of the weakest amongst them.

Finally, the 'rights approach' to state welfare provision may enhance the formal status and standing of the consumer, but it can provide no guarantees with regard to the substantive value of the services or benefits in question. If the introduction of the Benefits Agency will lead to the more efficient and congenial administra-tion of social security benefits, this may importantly affect some aspects of the claiming experience, but the 'customers' of that service will not be sovereign; they will be no less subject to the rules of the social security system and no less dependent upon the state for their means of subsistence.

The 'consumer' or 'customer' is no less socially constituted than is the 'client' or the 'claimant'. The change in terminology and emphasis serves only to conceal or deny the nature of the state welfare recipient's dependency. Recasting welfare provision in a form more closely resembling that of other commodities and insist-ing upon the consumer's status and formal rights of participation or appeal serves only to rebuild the illusion of individual auto-nomy: it masks the contradiction between the formal indepen-dence of the subject and the dependency of the state welfare recipient as object.

Basic income schemes

Arguably, the most radical alternative to the arrangements em-bodied in the existing welfare state would be the introduction of a basic income guarantee or social dividend (Ashby 1984; Green Party 1988; Parker 1989). The most radical justification for such a scheme has been proposed by Bill Jordan (1985, 1987). A basic income guarantee or social dividend (to which we shall refer generically as 'basic income schemes') would provide a single universal social security benefit which would be paid, without means-test or contribution conditions, to every man, woman and child. Jordan's justification arises from his analysis of the inherent tensions between individual autonomy and state authority. Implicit in his analysis is a recognition of the dependency of all social beings upon the family, the market and/or the state. His argument is that a basic income scheme would enable the individual to transcend such dependency. By guaranteeing the individual's needs before she/he enters the family or the market, a basic income scheme would give effect to individual autonomy (1987: 216). By removing means-tests and contribution conditions, it would also dispense with the 'unpleasantness of state coercion and surveillance' (1985: 293), so resolving the problem of state authority and compulsion.

Jordan claims that this form of welfare provision would neutralise the state and operate in accordance with the same laws of co-operation which characterise everyday human interactions between family, relatives and friends. The 'hidden hand' of market forces, moved by the compulsion to acquire and accumulate, would be displaced by a 'hidden hand of welfare', moved by the compulsion to co-operate and to share. For the purposes of this book, the practical limitations of Jordan's vision (see Dean 1991) are less important than the questions he raises about the relationship between dependency and power.

The principles of sharing and co-operation which, according to Jordan, inform the actions and organisation of families and households stem less perhaps from 'natural' compulsions than from complex relations of power between individual household members; relations of power that rest upon equally complex patterns of dependency. The introduction of a basic state income for each member of a household might well change the balance of power within that household; it might alter the pattern of dependency and, by allowing reluctant members to leave, it might even affect the composition of the household; it could not, however, extinguish the basic interdependency of individuals within a household, nor the dimensions of dominance and submission which arise from such factors as gender, age and the differential distribution of physical, intellectual and emotional needs and capacities.

Nor would a basic income scheme significantly lessen people's dependency on the market. While the individual citizen might no longer be compelled to enter the labour-market, the scheme would leave capital in command of both the wage structure (and thereby the size of the tax base upon which the basic income is dependent) and commodity prices in the market-place (and thereby the costs of individual subsistence which the basic income must meet). The individual would be no less dependent in a cash economy for his/her food, clothing, shelter, etc. and would have no more power over the market than she/he did before.

Finally, a basic income scheme could undoubtedly change the relations of power between state and individual, but it would still leave the state in control of the final income and living standards of a substantial proportion of the population. The individual state welfare recipient would be discursively constituted, not as a 'claimant' or as a 'consumer', but as a 'citizen'. His/her status, while constructed in the ideal sense from his/her autonomous individuality or 'independence', would in the material sense be none the less determined by his/her inherent dependency.

We shall return to the question of citizenship in the final section of this chapter, when we shall also expand on the notion of 'dependency fetishism'. Our purpose here has been to illustrate the ways in which even radical reappraisals of state welfare are constrained by ideals of autonomous individuality which render our dependency upon the wage relation and the commodity form invisible or 'natural'. Our argument now, however, will shift towards that other 'natural' form within which relations of dependency are constituted (broached in fact by Jordan), namely, the family.

Dependency and the family

In 1983 the British Cabinet's Family Policy Group set out to inquire 'what more could be done to encourage families in the widest sense to reassume responsibilities taken on by the state . . . responsibility for the disabled, elderly [and] unemployed 16 year olds' (*Guardian*, 17 February 1983). In pursuit of such an aim the government has been promoting 'care in the community' for the disabled and elderly, and in most instances this will mean care in the family (Finch and Groves 1983; Department of Health 1989). The government first cut and finally removed the entitlement of 16- and 17-year-olds to social assistance benefits and has limited the benefit entitlements of young people under the age of 25, thus compelling many young people to remain with their families until such time as they are financially 'independent' (see Chapter 3 above).

By 1988, Margaret Thatcher was declaring that 'the family is the building block of society, it is a nursery, a school, a hospital, a leisure centre, a place of refuge and a place of rest' (quoted in G. Brown 1989: 149). In this way the New Right has been seeking to reverse the historical development of the family as a specialised institution. Although the New Right is often claimed to espouse Victorian values, its vision of the family has more in common with what Stone (1977) describes as the 'restricted patriarchal' family model characteristic of the seventeenth and eighteenth centuries when, as a centralised state began to develop, the family became less a unit of government in its own right and more an instrument of government. The subsequent development of the modern nuclear family has indeed, from the nineteenth century onwards, entailed the transfer of such instrumental functions as production, education and individual protection to either the market or the state, and the resulting institution is constituted more as a unit of consumption: Talcott Parsons' classic definition of the modern family is of a functionally specific set of personal relationships constructed around the processes of primary socialisation (of children) and the personality maintenance (of adults: see, for example, Morgan 1975).

The public/private divide

Such a view of the family, some little while before it was subject to criticism by the New Right, came under attack from feminists who claimed that the family is especially dysfunctional for women, confining and subordinating them within relations of dependency (Mitchell 1966, 1971); and from radical psychiatrists who pointed to the destructiveness of the claustrophobic web of relationships which is characteristic of the modern family and which distorts individuals' perceptions and denies them their liberty (Laing 1971; Cooper 1972). The New Right's agenda for the family did not, however, entail a fundamental restructuring of family relations, merely the reimposition of lost functions and a shift in the burden of dependency.

More recent feminist writing has sought to situate the question of women's dependency in relation to matters of social policy and, in particular, the separation of the domain of the 'public' from that of the 'private' (Pascall 1986; Lister 1991). The public domain is that which encompasses the market and the state: it is the sphere of productive activity and its regulation; of the wage relation, the commodity form, state administration and male dominance. The private domain, on the other hand, is that of the family and the home: it is the sphere of both social and biological reproduction, to which women are largely confined. The subordination of private power to public power has consistently been at the expense of women. From this perspective Pascall has argued that it is the issue of dependency which provides the common axis both for social policy and for the feminist agenda: the former is concerned with the supervision of dependency, while the latter is concerned with the dependency of women on men (1986: Ch. 1).

In seeking to promote independence and self-reliance through changes in the social security regime, the Conservative governments of the 1980s were concerned about public dependency on the state, not private dependency within families. As Sarah Benton observed, 'when this government speaks of individuals it unconsciously adds "and their families" as though women and children, the dependent aged, sick and disabled are not independent beings for whom citizenship was created' (quoted in Lister 1991: 448). The dependability of full-time parents and carers rests upon their dependency upon others within the family, if not upon the state, and it is therefore for women in particular that economic dependency may represent the 'cost' of unpaid caring and domestic work. Their dependent status in the home, as Hilary Graham puts it, 'is not absolute, but conditional upon their being simultaneously depended on by others' (1983: 24). There is nothing logical or necessary about the established sexual division of labour; it is the public–private divide which makes it appear as a 'natural' consequence of 'normal' family life.

In Chapters 4 and 5 we observed several ways in which dependency can have a different meaning for women to that which it has for men. We observed first of all that women were rather more likely than men to admit that managing on social security benefits was 'hard', and that this may be taken to reflect the fact that managing the household budget is more commonly the concern of women. For women rather than for men, involvement and expertise in managing is more characteristically a mark, not of their independence, but of their dependability.

Secondly, in common with other research (see, for example, Graham 1987) we found that some women found they were 'better off poorer' as lone parents and preferred dependency on the state to dependency on an unreliable (or violent) man. This preference arose because women found that state dependency in fact gave them more control over their money and their day-to-day lives (c.f. Lister 1991). There was a sense in which their enhanced dependability as managers ironically brought a degree of 'independence'.

Thirdly, we observed that women were (without prompting) rather more likely than men to describe the claiming experience as 'degrading', while men were more likely than women to say they felt 'guilty' about their dependency on benefits. Though no claims can be made for the statistical significance of this observation, it is none the less suggestive of gender-specific connotations of 'degradation' and 'guilt'. Could it be that for women rather than for men the excursion into the public sphere of the state and/or the intrusion of the state into the 'private' sphere of the family is experienced in some sense as a violation? Could it be that for men rather than for women the exclusion from the public sphere of the labour-market is a cause for self-recrimination? Research on gender roles suggests that the sense of obligation which women feel in relation to caring, in particular, for elderly or disabled relatives is more likely to be fuelled by feelings of 'guilt' rather than perhaps 'love' (Ungerson 1987). Women 'care' just as men 'work', because they feel guilty if they do not. The possibility mooted by this perhaps facile generalisation is that, just as the fetishised form of the wage relation can obscure the nature of dependency relations in the public sphere, so the artificial schism between the public and the private can obscure the nature of dependency relations within the private sphere of the family.

Going against the grain

As our earlier discussion of social change implied, the public–private divide is not static. Relations of dependency and perceptions of dependency have been changing as a result of various quite different processes. Increased labour-force participation by women, while not yet challenging the male domination of the public sphere, has created new tensions at the boundary between the public and the private (and new demands, for example, for child-care provision). Changes in the family itself, resulting from the increasing incidence of divorce, cohabitation without marriage and single parenthood, are reflected in changing expectations of both private relationships and the provisions of the public sphere, at the level of both civil society and the state.

It was demonstrated in Chapter 4 that the pressures exerted, whether directly or indirectly, by recent social security reforms which might incline people to turn more to their families in preference to the state would seem to be out of step with mainstream cultural values and to be potentially disruptive of contemporary, socially constructed life-cycle patterns. Our research evidence suggested that social security claimants by and large value the family in its individual nuclear manifestation primarily for its affective relationships and emotional rewards and that these things can be undermined or deflected by the imposition of financial obligations.

Janet Finch (1989) has persuasively argued that family and kinship obligations are indeed subject to change and renegotiation over time. She shows that past attempts by government to impose particular patterns of obligation (such as under the New Poor Law of 1834, through the tightening of Poor Law regulations in the late nineteenth century and the creation of the household means-test for the unemployed in the 1930s) were largely unsuccessful. Many families responded by developing avoidance strategies, by dispersing to different localities or households. In contrast, where government has assumed responsibility for individuals through, for example, the provision of old age pensions, the evidence suggests that this has freed people to develop closer, more supportive relationships with family and kin.

Recent research by Craig and Glendinning (1990a) suggests like our own that the impact of the latest social security reforms, by reducing dependency on the state, far from enhancing family responsibility and cohesion, may be straining family relationships. Their investigation of families in receipt of income support indicated that many such families were heavily dependent on relations for help, especially in acquiring the kinds of household item for which legal entitlements to single payments under the old supplementary benefit scheme were previously available. This shift to dependency on families is

> at least as humiliating and damaging to their [claimants'] self esteem as dependency on the state. Moreover, the attempt to reduce dependency on the state was also damaging relationships within families . . . [T]he stress of living on such low incomes inevitably took its toll on the quality of relationships between parents and partners and between parents and children . . . Paradoxically, therefore, the attempt to weaken a 'culture of dependency' on the state may well inflict profound and lasting damage . . . [I]t seems that parents' ability to fulfil what they perceive to be the normal responsibilities of parenthood have actually been undermined. (Craig and Glendinning 1990b: 27)

Looking beyond the tangible affects of low income on interpersonal relationships, there is also an emerging body of opinion amongst some family therapists which arguably contradicts the political truths espoused by the New Right: a body of opinion which purports to identify an adverse syndrome associated directly with excessive interdependency. Minuchin (1974) has characterised healthy family relationships as falling in the middle range of a continuum, at one extreme of which lies 'disengagement' and at the other extreme 'enmeshment': dependency, in other words, can be underdone or overdone. During the 1980s, however, in the United States a new concept has emerged, that of 'co-dependency' (for the most all-embracing version of the genre, see, for example, Wegscheider-Cruse 1988). The notion of co-dependency appears to have been forged through an enlargement of the notion of 'co-alcoholism'; a syndrome supposedly associated with the behaviour of spouses, partners and sometimes the children of alcoholics. Co-dependency is a term now being used to describe any dysfunctional interpersonal relationship between a damaged or inadequate person who is excessively dependent and a partner or carer who is addictively or compulsively preoccupied with caring for, ministering to and manipulating that person. Such relationships are seen as dysfunctional within the discourse of co-dependency theory because they deny the integrity and independence of both the dependent and the carer.

There is no evidence, of course, to suggest a direct relationship between the retrenchment of state welfare provision and the incidence of 'co-dependency', but it is significant (or at least ironic) that the emergence of the co-dependency concept in family therapy should have coincided with various attempts at the level of social policy to shift the burden of dependency away from the state and 'back' to the family. In so far as the modern nuclear family was originally founded in the ideology of bourgeois individualism, there remains as it were an inherent tension or contradiction between the objective of nurturing independence through the family and that of promoting dependence on the family.

Dependency, welfare and the state

The declared intention of the Conservative governments which have held power in the United Kingdom since 1979 has been to roll back the state, to wean the individual from state dependency. As Sir Keith (now Lord) Joseph, the then Education Secretary, put it, 'In as much as personal responsibility has been eroded by a shift of housing, education and welfare provision excessively to the state, we are trying to shift that balance' (*Guardian*, 19 February 1983). Thus public sector tenants, for example, were given the right to buy their council houses (under the Housing Act 1980) or to transfer to alternative landlords (under the Housing Act 1988). Attempts have been made under the Education Reform Act 1988 to empower parents to subject state schools to market forces through the introduction of 'open enrolment' and 'formula funding'. The shift, however, has not been a simple shift from the public to private, or from the state to the market, but a complex shift in the balance between the two.

The monetarist economics of the early 1980s gave birth to arguments for a new era of 'welfare pluralism' or the 'mixed economy of welfare' (Beresford and Croft 1986: 3). Such rhetoric is not always allied to the wholesale privatisation of state welfare, but often denotes a shift away from state welfare provision towards state subsidised and/or state-regulated forms of private welfare provision (Papadakis and Taylor-Gooby 1987).

Modes of dependency

The state remains important, if not always as a direct provider, then as an indirect provider or as an overseer of welfare. The role played by the state and by government policy is ultimately of secondary concern in the day-to-day lives of 'ordinary people'. Richard Rose makes the point that ordinary people necessarily subscribe to the egocentric philosophy espoused by Marx (Groucho Marx!), who quipped, 'take care of me, I'm the only one I've got' (Rose 1989: 2). Government is something which by and large goes on 'over people's heads' and is quite distant from the day-to-day satisfaction of their welfare needs. Thus it is the private benefits of public welfare, regardless of how they might be delivered, which are valued and matter most to ordinary people. Indeed, 90 per cent of households in Britain at any one time depend upon at least one major private benefit from the state, such as a social security benefit or pension, medical treatment, education or public transport (*ibid.*: 24).

The source of welfare makes no difference to the inseparable nature of welfare and dependency. Under feudal social relations, the household was the primary source and allocator of welfare. Under early capitalism, the market became increasingly important as the means to secure the necessities of life. Under state welfare capitalism in the twentieth century, government also plays a major role. For Rose's 'ordinary people', the mixed economy of welfare has become a daily and unquestioned reality. For example, most people still look to the household as the primary source of personal care; to the market for food, clothing, consumer durables and so on; and to the state for expert health care and education. As to cash income, Rose calculated that in 1984, 32 per cent of personal incomes depended on transfers within the household, 30 per cent depended upon the market (i.e. earnings, private and occupational pensions, etc.) and 38 per cent depended upon the state (although this figure included earnings from public sector employment as well as income from social security benefits and pensions: *ibid.*: 138).

In a mixed welfare economy, we have different modes of dependency; we depend for our welfare upon a mixture of sources. From which source will depend upon our circumstances: not everybody has access to domiciliary care from within a household; those with insufficient means are denied access to welfare goods from the market; those who do not qualify under the relevant bureaucratic rules will not obtain access to state welfare benefits. The basis of our dependency and the means by which the totality of our welfare needs may be met can be highly complex, as are the distinctions to be drawn between household, market and state dependency. While 'ordinary people' may be relatively indifferent to the ins and outs of public policy debate, they remain very much concerned with such distinctions.

Public attitudes in Britain, even in the late 1980s and 1990s, clearly favoured a generous and expanding welfare state (see Chapter 3). Although better-off people may wish to retain the option of recourse to a privately administered welfare sector, the point at which they might cease to support the principle of common state provision would not yet seem to have been reached (Taylor-Gooby 1990: 19). What is more, public opinion seems during the 1980s to have become less critical of the adverse moral impact attributed to state welfare by the New Right: the notion of state welfare that is valued is of a generous system, criticised for inducing stigma rather than prodigality.

None the less, within public opinion there is ambiguity, particularly in relation to cash benefits. A majority of people believe that substantial numbers of social security recipients are claiming falsely, but at the same time that substantial numbers of persons entitled to benefit do not claim (*ibid.*: 11). There is a continuing high level of priority accorded by public opinion to benefits for the elderly, a more modest but increasing level of priority being given to child benefit, but a low and declining level of priority being given to benefits for single parents and the unemployed (*ibid.*: 4). Implicit in public opinion are distinctions between deserving and undeserving groups of social security recipients. Attitudes to state welfare dependency, if they are not inconsistent, are somehow selective.

To understand this it is necessary to understand the limitations which, according to Beresford and Croft (1986), are inherent in public opinion survey data. Although Beresford and Croft's own research ostensibly concentrated upon the personal social services, the data from their unstructured interviews with a sample of residents drawn from a local authority social services 'patch' reveals an added dimension to 'ordinary people's' attitudes to welfare in general. Certainly, people value the idea of having social services (and are prepared by and large to pay taxes to support them), but such services are not necessarily valued as a preferred form of welfare provision: as one of Beresford and Croft's respondents put it, 'I'm glad they're there, but I don't want to have to use them' (*ibid.*: 43).

Members of Beresford and Croft's sample exhibited a mixture of non-committal, positive and negative opinions about the services provided by their local social services department:

> But negative, equivocal or mixed opinions accounted for 40% of responses . . . People's negative comments covered a wide range of concerns . . . of insufficient and inappropriate provision and services, inexperienced staff, not getting help when it was needed, stigmatic and degrading treatment, and the social services department's remoteness, lack of concern and understanding, errors, interference, failure to inform, and its lack of knowledge of certain problems. (*ibid.*: 37)

Although these respondents had been asked about the provision of personal social services, Beresford and Croft are at pains to emphasise that the members of their sample by and large knew little about these services or how they related to welfare provision in general, and some confused the personal social services with social security, health and other services. There is considerable justification, therefore, for treating the views expressed in a more generalised sense as popular perceptions of state welfare as a whole. As such, these perceptions are sceptical rather than hostile; they acknowledge state welfare as desirable, but somehow deficient.

When asked about the various sources from which they themselves received 'care and support', the vast majority (93 per cent) of Beresford and Croft's respondents cited their partners or family relations a a source; alternatively or additionally, 22 per cent mentioned friends, but 19 per cent in total said they got no care and support, or did not need any or provided it themselves; only 7 per cent in total mentioned either state services, professional support or social services. When 'welfare' is defined in terms of 'care and support', most people interpret their needs in relation to household and family and not the state. Yet when the same people were asked whether they were getting the 'care and support' they wanted, 20 per cent said they did not: these Beresford and Croft found were more likely to be single and/or to be dependent on means-tested social security benefits than other members of the sample (*ibid.*: 110).

The implication of this last finding is not clear, but it seems to suggest that, so far as personal welfare goes (i.e. having enough 'care and support'), independence or dependency on one's self is somehow second best to dependency within the household. Furthermore, dependency for income upon the state as a surrogate is similarly second best; it represents as it were a constraint upon one's capacity to satisfy one's welfare needs.

The problem of state dependency

One way of explaining why welfare dependency may be perceived as constraining or less than satisfying is to consider the 'opportunity costs' associated with the receipt of welfare benefits. Prottas (1979) has argued that there is inevitably a certain 'price' attaching to the 'free' goods provided by the welfare state in terms of the time, effort or psychological discomfort involved in claiming one's entitlement to such goods. Prottas maintains there are two types of 'charge' that may be levied for such things as cash benefits, public housing or 'free' health care. First, he says, there are 'system level charges': charges imposed by the rules of the welfare system which often dictate that recipients must already be subject to a certain level of deprivation in order to qualify for assistance; or charges imposed by the physical characteristics of the claiming process, such as filling out long and tedious forms or having to wait for long periods in unpleasant institutional waiting rooms. Second, there are what Prottas calls 'street level' charges: charges imposed unofficially by 'street level bureaucrats' (c.f. Lipsky 1976) through their hostile manner, disinformation and the arbitrary or capricious bending of rules (Prottas 1979: Ch. 8).

The principle of 'lesser eligibility' once explicit under the 1834 Poor Law is more or less implicit in the ways in which many modern state welfare services are delivered. Such an observation is in itself hardly new, but the purpose of drawing attention to Prottas' work is to highlight the ways in which the power of the state over the citizen is mediated through the power of the 'bureaucrat' over the 'client'. 'Ordinary people' for the most part have few principled or ideological objections to dependency on the state; it is the particular relations of power within which this particular form of dependency is often enmeshed which can in practice distinguish it from other forms of dependency and which, this book argues, shapes ordinary people's perceptions.

Officially inspired inquiries demonstrate that levels of dissatisfaction with the service provided to claimants by the DSS (and before it the DHSS) are relatively high (DHSS 1985b; National

Audit Office 1988). However, our own research, which explored the nature of claimants' feelings of anger towards the social security system and their perceptions of fairness and unfairness, suggests that such inquiries may indeed underestimate the extent of that dissatisfaction. Our evidence indicates that the majority of social security claimants experience some sense of resentment about their treatment at the hands of the social security system. We found that even those claimants who were grateful for the benefits they received were uncomfortable with or lacked faith in the system (see Chapter 4 above).

Other research which has focused on the local practices of social security staff has shown that

> a combination of resource constraints, staff attitudes and beliefs and claimant tactics gives rise to practices which sustain and reproduce categories of 'deserving' and 'undeserving' at the very same time that the staff insist that such practices are actually intended to vitiate this distinction. (Howe 1985: 49)

Claimants whose demands place pressure on staff are regarded as grasping, pushy or greedy and the practical priorities adopted are such as to 'impugn, by implication, the motives of most claimants' (*ibid*: 65), even those who demonstrate by their passivity or acquiescence that they are 'deserving'.

In such circumstances it is hardly surprising that, while people do want the collective security of the welfare state, they are inclined to regard the state as an external authority or adversary. People cannot value their citizenship because state intervention is experienced, not as collective reciprocity, but as at best a poorly observed, quasi-contractual service, and at worst as the most begrudging and parsimonious largess. This in itself may have consequences for the behaviour of claimants towards the system (see pp. 117–20 above), but it also raises fundamental questions about dependency and welfare on the one hand, and citizenship and the state upon the other.

Conclusion

In drawing together the threads of our argument, the first point to be made is that 'dependency' is the concrete foundation upon which 'welfare' is constructed. 'Independence', on the other hand, is something attainable only at a certain level of abstraction. When we speak of individual autonomy, or the sovereignty of the worker, the consumer or the citizen, we must remember that the human individual remains dependent upon other human individuals and social structures. The sovereign worker is dependent upon an employer for the means of labour and of his/her very subsistence; the sovereign consumer is dependent upon a supplier for goods and/or services which she/he cannot him/herself supply; the sovereign citizen is dependent upon the state for physical security and the regulation of other human individuals and social agencies. Beneath each sovereign or autonomous worker, consumer or citizen is a dependent human being.

In one sense it was classical Marxism which implicitly yet most clearly recognised that it is dependency rather than moral agency which lies at the basis of the human condition and that it is through 'praxis' or conscious struggle that human history is made. Under capitalism, that struggle is a struggle of workers for sovereignty, not as individuals, but as a class. Individual dependency is not thereby dissolved, but mutual interdependency becomes possible through collective control of the means of production, distribution and exchange.

Using an equally broad brush, we might characterise the classical liberal view in terms of the Kantian notion of moral agency and the injunction of respect for others as autonomous 'ends in themselves'. In this tradition, our individual goals are served through the accretion of rights – civil, political and (according to Marshall 1963) social. It is therefore citizenship which ameliorates the dependency of the individual. And competing notions of citizenship are jostling for public attention in the 1990s as each of the three main political parties in Britain seeks to advance its own version of a 'Citizens' Charter' (see, for example, *Guardian*, 24 July 1991).

The development of citizenship and the formal protection it offers against arbitrary power were both necessary to and expanded through the development of capitalism. However, as Turner points out, 'citizenship exists despite, rather than because of capitalist growth' (1986: 141). Classical Marxists may object that the rights of bourgeois citizenship are a sham, but E.P. Thompson, for example, has argued that such aspects as the rule of law, which may 'disguise the true realities of power', may 'at the same time curb that power and check its intrusions' (1975: 265): he counsels that while working-class power may yet liberate us from dependency on capital and the bourgeois state, we should 'watch this new power for a century or two before [we] cut [our] hedges down' (*ibid.*: 266). There exists, therefore, a tension, even upon the left, as to whether the dependent human individual is to be protected as an active human subject, or as an abstract individual; as a worker, as a consumer or as a citizen (see, for example, the discussion of citizenship in Hall and Held 1989).

Whether individuals are cast as workers or citizens can make a real difference. For example, the import of European Community directives on rights to minimum income provision under the Social Charter may be radically altered, depending upon whether they are so drafted as to apply narrowly to 'workers' or broadly to 'citizens'. However, the dichotomy between the politics of class (for example, Wood 1986) and the politics of discourse (for example, Laclau and Mouffe 1985) may divert our attention from the inherent dependency of the human subject, a dependency which is neither the result of class subjection, nor a mere phantom of discourse. A dependency relationship, as Walker rightly observed in relation to dependency in old age, is a power relationship (1982: 127). Although the relationship between the state and individuals of all ages has increasingly in the age of modernity been understood in terms of 'welfare' rather than power (see Garland 1981), it is historically specific relations of power which determine not necessarily the extent, but the meaning, of our dependency.

What we are arguing for, therefore, is a theory of dependency in place of a theory of human needs. An excellent attempt to engage with the considerable literature on human needs has been provided by Doyal and Gough (1984). In seeking to defend a conception of 'universal human needs', they stress the importance of societal as well as individual needs, and the historical process of liberation through the optimisation of human needs. Doyal and Gough assert that the need for such things as health and autonomy through knowledge are not subjective or relative and can be objectively determined within the social and environmental context upon which such needs are predicated. Yet the needs of which they speak remain universal in an a priori sense: they are abstract expressions arising from a concrete condition, namely the mutual interdependency of human subjects; they are constituted in fact as claims or demands, just as 'rights' are constituted, not as universal attributes inhering in the individual, but through the regulation of capacities for action (see Hirst 1980).

Needs and rights alike are only realised in the context of relations of power within historically specific relations of production, distribution and exchange. Optimising needs and giving expression to rights requires the co-operative struggle of interdependent human subjects and it is universal human interdependency, not universal human need, that characterises the basis of our social existence. It is in the process of defining needs and rights for the human subject that the subject is socially constituted as an individual and the individual is rendered dependent. Autonomy is not the ontological 'given' of the human subject and, to the extent that it is achievable rather than mythical, it requires the capacity to identify, negotiate and struggle co-operatively for the optimisation of need. Autonomy does not rest upon the capacity to satisfy prescribed needs and so *evade* dependency.

This, then, is the sense in which views of welfare and the state are conditioned by a kind of 'dependency fetishism' on the left as much as the right. Just as our experience of capitalist relations of production, distribution and exchange can blind us to the underlying exploitative significance of commodities and the wage relation, so our experience of dependency can blind us to the underlying disciplinary significance of particular forms of power, the power that is exercised by institutions of 'welfare' and indeed within the family. The struggle lies not against dependency, but against the exploitation and discipline which constitute the human subject as a passive object; against, for example, the disciplinary effects endemic to the social security system which, as we observed in Chapter 5, can render claimants 'captives' of the system. The quest is not for autonomy through independence, but through ensuring the *mutuality* of our interdependence.

It behoves us, therefore, to conclude with a few remarks about the importance of this incipient theory of dependency for social policy and the role of the welfare state. If the object of social policy is regarded in terms of guaranteeing the mutuality of the interdependence of active human subjects, rather than in terms of securing the independence of the abstract individual, this has clear implications for the boundaries, not only between the state and civil society, but also between the spheres of the public and the private.

John Keane (1988), in advancing a form of civil society social-ism, has already pointed to the possibility of a democratised civil society founded on complex and interdependent forms of equality, liberty and solidarity, in which the state would serve as a mediating force to underwrite and protect the voluntary co-operation and social needs generated through the decisions of producers and consumers. One of the authors of this book has recently explored the idea that, if the welfare state is to protect its citizens from 'moral hazard' (i.e. the foreseeable consequences of the actions of others and the risk of exploitation by the more powerful), then intervention should extend beyond the public and into the private sphere in ways which would vitiate the perverse incentives that perpetuate inequality in the sexual division of labour (Taylor-Gooby 1991a).

The myth of dependency culture which was contrived during the 1980s was a paradoxical phenomenon in so far as it simultaneously threatened both the principle of *universality* which had under-pinned a welfare state born in the age of modernity, and the *diver-sity* and difference of human subjects which it is said are being realised through the birth of post-modernity. The fundamental issue for social policy, as Fiona Williams has put it, is not to coun-terpose universality and diversity, but

> to resolve the tensions between universal principles and policies, on the one hand, and the recognition of diversity, on the other. In other words, how to have welfare provision which is universal in that it meets all people's welfare needs, but also diverse and not uniform, reflecting people's own changing definitions of difference, and not simply the structured differentiation of the society at large. (1991: 8)

One of the keys to such an enterprise, we submit, is a proper understanding and theory of dependency. What is required of a welfare state is not (to use the words of John Moore whom we quoted at the beginning of this chapter) 'to take ever greater con-trol over our individual lives', but to ensure the mutual basis of our interdependence as active human subjects. It is exploitation and disciplinary power, not dependency, that 'decrease human happi-ness and reduce human freedom' and, until such time as it *is* safe to cut our hedges down, it is necessary to engage both in theory and in practice with the substance of welfare citizenship and the form of the welfare state.

APPENDIX

This appendix provides a brief technical account of the research upon which Chapters 4 and 5 of this book have been based. We shall first describe how the sample was drawn and how it was composed; secondly, we shall outline the methodology of the investigation; and finally, we shall describe a separate sub-sample analysis which was used to check the general validity of our findings.

The sample

The sample consisted of 85 social security benefit recipients of working age. It was not intended that this should be a statistically representative sample, but it was important to ensure that it should be balanced, so that the main groups of claimants in whom we were interested were included in it.

Fifty-five of the respondents were from Kent (drawn principally from Canterbury and from the Sittingbourne/Sheppey area) and 85 were from south London (from the Inner London Boroughs of Lambeth and Southwark).

The age and gender composition of the sample was as set out in Table A.1. Eight of the 85 respondents were black or of ethnic minority origin (three men and five women).

The principal benefits received by the respondents (or claimed by the partners of the respondents) were as set out in Table A.2. As approximately 70 per cent of all claimants in these categories

Table A.1 Age and gender composition of sample

Gender	Age			Totals
	18–24	25–39	40–pension age	
Male	7	14	21	42
Female	12	17	14	43
Totals	19	31	35	85

are income support recipients (according to 1988 figures: DSS 1991b), income support recipients were in fact only slightly over-represented in the sample.

Given the gender ratio (male: female) of income support recipients as a whole in 1988 (approximately 42: 50 for claimants under age 40 and 57: 43 for claimants aged 40 to pension age), the gender ratio of the sample (approximately 50: 50 for claimants under age 40 and 67: 34 for claimants aged 40 to pension age) indicates that women were slightly over-represented among the younger respondents and men slightly over-represented among the older respondents. More significant, perhaps, the age ratio (as between

Table A.2 Composition of sample by main benefit and type of claimant

Type of claimant	Main benefit				Totals
	Income support	Unemploy-ment benefit	Invali-dity benefit	Family credit	
Single non-employed	26	2	6	–	34
Other non-employed or partner thereof	14	1	1	–	16
Single parent who has never had permanent partner	9	–	–	–	9
Single parent who is widowed, divorced or separated	24	–	–	–	24
Wife of low-paid worker	–	–	–	2	2
Totals	73	3	7	2	85

those under age 40 and those aged 40 to pension age) for the sample as a whole (which was 59: 41) compared with that of income support claimants as a whole (83: 17 in 1988), reveals that older claimants were somewhat over-represented.

This would seem to be primarily related to the way in which the sample was drawn. Seventeen respondents were referred by independent advice agencies (mainly Citizens Advice Bureaux). Our evidence suggests that older people are more likely than younger people to avail themselves of agencies such as Citizens Advice Bureaux, so that older claimants were slightly over-represented amongst those referred. Fourteen respondents contacted the research staff as a result of a radio broadcast and a local press news item, and these respondents were predominantly older claimants. Seventeen respondents were referred by other agencies (also in response to the media coverage), namely a local Cyrenians Hostel, a Canterbury based 'drop-in' centre called Mustard Seed and a women's group organised by the local probation service. The remaining 37 respondents were identified for the purposes of the research by the Department of Social Security and provided a more representative age spread.

While bearing these factors in mind in the interpretation of the data, it must be remembered that the research was intended to be primarily qualitative in nature and that the sample which was achieved satisfactorily encompasses a sufficient number of each kind of working age social security recipient likely to have been affected by recent changes in the social security regime. In this context, the sample was more than adequate and it should be stressed that this is the largest empirical study of welfare benefit dependency to date in the United Kingdom to be conducted on the basis of discursive interviews.

Of the 50 non-employed respondents, 39 were men and 11 were women. Within this non-employed group unemployed men aged 40+; 16 registered unemployed men aged 18–39; 6 registered unemployed women; 3 women who were the partners of registered unemployed men; 12 respondents (10 men and 2 women) who were either currently incapable of work through temporary illness or injury, or partially disabled but available for employment; 2 respondents (both men) were full-time carers for ill or disabled people. Of the 33 single-parent respondents, 30 were women and 3 were men.

Of the 85 respondents, 44 were council or housing association tenants, 21 were owner-occupiers, 11 were private tenants, lodgers or hostel residents and 9 were non-householders.

Six of the 85 respondents had been in receipt of benefit for less than six months and are referred to in the text as 'short-term' claimants. Twenty-five respondents, who are referred to as 'medium-term' claimants, had been in receipt of benefit for between six months and two years, or else had a current claim of less than six months' duration which none the less represented a part of a continuing pattern of intermittent or consecutive claims. Fifty-four respondents, a majority of the sample, could be described as 'long-term' claimants, having been in receipt of benefit (or different benefits) for a continuous period exceeding two years.

The structure and composition of the sample was not such as to enable any serious consideration to be given to the important issues of race and neighbourhood. Although the sample contained a representative minority of black claimants, their number was too small for it to be possible to detect any significant variations in the pattern of their responses. Similarly, although the sample contained a spread of claimants from inner-city, suburban, provincial and even semi-rural social environments, there were no significant concentrations of respondents in specific neighbourhoods and no basis upon which to be able to determine neighbourhood effects with confidence. A few minor sub-regional variations are none the less worthy of comment, in so far as respondents from London were proportionately slightly *more* likely than respondents from Kent to do or be as follows:

1. To be either short- or long-term claimants (rather than medium-term claimants).
2. To come from clerical/retail/catering occupational backgrounds and correspondingly less likely to come from skilled manual backgrounds.
3. To appear to some degree to lack involvement in social/ recreational pursuits.
4. To be essentially pragmatic rather than principled in their attitudes to family dependency and fraudulent behaviour.
5. To be essentially principled rather than pragmatic in their rejection of long-term state dependency.

However, they were proportionately slightly *less* likely to do as follows:

6. To associate predominantly with other social security claimants and to be tolerant of other social security claimants.
7. To feel dependent on the government.

For the most part, these slight variations, if they are not incidental, are intelligible either directly or indirectly in terms of labour-market and social structural factors. The scale and nature of the variations, however, are in themselves not such as to suggest any important cultural variations between London and Kent, although they may support the case for further research focused upon neighbourhood influences within the context of the claiming experience.

Methodology

The fieldwork for the project was carried out during the whole of 1990. The interviews were conducted by prior appointment, usually in the respondent's own home (but, in a few instances, at the premises of the referring agency). The interviews were informal and loosely structured around a schedule of questions. While the key elements of the interview schedule may be inferred from Table A.3, it is important to emphasise that questions were not necessarily put in any set order; the wording of questions was adapted to fit the circumstances of the respondent and/or the interview situation; questions which were evidently inappropriate were omitted altogether; additional questions or prompts were used at the interviewer's discretion in order to clarify or develop themes as they emerged; respondents were allowed the freedom to talk in their own terms about the issues which concerned them. The interviews varied in duration from around 20 minutes (for the least communicative respondent) to over one and a half hours: the median duration is estimated to have been around 45 minutes.

Interviews were tape-recorded (except in three instances where the respondent declined to be tape-recorded and the interviewer took contemporaneous notes) and the tapes transcribed. The resulting transcripts were checked against the original tapes by the interviewer to ensure optimum accuracy.

Table A.3 Summary of core data

Respondent's awareness of rules relating to work incentives (*re* self or partner):	1. Feels/has felt pressured and associates this with recent rule changes	21
	2. Feels/has felt generally pressured by the system (but not especially conscious of recent changes).	6
	3. Is immune to *or* unaware of any particular or specific pressure relating to work incentives.	44
	4. Is aware of rule changes or has been affected by them but does not consider them to be oppressive or does not think them effective.	7
	5. Is aware of pressures being placed on other claimants, but not immediately affected him/herself.	4
	6. No reply/not applicable/question not put/ did not arise.	3
Employment experience (respondent's own):	1. Has past record of continuous full-time employment.	49
	2. Has record of short-term, intermittent and/or part-time employment.	32
	3. Has negligible or no labour-market experience (other than e.g. YTS).	2
	4. No reply/not applicable/question not put/did not arise.	2
Current employment:	1. None.	6ð
	2. Has declared part-time employment.	5
	3. Has undeclared employment (regular or occasional).	4
	4. Does voluntary work (regular).	5
	5. 2. and 4.	2
	6. 2. and 3.	1
Attitude to training/ educational opportunities (*re* self or partner):	1. Is not aware of anything currently appropriate and not especially interested.	20
	2. Is interested in further training/education, but unable to obtain or not aware of anything suitable.	18
	3. Is currently, recently, shortly or planning to become engaged on a training scheme (including Restart and Enterprise Allowance 'awareness' courses) or non-recreational educational activity.	34
	4. Is aware of/has been offered training, but is not interested or did not regard the offer as appropriate.	2 ▶

Table A.3 Summary of core data (*continued*)

	5. No reply/not applicable/question not put/ did not arise.	11
Inability/difficulty in finding jobs is related to (may relate to respondent and/or partner):	1. Stigma/discrimination associated with claimant status/long-term unemployment and/*or* lack of money to get to interview.	9
	2. Age.	15
	3. Lack of experience/qualifications or inappropriate experience/qualifications or length of absence from labour-market.	17
	4. Caring responsibilities/child-care costs.	20
	5. Inadequate wages.	15
	6. Medical factors.	11
	7. Past criminal record or lack of references.	7
	8. More complex reasons.	2
	9. No reply/not applicable/question not put/ did not arise.	24

Note: 26 respondents cited a combination of factors: frequencies sum to more than 85.

Does respondent appear to be motivated to find paid work?	1. Not at all/not particularly.	14
	2. Respondent is anxious to work, but temporarily prevented or constrained.	29
	3. Respondent is anxious to work and is currently seeking or has recently sought employment/training, etc.	35
	4. Respondent is not immediately anxious to find work, but expects to do so at some later date or would do so if a suitable opportunity presented itself.	6
	5. No reply/not applicable/question not put/ did not arise.	1
How much longer on benefit?	1. Uncertain/don't know.	28
	2. Indefinitely.	15
	3. Respondent has *plans* to come off at some future time or stage.	25
	4. Respondent has firm *hope* of coming off in the foreseeable future.	13
	5. Respondent has very recently returned to work and ceased claiming (all other responses, however, related to experiences when claiming).	3
	6. No reply/not applicable/question not put/ did not arise.	1

Table A.3 Summary of core data (*continued*)

Unfulfilled aspirations:	1. Respondent would like some form of self-employment.	7
	2. Respondent would like to take up a particular (new) skilled occupation or trade.	15
	3. Respondent would like managerial responsibility.	2
	4. Respondent would like to work in a caring occupation (social work, child-care, etc.).	14
	5. No reply/not applicable/question not put/ did not arise.	47
Type of education or training undertaken:	1. Government training scheme (ET or YTS).	13
	2. Job Club, Enterprise Allowance awareness training, etc.	4
	3. GCSEs.	1
	4. Specific vocational training.	12
	5. Access course.	1
	6. Degree course.	2
	7. 1. and 2.	1
	8. No reply/not applicable/question not put/ did not arise.	51
Attitudes to government schemes:	1. Has found/considers them helpful.	2
	2. Has found/considers them unhelpful, unsatisfactory or irrelevant.	23
	3. No reply/not applicable/question not put/ did not arise.	60
Respondent's primary motivation to work:	1. Is related to the pressures of the claiming experience.	2
	2. Is pragmatic and/or related to the desire for a better standard of living and/or to provide for family.	23
	3. Is the result of some internal drive/ ambition or need for self-esteem/ satisfaction.	45
	4. No reply/not applicable/question not put/ did not arise.	15
Awareness of disincentive/poverty trap:	1. Respondent discusses how much she/he would have to earn before it would be worth while going to work and/or makes a case for higher earnings disregards – or displays an awareness of the limitations such disregards impose.	24 ▶

Table A.3 Summary of core data (*continued*)

	2. Respondent acknowledges that *if* benefits were 'too high' she/he might not want to work.	2
	3. Respondent approves of family credit system.	2
	4. Respondent says wages are too low and/ or disapproves of family credit.	5
	5. 1. and 4.	7
	6. 1. and 3.	3
	7. 1. and 2.	3
	8. No reply/not applicable/question not put/ did not arise.	39
Explicit instances of counterproductive deterrence:	1. Hassle of initial claim process (and/or perceptions of the voluntary unemployment rule/rules governing payment of mortgage interest) deter respondent from taking temporary or insecure employment (or encourage him/her to do so without declaring it) because of difficulty of getting back on benefit.	2
	2. Low level of earnings disregard or the hassle of declaring part-time earnings discourages respondent (or respondent's partner) from taking part-time work (or tempts him/her to do so without declaring it).	18
	3. Both the above.	2
	4. No reply/not applicable/question not put/ did not arise.	63
Attitude to seeking support from family/ relatives/friends:	1. Disapproves (whether impliedly or expressly) and would/could not do so.	34
	2. Disapproves (whether impliedly or expressly) but does so or has had to do so.	23
	3. Expressly approves but does not do so/ does not have to.	3
	4. Expressly approves and has done so.	1
	5. Expresses neither approval nor disapproval, but has not done so.	6
	6. Expresses neither approval nor disapproval but has done so.	12
	7. No reply/not applicable/question not put/ did not arise.	6

Table A.3 Summary of core data (*continued*)

Relatives, etc. to whom respondent can/could turn for extra help or to borrow:	1. Parents/in-laws.	22
	2. Brother(s)/sister(s).	5
	3. Son(s)/daughter(s).	9
	4. Ex-partner.	1
	5. Friends.	7
	6. Combination of above.	19
	7. Nobody (or nobody to whom she/he could turn other than with extreme reluctance/difficulty).	20
	8. No reply/not applicable/question not put/ did not arise.	2
Strength/nature of disapproval of idea of enforced family dependency:	1. Disapproves on principle.	41
	2. Disapproval arises on practical grounds.	19
	3. No reply/not applicable/question not put/ did not arise.	25
Maintenance received by single parents:	1. No or negligible maintenance.	19
	2. Informal/irregular maintenance.	3
	3. Formal maintenance arrangement that is badly observed.	4
	4. Formal maintenance arrangement that is satisfactorily observed.	4
	5. No reply/not applicable/question not put/ did not arise.	55
Dependency on men – (question put to some female respondents and, hypothetically, to the female partners of some male respondents):	1. Prefers/would prefer dependency on state to dependency on a man.	12
	2. Prefers/would prefer dependency on a man to dependency on state.	9
	3. Does/would not wish to be dependent on state, other than for the enforcement/ supplementation of maintenance from male ex-partner.	1
	4. No reply/not applicable/question not put/ did not arise.	63
What would respondent do if benefits were cut off (initial or principal reaction)?	1. Turn to family/friends or charity.	16
	2. Get a job/go out to work (legitimate or otherwise).	28
	3. Turn to crime or prostitution.	10
	4. Sell possessions/house and/or draw on savings.	8
	5. Suicide.	1
	6. Walk the streets/starve/resort to institutional care.	6
	7. No ideas (passive).	8

Table A.3 Summary of core data (*continued*)

	8. No ideas (go and shoot them/demand to know why).	5
	9. No reply/not applicable/question not put/ did not arise.	3
Effect of increase in benefits:	1. Less dependency on family/friends.	9
	2. Better/more comfortable standard of living.	33
	3. Combination of 1. and 3.	4
	4. No/not much difference.	8
	5. Would relieve anxiety/reduce indebtedness.	16
	6. Would assist with costs of job searching/ purchase of work tools/moving to another area *or* enable respondent to save up towards such ends.	4
	7. Ambiguous reply.	3
	8. No reply/not applicable/question not put/ did not arise.	8
Social Fund:	1. Has experienced it and approves.	1
	2. Has not experienced it but approves.	1
	3. Has experienced it and disapproves.	24
	4. Has not experienced it but disapproves.	10
	5. No reply/not applicable/question not put/ did not arise.	49
Dealing with problems/complaints/ grievances:	1. No significant problems.	5
	2. Has had problems, and has usually attempted to sort them out him/herself.	30
	3. Has appealed to a tribunal and/or sought independent advice/assistance.	49
	4. Has had problems but done nothing about them.	1
Forms of advice/ assistance:	1. CAB, independent advice/law centre or other voluntary agency.	28
	2. Social worker, probation service or local authority consumer adviser/debt counsellor.	2
	3. MP or local politician.	2
	4. More than one of the above.	14
	5. Family/friends.	6
	6. None.	31
	7. No reply/not applicable/question not put/ did not arise.	2
Type of problem upon which advice was originally sought:	1. Form filling.	1
	2. Uncertainty over entitlement or for information.	19

Table A.3 Summary of core data (*continued*)

	3. Difficulty with budgeting/debt counselling.	5
	4. Assistance with challenging a specific decision or addressing a particular problem.	20
	5. No reply/not applicable/question not put/ did not arise.	40
Tribunal experience (including appeals on medical adjudications):	1. Never appealed.	55
	2. Appealed, but appeal aborted or superseded.	13
	3. Appealed, but did not attend hearing.	3
	4. Appealed and attended hearing unrepresented.	8
	5. Appealed and attended hearing with a representative.	2
	6. Appeal hearing pending.	3
	7. No reply/not applicable/question not put/ did not arise.	1
Strategies for dealing with social security (where consciously used in personal dealings with DSS, etc.):	1. Through displays of anger, threats (e.g. to leave children), etc.	5
	2. Through persuasion/argument.	12
	3. Through writing letters.	4
	4. Through manipulation (e.g. pre-emptive partial admissions, misleading information, etc.).	2
	5. Multiple strategies.	1
	6. Through compliance.	3
	7. No reply/not applicable/question not put/ did not arise.	58
Anger towards system:	1. Never been angry or annoyed.	3
	2. Principal cause of anger is the rules of the system or the tightening of the rules.	26
	3. Principal cause of anger is treatment received.	52
	4. Principal cause of anger is the amount of benefit.	26
	5. Some other cause.	4
	6. No reply/not applicable/question not put/ did not arise	2

Note: 19 respondents cited more than one cause: frequencies sum to more than 85.

Aspect of treatment which is cause of anger:	1. Degrading nature of treatment.	46
	2. Inefficiency of DSS.	15
	3. No reply/not applicable/question not put/ did not arise.	24

Table A.3 Summary of core data (*continued*)

Ease/difficulty of claiming process:	1. Easy/relatively straightforward.	23
	2. Respondent found it easy, but recognises that others might find it difficult.	8
	3. Difficult.	39
	4. Initially difficult, but becomes easier.	3
	5. Neither easy nor difficult (but perhaps annoying, tedious or ridiculous).	4
	6. Easy if you know what you are doing or have someone to help you (otherwise difficult).	3
	7. Easy in some instances but difficult in others.	2
	8. No reply/not applicable/question not put/ did not arise.	3
Overall fairness or unfairness of system:	1. Fair or 'fairish'.	7
	2. Unfair.	43
	3. Fair to respondent, but unfair to other claimants.	9
	4. Ambivalent/don't know/can't say.	18
	5. Unfair to claimant, but fair to some people.	5
	6. No reply/not applicable/question not put/ did not arise.	3
Cause of unfairness	1. Unfair as between different claimants (i.e. some people get more than others – or people who should get it do not and people that should not get it do).	15
	2. Because system treats everyone the same regardless of circumstances (or is insensitive to individual need).	6
	3. Because of the way claimants are treated.	14
	4. Because of the inadequacy of benefits.	5
	5. Other reasons.	9
	6. Combination of reasons.	1
	7. No reply/not applicable/question not put/ did not arise.	35
Managing on social security (respondent's experience):	1. Usually OK (or OK if you are frugal/ careful/adaptable).	13
	2. Always hard, difficult or impossible.	56
	3. Can be OK, but usually hard.	4
	4. Sometimes OK/sometimes hard (or 'a bit hard').	8
	5. Gets harder over time.	2
	6. No reply/not applicable/question not put/ did not arise.	2

Table A.3 Summary of core data (*continued*)

Activity/participation:	1. Respondent expresses or implies relative isolation from family/friends a lack of involvement in social/recreational pursuits and a lack of involvement in community activity.	17
	2. Respondent has some contact with family/friends, but lacks involvement in social/recreational pursuits and community activity.	27
	3. Respondent has some contact with family/friends and some involvement in social/recreational pursuits, but lacks involvement in community activity.	14
	4. Respondent has some contact with family/friends and some involvement in community activity, but lacks involvement in social/recreational pursuits.	14
	5. Respondent has some involvement in community activity and/or social/recreational pursuits, but expresses relative isolation from family/friends.	5
	6. Respondent has some contact with family/friends and some involvement in both social/recreational pursuits and community activity.	6
	7. No reply/not applicable/question not put/did not arise.	2

Note: 'Contact with family/friends' implies reasonably regular contact with a chosen circle of family and/or friends; 'social/recreational pursuits' implies some reasonably regular organised social, sporting, leisure or entertainment activity; 'community activity' implies some reasonably regular involvement in a community, voluntary, charity, political or religious organisation or group (whether on a formal or informal basis).

Cause/nature of social isolation:	1. Respondent is physically separated from family/friends or is isolated through financial or practical considerations.	22
	2. Respondent suffers from sense of social inhibition (through embarrassment, inability to reciprocate, diminished self-image, etc.).	19
	3. Respondent professes temperamental preference for 'keeping to him/herself'.	8
	4. No reply/not applicable/question not put/did not arise.	36

Political involvement:	1. Has seldom/never/not recently voted and is not politically active.	23

Table A.3 Summary of core data (*continued*)

	2. Always/usually votes but is not politically active.	40
	3. Always/usually votes and has (or has recently) had some formal political allegiance or involvement in political (including non-party political) activity or campaigning.	10
	4. Has seldom/never/not recently voted but has (or has recently) had some formal political allegiance or involvement in political (including non-party political) activity or campaigning.	7
	5. No reply/not applicable/question not put/ did not arise.	5
Politicising effects of the claiming experience:	1. Respondent has become more politically and/or consciously critical/mistrusting of the government and/or more left-wing.	8
	2. Respondent once supported, but has become disenchanted with, Thatcher(ism).	9
	3. Respondent expresses personal animosity (or even violent intentions) towards specific members of the Conservative Party/ government).	3
	4. Respondent expresses explicitly anarchic or extremist sentiments.	2
	5. No reply/not applicable/question not put/ did not arise.	63
Does respondent buy newspapers?	1. Regularly/usually.	34
	2. Never/seldom – cannot afford it.	11
	3. Never/seldom – cannot be bothered (or cannot read very well).	17
	4. Never/seldom but has access.	7
	5. Sometimes.	3
	6. No reply/not applicable/question not put/ did not arise.	13
Constraints on social life/participation etc.:	1. Not bothered/happy as she/he is.	14
	2. Would like to do more and blames/is conscious of lack of income/being on social security as a constraint.	55
	3. Would like to do more but attributes constraints primarily to other circumstances.	7
	4. Being on social security provides opportunities to do things (especially educationally) which respondent would not	▶

Table A.3 Summary of core data (*continued*)

	otherwise have been able to do.	1
	5. Ambiguous reply.	1
	6. No reply/not applicable/question not put/ did not arise.	7
Respondent's immediate social circle:	1. Composed mainly of (or includes many) other social security recipients.	21
	2. Includes a mixture of social security recipients and other persons (or else respondent claims to have a limited social circle and/or to be unaware of whether or not the people she/he has most to do with are on social security).	24
	3. Composed mainly of (or includes many) non-social security recipients.	37
	4. No reply/not applicable/question not put/ did not arise.	3
Feelings about negative imagery/ stereotypes:	1. Angered/distressed/annoyed.	36
	2. Disturbed but tolerant (i.e. indignant/ upset at being so identified, but not inclined to defend claimants as a whole).	16
	3. Considers them justified/partly justified.	10
	4. Not bothered or by and large dismissive.	18
	5. Contradictory responses (1. and 4. combinations).	2
	6. No reply/not applicable/question not put/ did not arise.	3
Feelings about living on social security for a long time:	1. Positive/comfortable.	4
	2. Neutral/resigned.	15
	3. Negative/uncomfortable.	54
	4. Ambivalent.	6
	5. No reply/not applicable/question not put/ did not arise.	6
Reasons for negative/ uncomfortable feelings *re* long-term claiming:	1. Financial/material.	18
	2. Moral/self-esteem.	47
	3. No reply/not applicable/question not put/ did not arise.	20
View of other claimants:	1. Generally negative/punitive/intolerant.	6
	2. Discriminates between deserving and undeserving groups of claimants.	23
	3. Generally positive/sympathetic/tolerant.	38
	4. Generally ambivalent/indifferent.	15
	5. No reply/not applicable/question not put/ did not arise.	3

Table A.3 Summary of core data (*continued*)

Changes in feeling resulting from claiming experience:	1. Has become more sympathetic to other claimants.	5
	2. Feels more justified about own situation/ more aware of the advantages of the welfare state.	4
	3. Has begun to feel liberated from old prejudices/moral constraints *or* fears that these are in danger of being eroded.	6
	4. Has become more passive/accepting of DSS authority or less inclined to question/ study its workings.	3
	5. Feels less comfortable about/at peace with the welfare state than in the past.	1
	6. No reply/not applicable/question not put/ did not arise.	69

Note: 3 respondents cited a combination of changes: frequencies sum to more than 85.

Beliefs regarding fraud and abuse:	1. A lot goes on or expects or supposes there is a lot.	40
	2. There is/will always be 'some' or 'quite a bit'.	25
	3. Less now than before (or, for example, 'a lot goes on but it's getting harder' or 'there used to be a lot, but I don't know about now').	6
	4. Very little goes on or it's not a big/ significant problem.	8
	5. No reply/not applicable/question not put/ did not arise.	6
Would respondent fiddle the system?	1. No – on principle.	16
	2. No – too frightened/anxious.	8
	3. No – not worth it/too difficult.	10
	4. Yes – in certain circumstances.	27
	5. Yes – is doing/has done so.	15
	6. No – but has done so in the past.	2
	7. Contradictory reply (respondent says no but has already admitted fraudulent conduct).	1
	8. No reply/not applicable/question not put/ did not arise.	6
Views of changes to the system:	1. Has no views/ideas or does not think changes make any difference.	20
	2. Has experienced recent changes as an improvement.	3

Table A.3 Summary of core data (*continued*)

	3. Is aware and approves of moves towards a more residual welfare state.	3
	4. Has experienced recent changes as a deterioration or regards them as flawed.	18
	5. Is aware but disapproves of moves towards a more residual welfare state.	14
	6. Believes there is an intention/conspiracy to phase out or abolish the social security system.	12
	7. Is aware of but indifferent/ambivalent about moves to a more residual welfare state.	3
	8. Believes that current social/economic trends are overloading/overburdening the system.	2
	9. No reply/not applicable/question not put/ did not arise.	10
Views on poverty:	1. There is no poverty.	4
	2. There is poverty, but it is attributable to the behaviour of the poor – bad management, fecklessness, overfecundity, etc.	9
	3. There is poverty, but it applies to the roofless, homeless, destitute or ex-psychiatric patients (or to some minority who slip through the net) and not necessarily to ordinary social security claimants.	25
	4. There is poverty, but it applies to certain other groups (e.g. old people, young people, the low-paid, large families and/or single parents) and not necessarily the respondent.	14
	5. The respondent believes or implies that she/he is poor (or that all social security claimants or 'most people' are poor).	27
	6. Respondent would be poor but for help received from family.	2
	7. No reply/not applicable/question not put/ did not arise.	4
Feelings regarding dependency on state:	1. Feels unequivocally dependent.	22
	2. Recognises a sense in which benefits give/ could give independence but feels more dependent than independent.	23
	3. Completely ambivalent.	12

Table A.3 Summary of core data (*continued*)

	4. Recognises a sense in which benefits make/could make him/her dependent, but feels more independent than dependent.	12
	5. Feels unequivocally independent.	8
	6. Don't know/don't understand.	2
	7. No reply/not applicable/question not put/ did not arise.	6
Explicit references to being 'trapped':	1. Respondent says she/he has become lethargic or has become inured to/ comfortable with life on social security and is reluctant to come off it (or recognises this as a danger).	9
	2. Respondent says she/he is too busy or preoccupied with or exhausted by the mechanics and rhythms of the claiming process to be able to break out of the cycle *or* that pressure to comply with the rules and requirements of the system stifles self-motivation.	4
	3. Respondent says she/he is afraid of the insecurity/uncertainty of the labour-market and prefers the predictability of claiming social security.	5
	4. Respondent says she/he feels 'trapped', 'caged', 'caught in a vicious circle' or that, in some ill-defined way, attempts to 'get off it' are frustrated by the system itself.	7
	5. No reply/not applicable/question not put/ did not arise.	64

Note: 5 respondents cited more than one factor: frequencies sum to more than 85.

Key words (where used by respondent in relation to claiming):	1. Degraded/degrading.	16
	2. Humiliated/humiliating.	4
	3. Sponge/sponging.	5
	4. Ponce/poncing.	2
	5. Guilt/guilty.	9
	6. Embarrassed/embarrassing.	8
	7. Others – demeaning/demoralising/ distressing/ashamed.	6
	8. No reply/not applicable/question not put/ did not arise.	50

Note: 12 respondents used more than one word: frequencies sum to more than 85.

Table A.3 Summary of core data (*continued*)

Key images/ stereotypes (where used *pejoratively* by respondents in relation to 'others'):	1. Dossers/tramps/winos/down-and-outs/ drug addicts/alcoholics.	9
	2. Young layabouts.	7
	3. Claimants who spend their money on drink or in the pub.	12
	4. Families with 'too many' children.	8
	5. People from abroad/black people.	7
	6. Others – rough/problem families, gypsies, etc.	4
	7. No reply/not applicable/question not put/ did not arise.	49

Note: 10 respondents used more than one image: frequencies sum to more than 85.

Key attributes (claimed or valued by respondents):	1. Cleanliness/hygiene.	12
	2. Abhorrence of debt/carefulness with money.	9
	3. Temperance/sobriety.	3
	4. Aversion to idleness/desire to keep busy.	14
	5. Being 'genuine'.	10
	6. No reply/not applicable/question not put/ did not arise.	52

Note: 10 respondents claimed more than one attribute: frequencies sum to more than 85.

Overall assessment of claimant's knowledge and awareness of or 'competence' with the system:	1. Confused/uncertain about entitlement.	24
	2. Confident about entitlement but exhibiting significant confusions or holding materially mistaken beliefs.	30
	3. Generally knowledgeable about own entitlement (or no evidence to the contrary).	31

The transcripts were coded in accordance with a coding frame which was gradually developed and extended in the course of the reading and re-reading of the transcripts so as to ensure the accommodation of as much data as possible and to maximise the sensitivity of the analysis. Finally, the transcripts were read again using an inductive analysis technique to test the emerging hypotheses of the research.

Table A.3 is a basic frequency table which provides a partial summary of the core data.

Sub-sample analysis

In order to determine whether the results of the investigation had been unduly influenced by the inclusion in the sample of respondents from groups which might be regarded as being outside the influence of a 'dependency culture', a sub-sample was established from which the following types of respondent were excluded: family credit recipients; other claimants who were back in employment at the time of interview; short-term claimants (i.e. those who had been claiming for less than six months and whose claim did not constitute a part of a pattern of consecutive or intermittent benefit claims); claimants who were temporarily sick or partially disabled or who were carers for adult sick or disabled persons. The remaining 'core' or sub-sample consisted of 64 respondents, 22 from London and 42 from Kent (i.e. almost exactly the same proportion as in the main sample).

Women and, of course, single parents were more heavily represented in this sub-sample. The sub-sample included all but one of the black respondents from the main sample and the sub-sample was also proportionately slightly younger than the main sample. The full demographic breakdown of the sub-sample was as set out in Table A.4.

All but one member of the sub-sample (who was on unemployment benefit) were income support recipients, and the sub-sample

Table A.4 Composition of sub-sample

	Age	Unemployed claimants (inc. 3 female partners of male claimants			Single-parent claimants			Totals
		Male	Female	(All)	Male	Female	(All)	
Medium-	18–24	0	2	(2)	0	2	(2)	(4)
term	25–39	2	2	(4)	1	2	(3)	(7)
claimants	40+	2	2	(4)	2	3	(5)	(9)
	(all)	(4)	(6)	**10**	(3)	(7)	**10**	**20**
Long-	18–24	4	0	(4)	0	7	(7)	(11)
term	25–39	6	0	(6)	0	11	(11)	(17)
claimants	40+	9	2	(11)	0	5	(5)	(16)
	(all)	(19)	(2)	**21**	(0)	(23)	**23**	**44**
Totals		(23)	(8)	**31**	(3)	(30)	**33**	**64**

contained proportionately slightly more respondents with a clerical/retail/catering occupational background (26/64 [41 per cent]: c.f. 29/85 [34 per cent]) and slightly fewer respondents from a skilled manual occupational background (8/64 [13 per cent]: c.f. 16/85 [19 per cent]) than did the main sample.

In terms of the patterns of the responses given by respondents in the sub-sample, there were no substantial or striking variations between these and those observed for the main sample and such slight variations as could be detected did not in any way support the idea that this 'core' sample might be more subject to a 'dependency culture'. Indeed, the sub-sample appeared as a whole to be proportionately slightly more highly motivated to work and/or to seek education/training than was the main sample (e.g. 50/64 [78 per cent] of the sub-sample were clearly anxious to work: c.f. 64/85 [75 per cent] of the main sample; and only 12/64 [19 per cent] of the sub-sample were not aware of and not interested in education/training opportunities: c.f. 20/85 [24 per cent] of the main sample). Although the sub-sample as a whole was just as likely as the main sample to disapprove of enforced family dependency, its members were slightly but noticeably more likely actually to have resorted to receiving help from family or friends (32/64 [50 per cent] of the sub-sample: c.f. 36/85 [42 per cent] of the main sample). Surprisingly perhaps, the sub-sample as a whole was proportionately slightly less likely than the main sample to mix predominantly with other social security claimants (13/64 [20 per cent] of the sub-sample: c.f. 21/85 [25 per cent] of the main sample). Moreover, sub-sample respondents were more likely than those in the main sample to have expressed negative or uncomfortable feelings about long-term dependency on benefits (none of the sub-sample had positive or comfortable feelings: c.f. 4/85 [5 per cent] of the main sample) and they were proportionately less likely to express sympathetic or tolerant views towards other social security claimants (26/64 [41 per cent] of the sub-sample: c.f. 38/85 [45 per cent] of the main sample).

Plainly, variations of this order in overlapping samples of this size will not be statistically significant, but they suggest none the less that the 'core' sample was in some ways actually less well accommodated to life on benefits than the main sample. Certainly, sub-sample respondents were proportionately slightly more likely than main sample respondents to feel dependent on the government (38/64 [59 per cent]: c.f. 45/85 [53 per cent]), but they were also proportionately more likely to exhibit awareness of a disincentive trap attributable to the workings of the benefits system (33/64 [50 per cent]: c.f. 37/85 [44 per cent]).

Many of these minor effects may be attributable in some measure to the 'core' sample's greater and/or harsher experience of the social security system. Interestingly, however, the sub-sample respondents were no more inclined than those of the main sample to express a willingness to 'fiddle' the benefits system; although the sub-sample contained all of the eight respondents who indicated (in spite of the way in which the relevant question had been put) that they would be 'too afraid' to try and fiddle the system, suggesting quite possibly that the sub-sample as a whole felt more deterred by the system. There was, moreover, no evidence that the sub-sample tended as a whole to be any more pragmatic or morally hardened than the main sample: on the contrary, members of the sub-sample were more likely to give principled rather than pragmatic reasons for their disapproval of enforced family dependency (33/64 [52 per cent]: c.f. 41/85 [48 per cent] for the main sample) and for being uncomfortable about long-term benefit dependency (37/64 [58 per cent]: c.f. 47/85 [55 per cent] for the main sample).

Other variations were even more minute in order (usually 2 per cent or less), but to the extent that the *direction* of these variations was intelligible and/or of interest, it can be reported that, proportionately, the sub-sample relative to the main sample contained fractionally fewer owner-occupiers and more council tenants, and on the whole its members: tended to give more complex explanations of their inability to find jobs; in the event of a sudden cessation of benefits were more likely to try and find work and less likely to turn to family or friends or to be able to sell property or use savings; were more likely to appreciate the difference an increase in benefits would make and/or to use such an increase to reduce their dependency on their families; found the mechanics of claiming slightly easier; were less likely to say they thought the social security system was unfair, but more likely to say they did not know whether the system was fair or not; were more socially isolated and more likely to feel constrained from social participation by reason of being on social security; were more likely to believe that 'a lot of fiddling goes on'; were more likely to believe in the existence of a conspiracy to phase out or abolish the social security system; were less likely to blame poverty upon the behaviour of the poor but more likely to attribute poverty to residual social groups.

REFERENCES

Ainley, P. (1988) *From School to YTS* Open University Press, Milton Keynes.

Ashby, P. (1984) *Social Security After Beveridge – What Next?* Bedford Square Press/NCVO, London.

Ashford, S. (1987) 'Family matters' in Jowell, R., Witherspoon, S. and Brook, L. (eds.) *British Social Attitudes: the 1987 report* Gower, Aldershot.

Atkinson, A.B. (1988) *Income Maintenance for the Unemployed in Britain and the Response to High Unemployment* Welfare State Paper no. 37, Suntory-Toyota International Centre for Economics and Related Disciplines, London.

Auletta, K. (1982) *The Underclass* Random House, New York.

Ball, M., Gray, F. and McDowell, L. (1989) *The Transformation of Britain* Fontana, London.

Barr, N. and Coulter, F. (1990) 'Social security: solution or problem?' in Hills, J. (ed.) *The State of Welfare: The welfare state in Britain since 1974* Clarendon Press, Oxford.

Bassett, P. (1989) 'All together now' *Marxism Today* vol. 33, no. 1 (January).

Bateson, N. (1984) *Data Construction in Social Surveys* George, Allen and Unwin, London.

Becker, S. and Silburn, R. (1990) *The New Poor Clients* Nottingham University/Community Care, Nottingham.

Bennett, F. and Chapman, V. (1990) *The Poverty of Maintenance* Child Poverty Action Group, London.

Beresford, P. and Croft, S. (1986) *Whose Welfare: Private care or public services?* Lewis Cohen Urban Studies Centre, Brighton.

Beveridge, W. (1942) *Social Insurance and Allied Services* Cmd. 6404, HMSO, London.

Bird, D. (1991) 'Industrial stoppages in 1990' *Department of Employment Gazette* vol. 99, no. 7, pp. 379–90.

Blaug, M. (1963) 'The myth of the old poor law and the making of the new' *Journal of Economic History* vol. 23, no. 2, pp. 151–73.

Booth, C. (1887) 'The inhabitants of the Tower Hamlets (School Board Division), their condition and occupations' *Journal of the Royal Statistical Society* vol. L.

Booth, C. (1902) *Life and Labour of the People of London* (17 volumes) Macmillan, London.

Bosanquet, N. (1987) 'Buying care' in Clode, D., Parker C. and Etherington, S. (eds.) *Towards the Sensitive Bureaucracy* Gower, Aldershot.

Bradshaw, J. and Holmes, H. (1989) *Living on the Edge: The living standards of low income families in Tyne & Wear* Tyneside CPAG, Newcastle.

Bradshaw, J. and Millar, J. (1991) *Lone-Parent Families in the UK* DSS Research Report no. 6, HMSO, London.

Brown, G. (1989) *Where there is Greed* Mainstream Publishing, Edinburgh.

Brown, J. (1989) *Why Don't they Go to Work? Mothers on benefit* Social Security Advisory Committee/HMSO, London.

Brown, J. (1990) 'The focus on single mothers' in Murray, C. *The Emerging British Underclass* Institute of Economic Affairs, London.

Brown, M. and Madge, N. (1982) *Despite the Welfare State* Heinemann, London.

Brown, P. and Sparks, R. (eds.) (1989) *Beyond Thatcherism: Social policy, politics and society* Open University Press, Milton Keynes.

Buck, N. (1991) 'Labour market inequality and polarisation: A household perspective on the idea of an underclass' paper given to a conference on 26 February, 'The idea of an underclass in Britain', organised by Policy Studies Institute, London.

Campaign Against Poverty (1991) *Newsletter no. 32* (May), CAP, Manchester.

Campbell, B. (1984) *Wigan Pier Revisited* Virago, London.

Carey, K. (1987) 'Rights to welfare' in Clode, D., Parker, C. and Etherington, S. (eds.) *Towards the Sensitive Bureaucracy* Gower, Aldershot.

Central Statistical Office (CSO) (1990) *Family Expenditure Survey 1989* HMSO, London.

Central Statistical Office (CSO) (1991a) *Social Trends* HMSO, London.

Central Statistical Office (CSO) (1991b) *Family Expenditure Survey 1990* HMSO, London.

Central Statistical Office (CSO) (1991c) *Annual Abstract of Statistics 1991* HMSO, London.

Clode, D., Parker, C. and Etherington, S. (eds.) (1987) *Towards the Sensitive Bureaucracy: Consumers, welfare and the new pluralism* Gower, Aldershot.

Cook, T. (1987) 'Participation' in Clode, D., Parker, C. and Etherington, S. (eds.) *Towards the Sensitive Bureaucracy* Gower, Aldershot.

Cooper, D. (1972) *The Death of the Family* Penguin, Harmondsworth.

Coote, A., Harman, H. and Hewitt, P. (1990) *The Family Way* Institute for Public Policy Research, London.

Cox, G. (1990) *Actively Seeking What?* Campaign Against Poverty, Manchester.

Craig, G. (1990) 'Watching the Fund' in Manning, N. and Ungerson, C. (eds.) *Social Policy Review 1989–90* Longman, Harlow.

Craig, G. (1992) 'Managing the poorest: The social fund in context' in *Social Work and Welfare Yearbook* (forthcoming).

Craig, G. and Glendinning, C. (1990a) *The Impact of Social Security Changes: The views of families living in disadvantaged areas* Barnardo's Research and Development, Ilford.

Craig, G. and Glendinning, C. (1990b) 'Parenting in Poverty' *Community Care* (15 March).

Dahrendorf, R. (1987) 'The underclass and the future of Britain', lecture delivered at St George's Chapel, Windsor Castle, 27 April.

Davies, C. and Ritchie, J. (1988) *Tipping the Balance: A study of non-take up of benefit in an inner city area* DHSS/HMSO, London.

Deacon, A. and Bradshaw, J. (1983) *Reserved for the Poor: The means test in British social policy* Basil Blackwell and Martin Robertson, Oxford.

Dean, H. (1989/90) 'Disciplinary partitioning and the privatisation of social security' *Critical Social Policy* issue 24 (vol. 8 no. 3).

Dean, H. (1991) *Social Security and Social Control* Routledge, London.

Dean, H. and Taylor-Gooby, P. (1990) 'Statutory sick pay and the control of sickness absence' *Journal of Social Policy* vol. 19, no. 1.

Dean, H. and Taylor-Gooby, P. (1991) *Dependency Culture: The image and reality of the claiming experience*, report of an empirical investigation funded by the Economic and Social Research Council – grant ref. R 00023 1776, University of Kent at Canterbury (unpublished).

Department of Employment (DE) (1972) *Gazette* vol. 80, no. 5 (May).

Department of Employment (DE) (1979) *Family Expenditure Survey 1979* HMSO, London.

Department of Employment (DE) (1988) *Employment in the 1990s* Cm. 540, HMSO, London.

Department of Employment (DE) (1991a) *Gazette* vol. 99, no. 8 (August).

Department of Employment (DE) (1991b) *Gazette* vol. 99, no. 6 (June).

Department of Employment/Department of Health and Social Security (1981) *Payment of Benefits to Unemployed People* HMSO, London.

Department of Health (1989) *Caring for People: Community care in the next decade and beyond* White Paper, Cm. 849, HMSO, London.

Department of Health and Social Security (DHSS) (1982) *Social Security Statistics 1981* HMSO, London.

Department of Health and Social Security (DHSS) (1985a) *The Reform of Social Security* vol. 1, Green Paper, Cmnd. 9517, HMSO, London.

Department of Health and Social Security (DHSS) (1985b) *The Reform of Social Security* vol. 3, Green Paper, Cmnd. 9519, HMSO, London.

Department of Health & Social Security (DHSS) (1986) *Low Income Families 1983* HMSO, London.

Department of Social Security (DSS) (1989) *Social Security Statistics 1988* HMSO, London.

Department of Social Security (DSS) (1990) *Children Come First* Cm. 1264, HMSO, London.

Department of Social Security (DSS) (1991a) *Social Security: The government's expenditure plans, 1991/92–1993/94* Cm. 1514, HMSO, London.

Department of Social Security (DSS) (1991b) *Social Security Statistics 1990* HMSO, London.

Disney, R. (1985) 'Should we afford SERPs?' *New Society* (21 June).

Donnison, D. (1991) *The Radical Journey: After the New Right and the Old Left* Rivers Oram Press, London.

Donzelot, J. (1979) *The Policing of Families* Hutchinson, London.

Doyal, L. and Gough, I. (1984) 'A theory of human needs' *Critical Social Policy* no. 10 (Summer).

Durkheim, E. (1964) *The Social Division of Labour* Free Press, New York.

Economic and Social Research Council (ESRC) (1987) *Newsletter* no. 61 (November).

Edwards, S. (1989) *Policing Domestic Violence: Women, the law and the state* Sage, London.

Ellwood, D. (1989) 'The origins of "dependency": Choices, confidence or culture?' in 'Defining and Measuring the Underclass' (special issue) *Focus* vol. 12, no. 1, University of Wisconsin/Madison Institute for Research on Poverty.

Employment Department Group (1991) *The Government's Expenditure Plans 1991/92–1993/94* Cm. 1506, HMSO, London.

Ermisch, J. (1990) *Fewer Babies, Longer Lives* Joseph Rowntree Foundation, York.

Evandrou, M. (1990) *Challenging the Invisibility of Carers: Mapping informal care nationally* Welfare State Paper 49, STICERD, London School of Economics.

Falkingham, J. (1989) 'Dependency and ageing in Britain' *Journal of Social Policy* vol. 18, no. 2 (April).

Family Policy Studies Centre (FPSC) (1989) *Family Policy Bulletin* no. 6 (Winter), FPSC, London.

Family Policy Studies Centre (FPSC) (1991) *Family Policy Bulletin* (March), FPSC, London.

Field, F. (1989) *Losing Out: The emergence of Britain's underclass* Blackwell, Oxford.

Field, F. (1990) 'Britain's underclass: countering the growth' in Murray, C. *The Emerging British Underclass* Institute of Economic Affairs, London.

Finch, J. (1989) *Family Obligations and Social Change* Polity Press, Cambridge.

Finch, J. and Groves, D. (eds.) (1983) *A Labour of Love: Women, work and caring* Routledge and Kegan Paul, London.

Finn, D. (1985) 'The Manpower Services Commission and the Youth Training Scheme: A permanent bridge to work?' in Dale, R. (ed.) *Education, Training and Employment* Pergamon Press, Oxford.

Foucault, M. (1976) *The History of Sexuality: An introduction* Penguin, Harmondsworth.

Foucault, M. (1977) *Discipline and Punish: The birth of the prison* Penguin, Harmondsworth.

Gallie, D. and Vogler, C. (1990) *Unemployment and Attitudes to Work* Working Paper no. 18 in The Social Change and Economic Life Initiative, Nuffield College, Oxford.

Garland, D. (1981) 'The birth of the welfare sanction' *British Journal of Law and Society* vol. 8, no. 1.

George, V. and Howards, I. (1991) *Poverty Amidst Affluence* Edward Elgar, Cheltenham.

George, V. and Wilding, P. (1985) *Ideology and Social Welfare* Routledge and Kegan Paul, London.

Giddens, A. (1990) *The Consequences of Modernity* Polity Press, Cambridge.

Golding, P. and Middleton, S. (1982) *Images of Welfare: Press and public attitudes to poverty* Martin Robertson, Oxford.

Gough, I. (1990) *International Competitiveness and the Welfare State: The case of the UK*, 'Reports and Proceedings', no. 85, Social Policy Research Centre, Sydney, Australia.

Graham, H. (1983) 'Caring: A labour of love' in Finch, J. and Groves, D. (eds.) *A Labour of Love: Women, work and caring* Routledge and Kegan Paul, London.

Graham, H. (1987) 'Being poor: Perceptions of coping strategies of lone mothers' in Brannen, J. and Wilson, G. (eds.) *Give and Take in Families* Allen and Unwin, London.

Green Party (1988) *Manifesto for a Sustainable Society* London: Green Party.

Greve, J. and Currie, E. (1990) *Homelessness in Britain* Joseph Rowntree Memorial Trust, York.

Habermas, J. (1987) *The Theory of Communicative Action* vol. 2, Polity Press, Cambridge.

Hakim, C. (1989) 'Workforce restructuring, social insurance coverage and the black economy' *Journal of Social Policy* vol. 18, no. 4.

Hall, S., Critcher, C., Jefferson, T., Clarke, J. and Roberts, B. (1978) *Policing the Crisis* Macmillan, London.

Hall, S. and Held, D. (1989) 'Citizens and citizenship' in Hall, S. and Jacques, M. (eds.) *New Times: The changing face of politics in the 1990s* Lawrence and Wishart, London.

Halsey, A.H. (1991) 'Citizens of the future' *Guardian*, 20 September, p. 17.

Harrington, M. (1962) *The Other America: Poverty in the United States* Penguin, Harmondsworth.

Harrison, M. (1991) 'Evaluation of the child support scheme, stage 1' in Whiteford, P. (ed.) *Sole Parents and Public Policy* 'Reports and Proceedings', no. 89, Social Policy Research Centre, Sydney, Australia.

Heath, A. (1991) 'The attitudes of the underclass', paper given to a conference on 26 February, 'The idea of an underclass in Britain', organised by Policy Studies Institute, London.

Heath, A., Jowell, R. and Curtice, J. (1985) *How Britain Votes* Pergamon Press, Oxford.

Hegel, G. (1966) *The Phenomenology of Mind* George Allen and Unwin, London.

Hirst, P. (1980) 'Law, socialism and rights' in Carlen, P. and Collison, M. (eds.) *Radical Issues in Criminology* Martin Robertson, Oxford.

Hoinville, G., Jowell, R. and associates (1980) *Survey Research Practice* Heinemann, London.

Holloway, J. and Picciotto, S. (eds.) (1978) *State and Capital: A Marxist debate* Arnold, London.

Howe, L. (1985) 'The "Deserving" and the "Undeserving": Practice in an urban local social security office' *Journal of Social Policy* vol. 14, pp. 49–72.

Hutson, S. and Liddiard, M. (1989) *Street Children in Wales?* The Children's Society, Cardiff.

Jenkins, P. (1977) contribution to *Man Alive*, BBC Television.

Johnson, P. and Webb, S. (1990) *Poverty in Official Statistics: Two reports* Commentary no. 24, Institute for Fiscal Studies, London.

Johnston, M. (1988) 'The price of honesty' in Jowell, R., Witherspoon, S. and Brook, L. (eds.) *British Social Attitudes: The fifth report* Gower, Aldershot, Hants.

Jordan, B. (1973) *Paupers: The making of the claiming class* Routledge and Kegan Paul, London.

Jordan, B. (1974) *Poor Parents: Social policy and the 'cycle of deprivation'* Routledge and Kegan Paul, London.

Jordan, B. (1985) *The State: Authority and autonomy* Blackwell, Oxford.

Jordan, B. (1987) *Rethinking Welfare* Blackwell, Oxford.

Joseph, K. (1972) speech to the Pre-School Playgroups Association, 29 June.

Jowell, R., Witherspoon, S. and Brook, L. (1990) *British Social Attitudes: The Seventh Report* Gower, Aldershot.

Keane, J. (1988) *Democracy and Civil Society* Verso, London.

Labour Party (1989) *Meet the Challenge, Make the Change: Final report of Labour's policy reviews for the 1990s* Labour Party, London.

Laclau, E. and Mouffe, C. (1985) *Hegemony and Socialist Strategy* Verso, London.

Laing, R.D. (1971) *The Politics of the Family and Other Essays* Tavistock, London.

Layard, R. and Nickell, S. (1990) 'The Thatcher miracle?' *Centre for Labour Economics: Unemployment seminar, 9th December* Centre for Labour Economics, London.

Le Grand, J. (1990) 'The state of welfare' in Hills, J. (ed.) *The State of Welfare: The welfare state in Britain since 1974* Oxford, Clarendon Press.

Leibfried, S. (1991) 'Europe's could-be social state', paper presented at a conference on 6 September, 'Europe after 1992', Ann Arbor, Michigan.

Lemann, N. (1986) 'The origins of the Underclass' *Atlantic Monthly* (June).

Levy, D. (1988) 'The welfare revolution: Moore's American cure for Britain's "dependency" habit' *The Listener*, 18 February.

Lewis, O. (1965) *The Children of Sanchez* Penguin, Harmondsworth.

Lewis, O. (1966) 'The culture of poverty' *Scientific American* vol. 215, no. 4.

Lewis, O. (1968) *La Vida* Panther, London.

Liebow, E. (1967) *Tally's Corner: A study of Negro streetcorner men* Routledge and Kegan Paul, London.

Lipsky, M. (1976) 'Towards a theory of street-level bureaucracy' in Hawley, W. and Lipsky, M. (eds.) *Theoretical Perspectives on Urban Politics* Prentice Hall, Englewood Cliffs, N.J.

Lister, R. (1991) 'Women, economic dependency and citizenship' *Journal of Social Policy* vol. 19, no. 4.

Low Pay Unit (1991) *New Review* no. 9.

Macnicol, J. (1987) 'In pursuit of the underclass' *Journal of Social Policy* vol. 16, no. 3.

MacPherson, C. (1962) *The Political Theory of Possessive Individualism* Oxford University Press, London.

Manning, N. (1989) 'Lessons from the USA: The legacy of Reagan's social policy', paper given to the Annual Conference of the Social Policy Association, University of Bath, 10–12 July.

Marsh, C. (1982) *The Survey Method* George, Allen and Unwin, London.

Marshall, T.H. (1963) 'Citizenship and social class' in Marshall, T.H. (ed.) *Sociology at the Crossroads and Other Essays* Heinemann, London.

Marx, K. (1970) *Capital* vol. 1, Lawrence and Wishart, London.

Marx, K. and Engels, F. (1970) *The Communist Manifesto* Pathfinder Press, New York.

Massey, D. (1984) *Spatial Divisions of Labour* Macmillan, London.

Mayhew, H. (1861) *London Labour and the London Poor* (4 volumes) Charles Griffin and Co., London.

McGlone, F. (1990) 'Away from the dependency culture' in Savage, S. and Robins, L. (eds.) *Public Policy under Thatcher* Macmillan, London.

McLaughlin, E., Millar, J. and Cooke, K. (1989) *Work and Welfare Benefits* Avebury, Aldershot.

Mead, L. (1986) *Beyond Entitlement: The social obligations of citizenship* Free Press, New York.

Minford, M. (1990) 'The odd one out in Europe' *New Review of the Low Pay Unit* no. 11 (August/September).

Minuchin, S. (1974) *Families and Family Therapy* Tavistock, London.

Mishra, R. (1984) *The Welfare State in Crisis* Harvester Wheatsheaf, Hemel Hempstead.

Mitchell, J. (1966) 'Women: the longest revolution' *New Left Review* no. 40.

Mitchell, J. (1971) *Woman's Estate* Penguin, Harmondsworth.

Moore, J. (1987) 'Welfare and dependency', speech to Conservative Constituency Parties' Association, September.

Morgan, D. (1975) *Social Theory and the Family* Routledge and Kegan Paul, London.

MORI (1991) *Survey of Applicants for Severe Hardship Allowances* MORI, London (quoted in the *Guardian*, 17 July).

Morris, L. (1991) *Social Security Provision for the Unemployed* Social Security Advisory Committee/HMSO, London.

Mount, F. (1982) *The Subversive Family* Jonathan Cape, London.

Moynihan, D. (1965) *The Negro Family: The case for national action* Office of Planning and Research, US Department of Labor, Washington DC.

Murray, C. (1984) *Losing Ground: American social policy 1950–1980* Basic Books, New York.

Murray, C. (1990a) 'Underclass' *Sunday Times Magazine*, 26 November 1989, reprinted in Murray, C. *The Emerging British Underclass* Institute of Economic Affairs, London.

Murray, C. (1990b) 'Rejoinder' in *The Emerging British Underclass* Institute of Economic Affairs, London.

National Audit Office (1988) *DHSS: Quality of service to the public at local offices*, Report by the Controller and Auditor General, no. 451, HMSO, London.

National Children's Home (1991) *Poverty and Nutrition Survey 1991*, NCH, London.

National Institute for Economic and Social Research (NIESR) (1991a) *Review* no. 136 (May).

National Institute for Economic and Social Research (NIESR) (1991b) *Review* no. 137 (August).

Office of Population Censuses and Surveys (OPCS) (1987) *General Household Survey 1985* HMSO, London.

Office of Population Censuses and Surveys (OPCS) (1990a) *General Household Survey 1988* HMSO, London.

Office of Population Censuses and Surveys (OPCS) (1990b) *General Household Survey for 1989: Preliminary results* OPCS Monitor SS 90/3, 30 October, HMSO, London.

O'Higgins, M. and Jenkins, S. (1989) 'Poverty in Europe: Estimates for 1975, 1980 and 1985', paper presented at EC Seminar on 'Poverty statistics in the European Community', 26 October.

O'Mahony, B. (1988) *A Capital Offence: The plight of single young homeless people in London* Routledge, London.

Oppenheim, C. (1990) *Poverty: The facts* Child Poverty Action Group, London.

Organisation for Economic Co-operation and Development (OECD) (1988) *The Future of Social Protection* OECD, Paris.

Pahl, J. (1989) *Money and Marriage* Macmillan, London.

Pahl, R. (1984) *Divisions of Labour* Blackwell, Oxford.

Pahl, R. (1988) 'Some remarks on informal work, social polarization and the social structure' *International Journal of Urban and Regional Research* vol. 12, no. 2.

Papadakis, E. and Taylor-Gooby, P. (1987) *The Private Provision of Public Welfare* Wheatsheaf, Brighton.

Parker, H. (1989) *Instead of the Dole: An inquiry into the integration of the tax and benefit system* Routledge, London.

Pascall, G. (1986) *Social Policy: A feminist analysis* Tavistock, London.

Pashukanis, E. (1978) *General Theory of Law and Marxism* Ink Links, London.

Plant, R. (1991) 'Welfare and the enterprise society' in Wilson, D. and T, (eds.) *The State and Social Welfare* Longman, London.

Price, R. and Bain, G. (1988) 'The labour force' in Halsey, A.H. *British Social Trends since 1900* Macmillan, London.

Prottas. J, (1979) *People Processing* Lexington Books, Lexington, MA.

Raison, T. (1991) 'Family policy' in Wilson, D. and T. (eds.) *The State and Social Welfare* Longman, Harlow.

Ringen, S. (1987) *The Possibility of Politics* Clarendon Press, Oxford.

Ritchie, J. (1990) *Thirty Families: Their living standards in unemployment* Department of Social Security Research Report no. 1, HMSO, London.

Roberts, B., Finnegan, R. and Gallie, D. (eds.) (1985) *New Approaches to Economic Life: Economic restructuring, employment and the division of labour* Manchester University Press, Manchester.

Room, G. (ed.) (1991) *European Developments in Social Policy* Bristol University Press, Bristol.

Rose, R. (1989) *Ordinary People in Public Policy* Sage, London.

Runciman, W.G. (1990) 'How many classes are there in contemporary British society?' *Sociology* vol. 24, no. 3.

Salvation Army (1989) 'Sleeping rough in London', press release (July).

Sarre, P. (1989) 'Recomposition of the class structure' in Hamnett, C., McDowell, L. and Sarre, P. (eds.) *The Changing Social Structure* Sage, London.

Scott, A. (1991) 'And never the twain shall meet? Life-time segregation of men and women' mimeo, to be published in Scott, A. (ed.) *Gender Segregation in British Labour Markets* (forthcoming) Cambridge University Press, Cambridge.

Smith, D. (1989) *North and South* Penguin, Harmondsworth.

Smith, R. (1985) 'Whose fiddling? Fraud and abuse' in Ward, S. (ed.) *DHSS in Crisis: Social security under pressure and under review* Child Poverty Action Group, London.

Social Security Benefits Agency (1991) *Framework Document* DSS/HMSO, London.

Social Security Research Consortium (SSRC) (1991) *Cash Limited – Limited Cash* Association of Metropolitan Authorities/SSRC, London.

Social Services Select Committee (1991) *Low Income Statistics: Households below average income tables 1988* HCP 401, 1990–1, HMSO, London.

Social Services Select Committee (1989) *Report on the Social Security Changes Implemented in April 1989* HCP 437-i, 1988–9, HMSO, London.

Stedman-Jones, G. (1971) *Outcast London* Clarendon Press, Oxford.

Stone, L. (1977) *Family, Sex and Marriage in England* Weidenfeld and Nicolson, London.

Svenson, M. and MacPherson, S. (1988) 'Real losses and unreal figures: the impact of the 1986 Social Security Act' in Becker, S. and MacPherson, S. (eds.) *Public Issues and Private Pain: Poverty, social work and social policy* Social Services Insight Books, London.

Taylor-Gooby, P. (1990) 'Social welfare: The unkindest cuts' in Jowell, R., Witherspoon, S. and Brook, L. (eds.) *British Social Attitudes: The seventh report* Gower, Aldershot.

Taylor-Gooby, P. (1991a) 'Scrounging, moral hazard and unwaged work', paper given to the 25th annual conference of the Social Policy Association, 9–11 July, University of Nottingham.

Taylor-Gooby, P. (1991b) *Social Change, Social Welfare and Social Science* Harvester Wheatsheaf, Hemel Hempstead.

Thompson, E.P. (1975) *Whigs and Hunters* Parthenon, New York.

Titmuss, R. (1963) 'The social division of welfare' in Titmuss, R. (ed.) *Essays on the Welfare State* Allen and Unwin, London.

Townsend, P. (1974) 'The cycle of deprivation: The history of a confused thesis' in *The Cycle of Deprivation*, Papers presented to a national study conference at Manchester University, March, British Association of Social Workers, Birmingham.

Townsend, P. (1979) *Poverty in the United Kingdom* Penguin, Harmondsworth.

Townsend, P. (1991) *The Poor are Poorer* Statistical Monitoring Unit, University of Bristol.

Treasury (1983) *The Government's Expenditure Plans*, 1983/4 to 1985/6, Cmnd. 8789, HMSO, London.

Treasury (1988) *The Government's Expenditure Plans*, 1988/9 to 1991/2, Cmnd. 288, vol. ii, HMSO, London.

Turner, B. (1986) *Citizenship and Capitalism: The debate over reformism* Allen and Unwin, London.

Unemployment Unit (1991) *Working Brief* (August/September) Unemployment Unit, London.

Ungerson, C. (1987) *Policy is Personal: Sex, gender and informal care* Tavistock, London.

Valentine, C. (1968) *Culture and Poverty: Critique and counterproposals* University of Chicago Press, Chicago.

Wacquant, L. and Wilson, W.J. (1989) 'The cost of racial and class exclusion in the inner city' in Wilson, W.J. (ed.) 'The Ghetto Underclass: Social Science Perspectives' (special issue) *Annals of the American Academy of Political and Social Science* no. 501.

Walker, A. (1982) 'Dependency and old age' *Social Policy and Administration* vol. 16, no. 2.

Walker, A. (1990) 'Blaming victims' in Murray, C. *The Emerging British Underclass* Institute of Economic Affairs, London.

Wegscheider-Cruse, S. (1988) *The Co-Dependency Trap* Nurturing Networks Inc., Rapid City, S.D.

Wicks, M. (1991) 'Social politics 1979–92: Families, work and welfare', paper given to the 25th annual conference of the Social Policy Association, 9–11 July, University of Nottingham.

Williams, F. (1991) 'Somewhere over the rainbow: Universality and selectivity in social policy', paper given to the 25th annual conference of the Social Policy Association, 9–11 July, University of Nottingham.

Wilson, W.J. (1987) *The Truly Disadvantaged: The inner city, the underclass and public policy* University of Chicago Press, Chicago.

Wilson, W.J. (1991) 'Studying inner-city social dislocations: The challenge of public agenda research', 1990 Presidential Address, *American Sociological Review* vol. 56 (February).

Wood, E.M. (1986) *The Retreat from Class* Verso, London.

Name Index

213

Subject Index